Rebels in Law

For
Gregory A. White
with
respect +
admiration

J. Clay Smith

Rebels

Voices in History

in *Law*

of Black Women Lawyers

Edited by J. Clay Smith Jr.

Ann Arbor
The University of Michigan Press

The Jack and Lovell Olender Foundation made a generous contribution toward the publication of this book so that it could be made available to a wider audience.

First paperback edition 2000
Copyright © by J. Clay Smith, Jr. 1998
All rights reserved
Published in the United States of America by
The University of Michigan Press
Manufactured in the United States of America
⊗ Printed on acid-free paper

2003   2002   2001   2000   5   4   3

A CIP catalog record for this book is available from the British Library.

Library of Congress Cataloging-in-Publication Data

Rebels in law : voices in history of Black women lawyers / J. Clay
   Smith Jr., editor.
     p.   cm.
   Includes bibliographical references and index.
   ISBN 0-472-10883-2 (cloth : acid-free paper)
     1. Afro-American women lawyers—History.   2. Afro-American women
lawyers—Biography.   3. Afro-Americans—Legal status, laws, etc.
4. Afro-Americans—Social conditions.   I. Smith, J. Clay, (John
Clay), 1942–   .
   KF299.A35R43   1998
   340'.0896073—dc21   97-45269
                                                           CIP

ISBN 0-472-08646-4 (pbk. : alk. paper)

Title page photograph:
Black Women Lawyers at the Annual Bar Association Convention in 1947. *Seated, left to right:* Mrs. Jeanne Murrell Capers, Cleveland; Lula Morgan Howard, Lincoln University, MO; *(with glasses)* Mrs. Rachel E. Pruden Herndon, Atlanta; *(lady with face hidden)* unknown; Ms. Margaret Haywood, Washington, DC; Ollie May Cooper, Washington, DC; Ms. Sadie T. M. Alexander, Philadelphia; Wilhelmina Jackson, Washington, DC; *(lady with oval hat)* Helen Elsie Austin; Ms. Isadora Augusta Letcher, Washington, DC. *Standing, left to right:* Sopolia Fanil Parker, Washington, DC; Bessie Samuels Chase, Washington, DC; Charlotte Pinkett, Washington, DC; and Lucia Theodosia Thomas, Chicago. *Courtesy of Ollie May Cooper and Mr. and Mrs. Paul F. Cooper.*

For

Ollie May Cooper
Who guided me to Black women legal scholars

and

Emily Williams Smith-Martin
My Mother, who taught me the meaning of life

Contents

Illustrations following page 110

Preface

The history of black women lawyers is a rich compilation of resonating and diverse voices.

The need for a collection of articles that includes the voices of early black women in the law is long overdue. This book was conceived in 1976 during an interview with Ollie May Cooper, a 1921 law graduate of Howard University. As I sat in her modest apartment looking through her scrapbook of memories, I could not recall being assigned to read anything by or about a black woman lawyer at any level of my education. As I listened to her talk about the "men of the law"—men such as Charles Hamilton Houston, Thurgood Marshall, and Clarence Darrow—I realized that Cooper was aware that she, as much as the men whom she affectionately referred to, was also an interpreter of the law. Yet, I wondered, who knows about the "black women of the law," their ideas and opinions about law, politics, and social policy, and what canons they birth? I wondered to what extent black women lawyers have interpreted the law in a way that has forged new and recognized paths.

The impetus to collect the writings of black women lawyers was instilled by Ollie May Cooper. Before I left her home, she gave me a copy of an article entitled, "Women and the Law," which had been published in the *Washington Afro-American* in 1963.

Ollie May Cooper had been retired as secretary to the law dean at Howard University for three years before I enrolled as a law student in 1964, but she maintained a small office adjacent to the Dean's office where she talked to me about the legal history of black lawyers. This was the first time that a woman lawyer had talked to me about the significant role that black lawyers had played to advance the status "of Negroes" in America. As a law student, and years after I left law school, I did not realize that Cooper and the lawyers, whom she referred to as "legal scholars," would lead me to write about their ideas on law, politics, race, and social and international concerns.

The need for this book is generated and enhanced by the number of books and articles available today by contemporary black, white, and other women of color on law and social policy, particularly those writing under the broad subjects of feminist jurisprudence and critical race theory. *Rebels in Law* is intended not only to introduce new voices to ongoing scholarship on these themes by women in the legal academy, but beyond, to social and political scientists who have ignored the voices of black women lawyers when they have contested political and social science issues in writing about their struggles to gain equality. In addition, this book can be helpful to teachers in African-American studies and women's studies programs who may wish to expand the message of the struggle of women by including the voices in history of black women lawyers.

Twenty-four of the sixty-two articles in the book have never been published, and many of the articles published have appeared in nonlegal publications. Thus, *Rebels in Law* provides a rare and rich reservoir of original thoughts by pioneer and contemporary black women lawyers never before assembled.

The articles in this book share stories, philosophies, beliefs, and disbeliefs about the law and provide a window through which the reader can see how black women lawyers shaped the law and challenged its framework and its legal institutions.

The rationale for the organization of *Rebels in Law* is drawn from the logic of the subject matter of their voices. Hence, in parts 1 through 4, we discover the context of the calling of black women to the law through their stories and expositions. We also discern that black women recognize their power in their march to gain equality and respect. Beyond wielding power, these authors reveal the struggles of women to enter law schools, gain employment as lawyers, become and sustain themselves as law teachers, and demonstrate their responsibility to speak out on behalf of the black lawyer in public forums. These women lawyers reveal an astute recognition of the politics of the presidency and the impact that appointments to, and decisions of, the U.S. Supreme Court have on black Americans and women.

Parts 5 through 7 are organized to show how black women lawyers address more specific themes, such as race, equality, justice, freedom, criminal justice, and international concerns.

Finally, the appendixes provide new facts about the role that black women have played in the profession of law in spite of 1950–90 census data that demonstrate that even with the benefit of affirmative action, the progress of black women lawyers has not kept pace with the steady increase in the number of white women lawyers.

Acknowledgments

Many individuals and institutions were helpful in the completion of this book. It is a pleasure to acknowledge some of them. A year's leave from Howard University School of Law allowed me valuable time to finish a significant portion of this book. My thanks to Valerie A. Railey, Felicia Ayanbiola, and Iris M. Lee of the Reference Department of the Howard University School of Law Library, who helped assemble documents contained in this book. I received support from the Moorland-Spingarn Research Center at the Howard University Library (especially the curator of manuscripts, JoEllen EL Bashir, and Clifford Muse, the university archivist), the Schomburg Center for Research in Black Culture, and Daniel Williams and Raymond Trent of the Tuskegee University Library and Archives and the Biddle Law Library (University of Pennsylvania), respectively. During my leave, Karen Summerhill of the Georgetown Law Library provided me with excellent assistance.

Others who have been supportive are Associate Dean and Professor Elizabeth Hayes Patterson of the Georgetown Law School and Patti Grace Smith, the Acting Administrator for Commercial Space Transportation, Federal Aviation Administration, Department of Transportation, who read the manuscript and provided critical and useful recommendations that greatly enhanced the book. Carole Gaillard Watt and Johnine Waters Brown, both prolific writers and purveyors of life, and whose lives ended while this book was in process, were a great inspiration to me.

I am grateful to former Dean Henry Ramsey and Interim Dean Alice Gresham Bullock of the Howard University School of Law for providing summer research stipends to complete this book.

My thanks to the several colleagues, students, and organizations, like the National Bar Association and its affiliates, whose words, deeds, and encouragement reaffirmed the importance of this project. A special thanks to Professor

Hanes Walton Jr. of the political science department at the University of Michigan who first saw the dimension of black lawyers in the area of politics. I also thank Chinhayi Jai Coleman, Michelle R. Barrett, and Kirk Sinclair (Georgetown law students) for their able assistance in doing the census appendix, as well as Jason Crump, Sheila Harley, and Aquaretta Knight (Howard Law School students) for their support in the completion of this project. The administrative support of Delphyne Bruner, Rijan Ninan, Vita Walker, and Ivet Johnson (Howard University) and Jennifer Fairfax (Georgetown University) is acknowledged with gratitude.

Finally, my appreciation is extended to Charles T. Myers, the very able editor for political science and law at the University of Michigan Press, for his early recognition of the importance of *Rebels in Law;* and to Kevin M. Rennells, the copyediting coordinator, whose editorial suggestions improved the overall quality of the book.

The Press is grateful for permission to print and reprint the following copyright material and letters.

Afro-American Studies Program, Boston University: Marian Wright Edelman, "Dynamics of Change." *Afro-American Studies Series,* No. 1, at 7 (1970).

Afro-American Studies Program, Boston University: Pauli Murray, "Constitutional Law and Black Women." *Afro-American Studies Series,* No. 1, at 33 (1970).

The American Society of International Law: Goler Teal Butcher, "Women and Minorities in International Law." Reproduced with permission from 81 ASIL PROC 520 (1987), © The American Society of International Law.

H. Elsie Austin: "Racism is a Deadly Force." 1944 (unpublished).

Edgar S. Cahn: Jean Camper Cahn, "Antioch's Fight Against Neutrality in Legal Education." 1 *Learning and the Law* 40 (1974).

Jean Murrell Capers: "Lawyers are Leaders in the Community." Oct. 27, 1994 (unpublished).

Paul F. Cooper: Minutes, Epsilon Sigma Iota, 1938–1945 (unpublished).

Crisis Publishing Company: Constance Baker Motley, "The Role of Law in Effecting Social Change." *Crisis,* Jan. 1978, at 24.

Mahala A. Dickerson: "Jet Propelled into Law." Aug. 29, 1994 (unpublished).

Dillard University: Margaret Bush Wilson, "Minority Coalitions to Secure Civil Rights," in Donald W. Wyatt, ed., *Progress in Africa and of Developing Nations* 109 (Dillard University, New Orleans: 1972).

Anita Faye Hill: "The Power of Black Women To Tell Their Stories." Sept. 30, 1995, Carlson Lecture, University of Minnesota, Oct. 29, 1992 (unpublished).

Howard Law Journal, Howard University School of Law: Daisy G. Collins, "The United States Owes Reparations to its Black Citizens," 16 *Howard Law Journal* 84 (1970).

The Jane E. Hunter Scholarship Committee: Jane E. Hunter, A Nickel and a Prayer 184, excerpt from Chapter 16, "Looking Ahead," herein, "When American Democracy Becomes a Sham."

Issie L. Jenkins: "The Black Woman: Who Speaks for Her?" Oct. 13, 1994 (unpublished).

Johnson Foundation: Clarence Page's interview of Eleanor Holmes Norton, "Issues on Race: Employment and the Black Community," 1968 (unpublished audio tape transcription).

Barbara Jordan: "Erosion of Civil Rights," May 11, 1974 (unpublished).

Arthenia L. Joyner: "There is a Future For Black Lawyers." *Spectrum,* American Bar Association, Younger Lawyers Division newspaper, Fall, 1985, pages unnumbered.

Lambda Kappa Mu Sorority, Inc.: Pauli Murray, "The Negro Woman in Quest for Equality." *The Acorn,* June, 1964, pages unnumbered.

Law and Equality, University of Minnesota Law School: Constance Baker Motley, "Some Reflections of My Career." 6 *Law and Equality* 35 (1988).

Legal Defense and Education Fund: Elaine R. Jones, "African Americans Must Reject Anti-Semitism." *New York Times,* Jan. 28, 1994, at 7.

Jane M. Lucas: "Breaking New Ground with Grace: The University of Michigan's First Black Woman Law Graduate," Sept. 17, 1994 (unpublished).

Moorland-Spingarn Research Center, Howard University: "Pauli Murray's Appeal: For Admission to Harvard Law School," circa 1944 (unpublished); Mary Ann Shadd Carey, "Give Colored Women the Right to Vote," circa 1870; Zephyr A. Moore, "Law and Its Call to Women," in 1922 Year Book (V) (pages unnumbered); Ambassador Patricia Roberts Harris, "The Underdeveloped Resource," March 2, 1966.

National Association for the Advancement of Colored People: Althea T. L. Simmons, "The Japanese Buraku Problem: A Foreigner's Perspective," Dec. 4, 1982 (unpublished).

National Bar Association: Georgia Jones Ellis, "The Necessity of Universal Suffrage," Proceedings of the Eighth Annual NBA Convention 97 (1932); Sadie T. M. Alexander, "Women Practitioners of Law in the United States", 1 *National Bar Association* 56 (July 1941); Arnette R. Hubbard, "President's Message," 13 *National Bar Bulletin* 2 (Sept.–Nov. 1981), herein "Speaking Out Against Duplicity in Foreign Policy."

National Council of Negro Women, Inc. and the National Park Service: Mabel Haden Covington, "What Shall We Teach Our Children." *The Afraamerican Woman's Journal* (Summer/Fall 1947), pp. 20–21, 30. Records of the National Council of Negro Women- Series 13, Box 1 Folder 22, Mary McLeod Bethune Council House NHS, National Park Service, Washington, D.C.

National Public Radio: Lani Guinier, "President Clinton's Doubt; Lani Guinier's Certainty." © National Public Radio ® The News report ("Clinton Retracts

Nomination of Lani Guinier") by NPR's Neal Conan was originally broadcast on NPR's "Morning Edition" on June 4, 1993, and is used with the permission of NPR. Any unauthorized duplication is strictly prohibited.

New England Law Review: "Hon. Margaret A. Haywood." 27 *New England Law Review* 613 (1993), herein, "Lawyer, Law Teacher and Judge."

The New York Times: "The Next-to-Last Word on Political Correctness," Dec. 11, 1993, at 23, herein, "Political Correctness: Professor Linda S. Greene vs. Robert Bork."

The Pepperdine Law Review; Consuelo B. Marshall, "Women and the Criminal Justice System." 20 *Pepperdine Law Review* 1197–1205 (1993). Reprinted from the Pepperdine Law Review, Volume 20, Number 3; Copyright 1993 by the Pepperdine Law Review.

The Philadelphia Lawyer: Sadie T. M. Alexander, "Forty-Five Years a Woman Lawyer." 51 *Shingle* 20 (Winter 1988).

Glendora M. Putnam: Glendora M. Putnam, "Sheer Determination Brought Me Through," Dec. 2, 1994 (unpublished).

Temple Political & Civil Rights Law Review, Temple University School of Law: Karen Hastie Williams, "Thurgood Marshall and His Legacy." 2 *Temple Political & Civil Rights Law Review* 159 (Spring 1993).

Lucia T. Thomas: "Second Black Woman at University of Michigan's Law School," July 13, 1994 (unpublished).

Gloria E. A. Toote: "Black Political Power," Sept. 16, 1982 (unpublished).

Cora T. Walker: "Problems Within The Legal Profession." *Spectrum,* American Bar Association, Younger Lawyers Division newspaper, Fall, 1985, pages unnumbered.

Washington Afro-American Publishers: Juanita Jackson Mitchell, "The Most Dangerous Election in History," *Washington Afro-American,* Oct. 20, 1984, at 5.

Washington Afro-American Publishers: Ollie May Cooper, "Women in Law," July 29, 1961, at 6 (Supp.). Reprinted with permission of the Afro-American Co. of Baltimore City T/A The Washington AFRO-American Newspaper.

Washington Post: Pauli Murray, "Black Strategies: Responding to Thomas Sowell. I Know Where You're Coming From, but . . . ," © *Washington Post,* Feb. 26, 1981, at A19.

Grace Watson and the Schomburg Center for Research in Black Culture: Speeches by Barbara M. Watson, "Female Liberation and Human Survival," December 2, 1975; "Justice and Values In Government," Oct. 29, 1976; and Untitled Speech before unidentified group, November 26, 1968, herein "Human Rights and Social Relations."

Veva I. Young: Forty Years a Lawyer, May 1991 (unpublished).

Introduction: Law Is No Mystery to Black Women

J. Clay Smith Jr.

> When a white man teaches constitutional law, he teaches it from his particular insight. . . . His perspective might be different from that of a black woman, who might be more likely to talk about basic constitutional issues such as slavery and civil rights. . . . Black women are more often confronted with and have unique perspectives on the social areas of law that have been under-emphasized. . . . These are not the problems that white males, black males, or white women teaching in law schools are necessarily attuned to. They are problems that black women cannot escape.
>
> —Dean Marilyn V. Yarbrough

$\mathcal{T}$HE ENTRY OF BLACK WOMEN in the field of law introduced an unknown "colored gender" into the profession. The legal profession may have been ignorant of the black woman, but the law was no mystery to her.[1] During slavery, black women witnessed the cruel and unusual nature of the law and its application.[2] The metaphysical abstractions and the nature of law were introduced

---

Epigraph from *Black Female Law Professors Essential to Campus Diversity, Dean Says,* UPI, Sept. 5, 1990, *available in* LEXIS, NEXIS Library, UPI File. From 1987 to 1991, Yarbrough served as Dean of the School of Law at the University of Tennessee, becoming the third black woman in the nation to head a law school.

1. *A Mother Is Sold Away from Her Children, in* GERDA LERNER, ED., BLACK WOMEN IN WHITE AMERICA: A DOCUMENTARY HISTORY 10–12 (New York, Vintage Books 1972).

2. *See generally* MELTON A. MCLAURIN, CELIA: A SLAVE (Athens, The University of Georgia Press 1991); LINDA BRENT, INCIDENTS IN THE LIFE OF A SLAVE GIRL (San Diego, Jovanovich 1973); Dorothy Burnham, *The Life of the Afro-American Woman in Slavery,* 1 INT'L J. WOMEN'S STUD. 363 (1978). (Ms. Burnham states: "The institution of slavery fixed the status of the Black woman and closely defined the social and legal conditions under which she would live and function for a period of over 200 years in the United States.") *Id.* A. LEON HIGGINBOTHAM JR., IN THE MATTER OF COLOR:

to black women in ways that she could only describe as disagreeable to her nature and mind. The law was an instrument of her oppression, an obstruction to the formation of a family.[3] The law (and policies and customs of slavery) provided black women no voice to object to injustices against black men or her children. It provided no protection from uninvited intrusions to her vital sanctuaries by white and black men for which she could claim sanctions.[4]

Attempts of black women in the North to influence law during the slavery era may not have been much better than those of her sisters in the South, except for the rare experiences of women like Luce Terry. Luce Terry, a free black woman in the North, is likely the first female voice to argue before a court on which a member of the U.S. Supreme Court sat.

In 1796, in a case to protect the economic interests of her family, Luce Terry gained a national reputation during a series of lawsuits for ejectment, trespass, and actions to quiet title to land deeded to her husband in the 1760s prior to Vermont's statehood.[5] It is not known what role her husband played in his effort to protect the title to his land, but George Sheldon, a nineteenth-century historian, reports that the dispute was heard by Samuel Chase, a justice of the U.S. Supreme Court, who at the time was riding circuit in New England. Although Luce Terry's husband was represented by two white lawyers, she "argued the case at length before the court convened in Vermont. Justice Chase said that Luce made a better argument than he had heard from any lawyer at the Vermont bar."[6] Luce Terry's advocacy before Justice Chase makes hers the first voice of a black woman in the nation to influence law before a court on which a member of the U.S. Supreme Court sat.

RACE & THE AMERICAN LEGAL PROCESS—THE COLONIAL PERIOD 42–45, 252 (New York, Oxford University Press 1978).

3. Michael B. Chesson, *Slavery Denied Legal Marriage to Blacks,* N.Y. TIMES, April 9, 1995, at 14E, stating, "Couples were often allowed to live together, and might well fulfill all the responsibilities and have some privileges of matrimony, until death, but they never legally married, nor so regarded by any white institution." *See also* HERBERT G. GUTMAN, THE BLACK FAMILY IN SLAVERY & FREEDOM, 1750–1925, at xxi (New York, Pantheon Books 1976). *But see* JEANNE NOBLE, BEAUTIFUL ALSO ARE THE SOULS OF MY BLACK SISTERS: A HISTORY OF THE BLACK WOMAN IN AMERICA 39–40 (Englewood Cliffs, N.J., Prentice Hall 1978), suggesting there were cultural marriages during slavery. Laura F. Edwards reports that "[t]he law [did] not recognize slave marriages, and emancipation did not make them legal." Laura F. Edwards, "The Marriage Covenant is the Foundation of all Our Rights": The Politics of Slave Marriages in North Carolina after Emancipation, 14 LAW & HISTORY 81, 90 (Spring 1996).

4. *See* DEBORAH GRAY WHITE, AR'N'T I A WOMAN? FEMALE SLAVES IN THE PLANTATION SOUTH 152 (New York, W.W. Norton 1985); *The Breeder Woman, in* BLACK WOMEN IN WHITE AMERICA, *supra* note 1, at 47–48.

5. J. CLAY SMITH JR., EMANCIPATION: THE MAKING OF THE BLACK LAWYER, 1844–1944, at 70 n.74 (Philadelphia, University of Pennsylvania Press 1993), quoting George Shelton, *Negro Slavery in Old Deerfield,* 8 NEW ENGLAND MAG. 54 (March 1893).

6. *Id.* (EMANCIPATION).

In 1848, fifty-two years after Luce Terry presented argument before Justice Chase, the first Women's Rights Convention in the U.S. was held in Seneca Falls, New York. No black women are known to have attended this meeting. The meeting produced the Declaration of Sentiments,[7] a document stating that "the history of mankind is a history of repeated injuries and usurpations on the part of man toward women, having in direct object the establishment of an absolute tyranny over her."[8] Approximately sixty-four women and thirty-two men, including Frederick Douglass,[9] the only black male delegate at the convention, signed the Declaration.[10] While this Declaration was important to all women, during the 1840s "there was greater acceptance among Black men of women in activist roles than there was in the broader society."[11]

Whether the acceptance of black men or women in activist roles influenced black or white women to enter the legal profession cannot be determined either way, but given the activism of Luce Terry and the groundbreaking entry into the law by pioneer black women, it can reasonably be assumed that black women had the same ambitions as white women, white men, and black men. Because the study of black women lawyers has been ignored by legal historians,[12] only general assumptions can be made about the ambitions of black women lawyers by what they have said, written, and their "jobs outside of the home."[13] Two observations appear certain about the black woman, who was never "considered delicate or worthy of homage"[14] in the conception of her sphere: She never succumbed to the notion that she was unworthy of being treated the same as white

---

7. JOAN HOFF, LAW, GENDER, AND INJUSTICE: A LEGAL HISTORY OF U.S. WOMEN 383 (New York, New York University Press 1991) (Appendix 2).

8. *Id.* at 385–86. Years later, Alvah L. Stinson wrote that "[t]he condition of women at common law was little better than that of a slave." ALVAH L. STINSON, WOMEN UNDER THE LAW 1 (Boston, Hudson Printing 1914).

9. For the specific views of Douglass on women's rights, *see* 2 PHILIP FONER, ED., THE LIFE AND WRITINGS OF FREDERICK DOUGLASS 16–17 (New York, International Publishers 1975); WALDO E. MARTIN JR., THE MIND OF FREDERICK DOUGLASS 136–64 (Chapel Hill, University of North Carolina Press 1984).

10. Madelyn C. Squire, *Discovering Our Connections: Reflections on Race, Gender and the Other Tales of Difference*, 23 GOLDEN GATE U.L. REV. 795, 802 (1993).

11. PAULA GIDDINGS, WHEN AND WHERE I ENTER: THE IMPACT OF BLACK WOMEN ON RACE AND SEX IN AMERICA 59 (New York, William Morrow 1984). Darlene C. Goring states that "[t]he inestimable importance of the Seneca Falls Declaration was its role as the articulated consciousness of women's rights at midcentury . . . [T]he Declaration all but ignored . . . the condition of black women in the South and North alike." Darlene C. Goring, *Affirmative Action and Gender Law School Academic Support Programs*, 84 KY. L.J. 941, 972 n.94 (1994/1996).

12. *See* Appendix B, *infra*, regarding pioneering facts about black women lawyers and law teachers.

13. JEANNE L. NOBLE, THE NEGRO WOMAN'S COLLEGE EDUCATION 128 (New York, Bureau of Publications Teachers College, Columbia University 1956).

14. *Id.* at 16.

women, and "'[n]either economic necessity nor tradition . . . instilled in her the spirit of subordination to masculine authority.'"[15]

While many of the writings of pioneer black women lawyers have not been unearthed, it is inferred by one author that black women professionals, including black women lawyers, were published in "newspapers and journals of the day."[16] In general, the voices of black women and black women lawyers have been "'broad in the concrete as in the abstract'"[17] on legal, political, and social issues. For example, in 1867, Sojourner Truth, a black woman whose voice, no less than that of Frederick Douglass, spoke eloquently about the rights of "colored women," asserted her indignation at the "stir about colored men getting their rights, but not a word about colored women."[18] Truth believed that if only black men won the right to vote, black women would remain subordinate to them. Thus, she proclaimed, "I want women to have their rights. In the courts women have no rights, no voice; nobody speaks for them. I wish women to have their voice. . . ."[19] The extent to which communities in the nation have listened to the incredibly substantive and brilliant voices of black women lawyers is unmeasured and untold even with their impressive record of achievements to advance civil and human rights.[20]

Brilliant black women admitted to the Bar prior to 1900 were quite informed about the history and life conditions black women faced before courts of law during slavery and after Emancipation. They were likely aware of Maria W. Stewart, called by some, America's first black woman political writer, who urged the black woman to exert herself and lift "the rising generation."[21] Stewart's message to the black woman that her "example is powerful [and] influence great; extend[ing] over . . . husbands and . . . children, and throughout

---

15. *Id.*, quoting E. FRANKLIN FRAZIER, THE NEGRO FAMILY IN THE UNITED STATES 102 (New York, Dryden Press 1948).

16. Lucinda W. Gamble, *The Emancipation of Woman, in* AFRO-AMERICAN ENCYCLOPEDIA, OR THE THOUGHTS, DOINGS, AND SAYINGS OF THE RACE 274, 275 (Nashville, Tenn., Haley & Florida 1895). Still in modern times, "[t]he contributions of black women to the literature of America have not been fully realized, let alone researched or appreciated." LORRAINE ELENA ROSES & RUTH ELIZABETH RANDOLPH, EDS., HARLEM'S GLORY: BLACK WOMEN WRITING, 1900–1950, at 6 (Cambridge, Harvard University Press 1996).

17. BELL HOOKS, AIN'T I A WOMAN: BLACK WOMEN AND FEMINISM 193 (Boston, South End Press 1981), quoting Anna J. Cooper.

18. Sojourner Truth, *Keeping the Theory Going While Things are Stirring, in* MARLENE STEIN WORTMAN, ED., 1 WOMEN IN AMERICAN LAW: FROM COLONIAL TIMES TO THE NEW DEAL 196 (New York, Holmes & Meier Pub. 1985).

19. *Id.*

20. *See, e.g.,* J. Clay Smith Jr., *United States Foreign Policy and Goler Teal Butcher,* 37 How. L.J. 139 (1994).

21. MARILYN RICHARDSON, ED., MARIA W. STEWART, AMERICA'S FIRST BLACK WOMAN POLITICAL WRITER: ESSAYS AND SPEECHES 55 (Bloomington and Indianapolis, University of Indiana Press 1987).

the circle of [her] acquaintance"[22] may have inspired black women to rethink their roles as silent partners in a male-dominated society. For example, in 1875, a colored woman, residing in Richmond, Virginia, "fearing I shall not do my duty to my race if I remain silent," argued for the passage of civil rights legislation pending in Congress. Her letter was intended to inform Congress that "[n]othing can ever make [black women] equal with the white race while our daughters are forced to commit adultery by every white man and boy that chose to treat them as dogs."[23]

It is likely that the roots of black women lawyers are connected with the "feminist intelligentsia"[24] of the nineteenth century. Black women such as Anna J. Cooper, Victoria Earle Matthews, and Margaret Murray Washington help to define the contours of feminist discourse represented in this work. However, the quest to advance truth and combat irrational state and private conduct toward black women did not originate from a single source of feminism.[25] Anna J. Cooper suggests that women have the capacity to determine truth for the advancement of women and the power to reject irrationality that limits advancement through the force of intelligence. Expressing her opinion about the essential and peculiar differences between men and women, Cooper stated,

> [T]here is a feminine as well as masculine side to truth; that these are related not as inferior and superior, but as complements—complements in one necessary and symmetric whole . . . That while we not infrequently see women who reason, we say, with the coolness and precision of a man, and men as considerate of helplessness as a woman, still there is a general con-

---

22. *Id.*

23. 3 CONG. REC. 1006 (43d Cong., 2d Sess. 1875).

24. The term *feminist intelligentsia* is used by Barbara Omolade, who states: "The emergence of a Black feminist intelligentsia is one of the most important developments of the desegregated era of American life . . . Since the 1960s, enough Black female intellectuals have emerged to create an intelligentsia with several distinctive forms evidenced in books, articles, speeches, and plays, as well as in the visual and performing arts." BARBARA OMOLADE, THE RISING SONG OF AFRICAN AMERICAN WOMEN 117 (New York, Routledge 1994). This editor is in agreement with Omolade, but contends that the term *feminist intelligentsia* has broader reach, a reach that could include the voices in history of black women during segregated nineteenth- and twentieth-century eras. *See, e.g.,* Joanne Braxton, *Introduction, in* N. F. MOSSELL, THE WORK OF THE AFRO-AMERICAN WOMAN xxvii (New York, Oxford University Press 1988).

25. For the views of black women scholars on this theme today *see, e.g.,* Kimberlé Crenshaw, *Demarginalizing the Intersection of Race and Sex: A Black Feminist Critique of Antidiscrimination Doctrine and Anarchist Politics, in* KATHERINE T. BARTLETT & ROSANNE KENNEDY, EDS., FEMINIST LEGAL THEORY: READINGS IN LAW AND GENDER 66–67 (Boulder, Colo., Westview Press 1991); Angela P. Harris, *Race and Essentialism in Feminist Legal Theory, id.* at 235, 238; L. Amede Obiora, *Neither Here nor There:* Of the Female in America Legal Education, 21 LAW AND SOCIAL INQUIRY 395, 400–408 (1996); *see generally* ADRIEN KATHERINE WING, CRITICAL RACE FEMINISM: A READER (New York, New York University Press 1997).

sensus of mankind that one trait is essentially masculine and the other is peculiarly feminine . . . [T]he feminine factor can have its proper effect only through women's development and education so that she may fitly and intelligently stamp her force on the forces of her day, and add her modicum to the riches of the world's thought. . . .[26]

Black women of the nineteenth century determined that educated black women of the twentieth century would have something to say "to add her modicum to the riches of the world's thought."[27] Women such as Margaret Murray Washington opined that the voices in history of black women would be magnified through and supported by black women's groups, whose unity would force "the world to become acquainted with her."[28] The decision by black women to plow their own ground and to plant their own seeds to unify the voices of black women is likely to have influenced pioneer black women lawyers, such as Charlotte E. Ray and Lutie A. Lytle, to lend their considerable skills to the National Association of Colored Women's Clubs.[29]

For Cooper and other black women of her day, the essential question posed by Victoria Earle Matthews was "What part shall we women play in the Race Literature of the future?"[30] This book demonstrates that black women lawyers have answered this question, through the voices of black women, thus making their own case on the merits and the context of this book. Their voices and actions establish that they have "fitly and intelligently stamp[ed their] force on the forces of her day."[31]

During the twentieth century, the voices and the ideals of black women lawyers have evolved in spite of the jagged edges of social and legal culture that have attempted to assign her to historical oblivion by simply excluding her from the matrix of legal thought.[32] The entry of black women into the legal profes-

---

26. Anna J. Cooper, *The Higher Education of Women*, 2 THE SOUTHLAND 186, 192, April, 1891.

27. *Id.*

28. Mrs. Booker T. Washington (Margaret Murray Washington), *Club Work among Negro Women*, *in* J. L. NICHOLS & WILLIAM H. CROGMAN, EDS., THE NEW PROGRESS OF A RACE 177, 178 (Naperville, Ill., J. L. Nichols & Company 1920).

29. *Id.* at 200. *See also* Larry L. Martin, *Charlotte E. Ray*, *in* JESSIE CARNEY SMITH, ED., NOTABLE BLACK AMERICAN WOMEN 923 (Detroit, Gale Research 1992), stating that Ray "was an active member in the National Association of Colored Women." *Official Directory of the National Association of Colored Women*, 1926–1928, at 17 (1928), reports that in 1926 Lutie A. Lytle was an active member of the National Association of Colored Women, representing the northern region of the Transportation Committee.

30. Henry Louis Gates Jr., *Foreword*, Two BIOGRAPHIES BY AFRICAN-AMERICAN WOMEN xxi (New York, Oxford University Press 1991).

31. *The Higher Education of Women*, *supra* note 26, at 192.

32. *Compare* PATRICIA WILLIAMS, THE ALCHEMY OF RACE AND RIGHTS: DIARY OF A LAW SCHOOL PROFESSOR 1–44 (Cambridge, Mass., Harvard University Press 1991) *with* Richard Aynes,

sion has empowered them to etch new paradigms in law and politics, and to rebel against being viewed as frivolous. The extent to which black women lawyers have been "accorded juridical equality with men and the scholarly attention their historical legal status deserves"[33] is today a question being addressed by women of color.[34] Contemporary black women legal scholars recognize that they and practicing lawyers have been so unduly burdened attempting to gain recognition and protected rights under law that their efforts to achieve juridical equality has not kept pace.

Although the claim that the voice of the black woman lawyer has been silenced is substantially true, in her advocacy to discover truth, fair play, and justice, she has always "wrestle[d] herself free of the demons of the discipline of history which den[ied] her"[35] by introducing the forums to "new languages, new perspectives and knowledge."[36]

Fighting for identity, recognition of self has been more than a calling for black women lawyers;[37] the fight has been viewed by some as an obligation of black women to her people. In 1970 one scholar wrote that "[Black women] have an obligation as Black women to project [themselves] into the revolution to destroy . . . institutions which not only oppress Blacks but women as well, for if those institutions continue to flourish, they will be used against us in the continuing battle of mind over body."[38]

This book is about black women's voices, rebellious, strident voices in the law. The number of black women lawyers increased from 446 in 1970 to 11,006 in 1990. During the same period the number of white women lawyers increased from 11,664 to 161,044.[39] Many lawyers and laypersons, black and white, have never been exposed to the broad range of black women represented in these pages. This book focuses on the substance and the meaning of voices in history of black women lawyers. The voices of black women lawyers represented in this work advance concepts that spring from the roots of their womanhood, history, culture, and experiences. As patricians, black women lawyers are faced with a variety of contradictory ways of thinking resulting from the manner in which

---

Book Review, Reviews in Am. Hist. 290, 293 (1995), quoting BERNARD SCHWARTZ, MAIN CURRENTS IN AMERICAN LEGAL THOUGHT 614, 616 (Durham, N.C., Carolina Academic Press 1993).

33. LAW, GENDER AND INJUSTICE, *supra* note 7, at 3.

34. *Women of Color in Legal Academia: A Biographical and Bibliographic Guide,* 16 HARV. WOMEN'S L.J. 1 (Spring 1993); Paulette M. Caldwell, *A Hair Piece: Perspectives on the Intersection of Race and Gender,* 1991 DUKE L.J. 365.

35. THE RISING SONG OF AFRICAN AMERICAN WOMEN, *supra* note 24, at 110.

36. *Id.* at 104.

37. *See* Appendix A, *infra,* regarding the first black legal sorority.

38. Kay Lindsey, *The Black Woman as a Woman, in* TONI CADE, ED., THE BLACK WOMAN: AN ANTHOLOGY 89 (New York, The American Library 1970).

39. *See* Appendix C, *infra,* regarding census data, 1950–90.

the male-dominated society has defined the role of women and their legal interests.

Rebels in Law establishes that black women lawyers, like their white counterparts, did—and continue to—refute and define customary misconceptions about their presence, role, and interests in law and politics, as related to race, class, and gender.[40]

---

40. *Women of Color in Legal Academia, supra* note 34.

Part 1

Law and Its Call
to Black Women

Charlotte E. Ray is the first black woman lawyer in the nation's history. She was admitted to the District of Columbia bar in 1872, the year that she received her law degree from Howard University. Lutie A. Lytle's interview by the Topeka Daily Capital, *in "Miss Lutie Lytle Speaks in 1897" has the earliest known recorded words by a black woman lawyer. The interview was published the year that Lytle graduated from Central Tennessee Law School, a black law school founded in 1879. The interview reveals that pioneering black women made choices on where to practice law based, in part, on supply and demand, and on the success and failure of black male lawyers' attempts to practice law in certain regions of the nation.*

Three themes permeate part 1. First, it is clear that pioneering black women in law believe that men thwarted their efforts to enter and to succeed in the field of law; that law was the most conservative of all professions. Black women lawyers also believe that they see the world differently than men because they are detached from the vested interest and customs used by men to control them. Black women see law as an instrument to liberate themselves from the dominion and control of men and as a tool to protect women and their children.

A second theme evolves out of a belief on the part of black women that a record is needed to support the fact that black women can succeed, and have succeeded, in the law. This record demonstrates the fact that black women lawyers have historically worked to inspire other women to follow in their footsteps. It can provide the substance upon which injustice against women can be eliminated. The collective reflections of these black women lawyers, including a statement from an eighty-three-year-old lawyer, tell powerful and illuminating stories about their lives, hopes, dreams, disappointments, and aspirations; and they present expressions about their husbands, law school experiences, attitudes of male law students relative to women, and the expectations of their parents.

A third theme presented in part 1 is that black women lawyers are determined to overcome the barriers created by the legal profession and law. Some of these women have been lawyers for half a century and remain committed to the struggle of liberation of black women. Some share the view that black women should not go to law school solely to get a job, but to serve the community as well.

Miss Lutie Lytle Speaks in 1897

Lutie A. Lytle

(1897)

*A*N INTERVIEW APPEARED IN THE SEPTEMBER 15, 1897, *edition of the* Topeka Daily Capital. *In talking to the reporter [unidentified] in regard to her future work, Lutie Lytle, the first black woman admitted to the bar of the states of Tennessee and Kansas in 1897, told the reporter that she would open an office and commence the practice of law. The following questions and answers by Lytle ensued:*

Q: Do you expect to locate permanently in Topeka?

A: I think not . . . for there are so many lawyers here now. When I was graduated [from Central Tennessee College Law Department] in June [1897], I intended to commence practicing right away, but I found that a rest was what I needed. In the meantime I have been looking around for a field. Illinois is a good field for a female lawyer. One or two have started in Chicago, but have failed. It seems to me, however, that Chicago ought to furnish an opening for a female lawyer if she has lots of energy.

Q: How soon do you expect to leave Topeka?

A: I do not know. I have some other work I expect to finish before entering actively on the practice of my profession. I shall probably open a temporary office in Topeka next week to do some office work and carry on some unfinished business that must be attended to at once.

Q: To the principles of what political party do you subscribe?

A: I would rather not express my political proclivities at this time. Ever since a small girl in the High school I have been interested in politics, and hoped some day to be able to take an active part in shaping the great questions of the

---

Shortly after this interview, Lytle joined the law faculty of the Central Tennessee Law School in Nashville in 1897. *See* THIRTY-FOURTH ANNUAL CATALOGUE OF THE CENTRAL TENNESSEE COLLEGE 1899–1900, at 115 (1900), listing Professor Lytle as a "teacher in Law Department" and the librarian in 1897.

day. But just at this time for reasons of my own I would rather not publicly express myself.

Q [*The reporter stated*]: In speaking of the interest taken in the professions by her race, Miss Lytle said that more colored young people were studying the medical profession than that of law.

A: The Southern states offer a great field for the doctor. In Memphis alone there are twelve colored doctors, and they are not quacks, either. They have their diplomas. One of my friends who graduated from the [Central Tennessee College] medical department two years ago had built up a splendid practice in that city. She has bought and paid for a beautiful home and has one of the nicest furnished offices in the city.

Q [*The reporter concluded the interview*]: Miss Lytle is a great admirer of her own profession, and there is no question that success will crown her efforts at the bar.

Law and Its Call to Women

Zephyr Abigail Moore (Ramsey)

(1922)

> We are living, we are dwelling
> in a grand and an awful time,
> In an age on ages telling,
> To be living is sublime.

THESE WORDS, THOUGH UTTERED IN ANOTHER AGE, were never more appropriate than in this, the one in which we live, and while this is true, it becomes preeminently so when civilization with regard to the general status of woman is made the criterion of judgment.

The advantages and opportunities open to the women of today to prepare themselves for service in practically every branch of social and political endeavor are potent factors in the development of this present great democracy of which we boast.

For centuries there has been the widespread feeling among physicians and lawyers that theirs are men's professions and that women, no matter how well trained in these professions, are outsiders and intruders. Some of the leaders in each profession have not held this view; the war has done something to shake it, and the new political status of women is helping to do away with it.

This attitude on the part of professional men, however, has played its part in deterring women from entering medicine and law, together with the length and cost of training and the difficulty of establishing an independent practice.

Law is a profession much less commonly entered by women than is medicine. It being the most conservative of all professions, its standards and methods of training are far less well established, and it has been less affected by the modern social spirit. Yet, in spite of the fact that it suffers from being dominated

1922 YEAR BOOK (V), HOWARD UNIVERSITY (pages unnumbered).

by the spirit of precedent rather than by the spirit of scientific inquiry, there are signs that it is entering upon a period of reorganization, standardization, and socialization. It has always commanded the interest and services of men of the highest ability, and its professional contribution to public and social welfare, the securing of justice in human relations, has never been so imperatively needed.

There is a strong movement within the profession for the simplification of American legal procedure which is overburdened with precedent and detail, and for a clearer recognition of its public and social obligations, a greater emphasis upon its responsibilities as the guardian of essential human rights, and the furtherance of justice to every economic and social group.

These newer developments in the legal profession strengthen its appeal to women. Their own new political status tends to widen their legal opportunities, and will enable them to take a more active part both in the administration of justice and in the promotion of sound legislation.

The law needs imperatively men and women who are not merely class-minded and property minded, but who bring a trained and active intelligence to bear upon the difficult problems of justice in modern human relations.

The call to women for service in the legal profession is undeniable. Their relative detachment from vested interests and large property transactions leaves them free to devote themselves to the human and preventive side of law. Women lawyers are especially needed in matters concerning the protection and welfare of women and children. They are needed in legal aid societies. They are also needed as judges in juvenile courts, municipal courts, courts of domestic relations, small claims courts and the like. Just at present there is almost an obligation upon women lawyers of sound, liberal education, through professional training, strong character, and indisputable standing in the community, to become candidates for judicial and other public offices. New York has a woman assistant district attorney, and a woman city magistrate presiding over the women's court and the court of Domestic Relations. Washington, D.C., has a woman judge on the Juvenile court, and one in the Municipal court. Another has been elected judge in the court of Common Pleas in Ohio. Another has been federal probate attorney for Indians in Oklahoma. A California woman has just been appointed as assistant attorney general of the United States, the first to hold such a position.

Without doubt there is a steadily widening field for women with legal training and those who wish to enter the law should endeavor to secure preparation in a law school of high standing in which the training includes study by the case method, practice in moot court, and emphasis upon modern legal and social problems as well as technical legal procedure. This training should be based upon a comprehensive liberal education, including some Latin and a course in economics, sociology, philosophy, political government, and psychology with attention to its abnormal aspects. They should be women of robust health, clear and vigorous minds with ability to weigh evidence impartially, to handle detail, to reach practical decisions without losing idealism, and above all to manifest an inexhaustive interest in the workings of the body politic and the workings of the popular mind.

According to the census of 1920, there are now 1,500 women members of the bar. Of the seven law schools of highest entrance requirements, Harvard, Columbia, and Western Reserve do not as yet admit women. The Yale Law School was opened in 1919–20 for the first time to women with a satisfactory college degree. The University of Pennsylvania School of Law has been open to them since 1898, and there is little doubt that the next few years will find the three above mentioned universities opening their doors.

When we pause to consider the outlook, the scope, and opportunity for women to engage in earnest professional endeavor, and not the encouragement given them, together with their correspondingly awakening interest along these lines, we are forced to say ours is an age when to be living is indeed sublime, and whatever may be the fault of our democracy, it is still great.

Legal Profession Followed by Nation's Best Known Socialites

Edith Spurlock Sampson

(1935)

*W*OMEN HAVE STEADILY ENTERED THE LEGAL profession. Their entrance into this conservative profession is a part of that larger effort of women to become oriented in modern society, a society in which, whether praised or condemned, the profession of law plays one of the vivid parts.

The few years since women first entered into this new vocational field constitutes a pioneer period. Courage, persistence and faith have been shown in overcoming prejudice and in meeting the uncertainties of the new field. Law schools were not open to them in every instance, in fact, some of the leading universities of the country still bar their doors to women seeking the study of law.

The educational requirements for this study of the law and for the admission to the bar in the various states run the gauntlet. In some jurisdictions those who have studied in law offices under supervision and for a certain length of time, may submit themselves as candidates while in other jurisdictions the requirements are a sound pre-legal education followed by a course in an accredited law school. The women of color who thus far have been admitted in the various states are products of these various jurisdictions.

Too much stress cannot be laid on securing the proper preparation and education for this important field of endeavor. The law needs women who will bring a trained and active intelligence to bear upon the many and difficult problems of justice in modern human relations. Women's present political status tends to widen their legal opportunities and eventually they will be able to take a more active part in the administration of justice and in the promotion of sound legislation. Women as lawyers are needed in matters concerning the protection and welfare of women, children; as public defenders in specialized

---

THE CHICAGO DEFENDER, May 4, 1935, at 25.

women's courts; as probation officers in Juvenile Courts; as arbitrators on industrial accident boards; as judges in the Juvenile and Domestic Relations courts; as members of the state legislatures, etc.

The profession of law is concerned with the administration of justice. There are many branches of the law and women lawyers have thus far invaded all of them. They have not been especially active in the field of criminal law, yet practice of the criminal branch has great social significance and probably offers more opportunities for constructive work than any other branch. The profession is as broad and as far reaching as human activities. The same exact question and set of facts seldom, if ever occur in toto and human relationships are always involved. It is a profession which provides steady opportunity for growth. It opens the best possible method for constructive membership in the community, it develops an understanding of our social and civic institutions and offers a firm leverage for real effective citizenship and intelligent public service.

Professional women have many problems of their own to meet and to solve such as the problem of combining a professional career with marriage and parenthood. Women as newcomers in the professional field are having to make adjustments in their personal and social life. They have found in many instances that marriage is not incompatible with carrying on their professional work as compared with clerical and industrial work facilities, such continuance in many fields. The tendency toward group practice, consulting service and part time work suggests several types of adaptation.

There are many successful women in independent practice but the majority have salaried positions with firms; governmental services or with social service agencies. Legal training for those preparing for the social service field is strongly advised for the law is a key to many social problems.

The States in which women of color have thus far been admitted to practice are as follows:

California, Illinois, Indiana, Iowa, Massachusetts, Michigan, Minnesota, Missouri, Nebraska, New York, North Carolina, Ohio, Pennsylvania, Virginia and the District of Columbia and Kansas.

There have been more colored women admitted to practice law in the State of Illinois than in any other state in the Union . . .

An effort has been made by the writer to secure data on the women of our race who have secured their licenses and the following resume will give you some idea as to their training, admission and affiliations.

Mrs. Raymond Pace Alexander [Sadie T. M. Alexander] appears to be the only colored woman admitted to practice in the state of Pennsylvania. She received a B.S. degree from the University of Pennsylvania in 1918, an M.A. degree in Economics from that same institution in 1919 and a Ph.D. degree was awarded Mrs. Alexander from the University of Pennsylvania in 1921. She received her LL.B. degree in 1927 and in 1928 was admitted to practice. From 1921–23 she was the assistant actuary for the North Carolina Mutual Life Insurance company. She is the author of "Standard of Living Among One Hundred Negro Migrant Families of Philadelphia."

Mrs. Gertrude Rush of Des Moines, was admitted to practice in Iowa in 1918 and in that state she now engages in the general practice of law. She is identified with many civic, charitable and educational organizations.

Miss Zanzye Hill, appears to be the only colored woman ever admitted to practice law in the state of Nebraska. She attended the University of Nebraska, receiving an A.B. degree in 1927 and an LL.B. degree in June of 1929. During the existence of the Woodmen of the Union Life Insurance Company of Arkansas, she was employed as junior counsel. She specializes in corporation and real estate law.

Mrs. Lena O. Smith is probably the only woman of color ever admitted to practice in the state of Minnesota. She is engaged in the general practice of law in Minnesota where she maintains a magnificent office in the Palace Building. She graduated from the Northwestern College of Law[1] in Minneapolis and was admitted to practice in the state courts in June, 1921. She is president of the local branch of the N.A.A.C.P., president of the Business and Professional Women's Club and member of the Board of Directors of the Urban League.

Mrs. Ruth Whitehead Whaley was admitted to practice in the state of New York in June 1925. She had attended Livingstone College at Salisbury, North Carolina, receiving an A.B. degree in June 1919. She received an LL.B. degree from Fordham University School of Law, New York, in June 1924. For several years she engaged in the general practice of law in New York and was one of the most outstanding members of the profession. She was an active and vigorous politician. She changed her residence within the past few years and is now practicing in North Carolina.

Mrs. Ann Jones Robinson was also admitted to practice in New York state, receiving her license in April, 1923. Her practice is limited to real estate and such other matters as she can without interference with her position as a teacher in the Frederick Douglass junior high school of New York.

Mrs. Lisle Carter [Eunice Hunton Carter]. Mrs. Carter has an excellent education, having received her A.B. and A.M. degrees from Smith College. She studied law at Fordham University and in 1922 received an LL.B. degree. She is at present actively engaged in the general practice of law in New York. She is a member of the National Business and Professional Women's Club, National Association of College Women and is affiliated with a number of other organizations. She was the candidate on the Republican Fusion Ticket for the Assembly in 1924 and was defeated by a small number of votes. She was recently appointed by Mayor

---

1. The Northwestern College of Law merged into what is today the William Mitchell College of Law in Minneapolis.

Fiorello H. LaGuardia to serve as a member of the Bi-Racial Commission to study conditions in Harlem and she is serving as secretary of this body.

Mrs. Roscoe C. Bruce [Clara B. Bruce], has been admitted to practice in Massachusetts. She received her license in 1926, having prepared for the study of law in various institutions of learning. She attended Howard University, Radcliffe College, Boston University Law School and from this last named school was graduated in 1926. She was editor-in-chief of the Boston University Law Review in 1925–26. At the present time she is the assistant manager of the Dunbar apartment in New York.

Miss Bernice M. Grandison, a graduate of the Portia Law School of Boston, was admitted to practice in Massachusetts in 1927. She engages in such practice as will enable her to continue her duties as a teacher in the public schools of Lynn, Mass. She is a member of the Bar Association of Boston.

Mrs. Carrie Mason has been admitted to practice in the state of Indiana. She received her legal education at Howard University and is at present a school teacher in Gary, Indiana.

Mrs. Virginia Stephens Pendleton,[2] who was admitted to practice in California in 1929 attended University of California, receiving an LL.B. degree in 1929. She had previously received her B.S. degree from that same institution in May, 1924.

Mrs. Zephyr Moore Ramsey, was admitted to the bar in California in 1930. Mrs. Ramsey had been admitted to practice in the state of Missouri in 1925 and was the first colored woman ever allowed the privilege of practicing in the courts of Missouri. She is a graduate of Howard University, receiving her A.B. and LL.B. there. Although a resident of Pasadena, Calif., she is at the present time in Washington, D.C., working for the Government. She is a member of the Blackstone Club of Los Angeles and is also affiliated with the Women's Political Study Club of Pasadena and the Epsilon Sigma Iota Sorority.

Miss Tabytha Anderson has also been admitted to practice in the state of California. She received her legal training at the Hastings College in Calif., and at the Howard University Law School, graduating from the latter institution in 1931. She is engaged in the general practice of law and has recently been elected president of the San Francisco Branch N.A.A.C.P.

Mrs. Isadora A. Letcher has been admitted to practice in the state of Michigan. She is a graduate of Howard University Law School. She is, at present, living in Washington, D.C.

Mrs. L. Marian Poe was admitted to practice law in Virginia in 1925. She, too, was a graduate of Howard University and has the distinction of being the

---

2. For more on Annie Virginia Stephens Coker, *see* Brenda F. Harbin, *Black Women Pioneers in the Law*, 4 THE HISTORICAL REPORTER 6 (Spring 1987) (she is the first black woman admitted to the California bar).

first colored to ever be admitted to practice in Virginia. Prior to her entrance into the active practice of law she had been engaged as a clerk, a stenographer and a bank cashier. She is the president of the Women's Community League and is secretary of the Citizen's Voters League of Newport News, Virginia, in which city she resides.

Mrs. Inez Field Scott of Hampton, Virginia, has also been licensed to practice in Virginia.

Miss Bertha Douglas of Norfolk, Virginia, is another woman of color who has been admitted to practice in the courts of Virginia.

Miss Ollie M. Cooper was admitted to the Bar of the Supreme Court of the District of Columbia, Washington, D.C. in October, 1926. She is a resident of Washington and does not engage in the practice of law. She is the secretary to the Dean of the Howard University School of Law from which school she was graduated. She has been the assistant secretary of the National Bar Association.

Mrs. Thelma D. Ackiss was admitted to practice in the courts of the District of Columbia, Washington, D.C. in 1932. She received her legal training at Howard University, [graduating in 1931]. She is a member of the N.A.A.C.P. and the New Negro Alliance and is a resident of Washington. She is continuing her studies at Howard University working for an M.A. degree.

Mrs. N. K. Christopher. Mrs. Clara Christopher was admitted to practice in the courts of Ohio in 1922. She is a graduate of Baldwin Wallace Law College.[3] For several years, Mrs. Christopher was engaged in the real estate business and later accepted the position as Chief of the Department of Claims and assistant in the legal department of the National Benefit Life Insurance Company at Washington. At that time Mrs. Christopher was said to have been the highest salaried woman of color in the insurance field. At present she is in business with her husband in Cleveland where they conduct a funeral establishment. For this business she received her training at the Cleveland School of Embalming where she was graduated in 1933.

Mrs. Hazel Mountain Walker was licensed to practice in the courts of Ohio in 1921. She received her legal training at the Baldwin Wallace Law College. She has been a teacher in the public schools in Cleveland for many years. She is an active and vigorous politician and at the present time is the president of the Colored Women's Branch of the Democratic League of Ohio. She is a member of the Harlan Bar Association and of the Gilpin Players. For many years she took an outstanding part in the work of the N.A.A.C.P.

Mrs. Louise Pridgeon, (deceased) was licensed to practice in Ohio after her graduation from the Baldwin Wallace Law College in 1922. Mrs. Pridgeon until her death engaged in the general practice of law in Cleveland. She was the

---

3. The Baldwin Wallace Law College is the name of the law school at Case Western Reserve University (hereinafter Baldwin Law College).

founder and for several years the president of the Harlan Law Club, an organization composed of all the colored lawyers of Cleveland.

Miss Jane Edna Hunter was admitted to practice in the courts of Ohio in 1926. She had received her LL.B. degree from the Baldwin Wallace Law College. Miss Hunter is the executive secretary of the Phyllis Wheatley Association of Cleveland, and is a nationally known social worker.

Miss Helen Elsie Austin was admitted to practice law in the courts of Ohio in 1921 and she was also admitted to practice in the courts of Indiana in 1932. Miss Austin received her A.B. degree from the University of Cincinnati and her LL.B. degree from that same institution. She is engaged in the general practice of law and is a member of the executive committee of the N.A.A.C.P. of which organization she serves as chairman of the Legal Redress Committee. She also is a member of the National Society of University Women.

Mrs. Albert Johnson [Mrs. Violet Neatly Anderson Johnson] was the first colored woman to be admitted to the practice of law on examination by the Supreme Court of Illinois. She is a graduate of the Chicago Law School[4] having received her LL.B. degree in 1920. From 1905 to 1920 Mrs. Anderson conducted a Law Reporting Agency and from 1920 until the present time has been engaged in the general practice of law. She has a large clientele and is one of the outstanding members of the Bar. She is the National President of the Zeta Phi Beta Sorority. She has been admitted to practice in the United States District Court, Eastern Division and has also been admitted to practice before the Supreme Court of the United States. She is a member of the Cook County Bar Association and of the National Bar Association.

Mrs. Edward H. Morris [Jessica Morris] (deceased), a graduate of Northwestern University Law School was admitted to practice in the State of Illinois, but never was actively engaged in the profession.

Mrs. Leroy P. Johnson [Mable Johnson], was admitted to practice in the State of Illinois in 1926. She had attended the State Normal College in Alabama, and later enrolled as a student at the Kent College of Law in Chicago, where she received her LL.B. degree. Mrs. Johnson is associated with her husband in the general practice of law, but spends a considerable amount of her time in the field of research. She served successfully for two years as chairman of the committee of management of the Y.W.C.A.

Miss Anna Crisp, was admitted to practice in the State of Illinois in 1926. She attended the State Normal College at Nashville as well as Knoxville College. She later enrolled in the Chicago Law School where she received her LL.B. degree. At the present time she is engaged in the general practice of law as well as acting as a court reporter.

---

4. As result of a merger of two law schools, today this law school is named the Chicago-Kent Law School.

Mrs. Macon Huggins [Alice Huggins], was admitted to practice in the State of Illinois in 1929. She was a graduate of the Chicago Public Schools and the Chicago Normal College. She has been engaged for many years as a teacher in the public schools. In 1926 she received the LL.B. degree from the John Marshall Law School. At the present she is working for the Ph.D. degree in English at Loyola University. She engages in the practice of law and is associated with her husband in business. She is a member of the Cook County Bar Association, the Professional Women's Club and other organizations.

Mrs. Georgia Jones-Ellis was admitted to practice in the State of Illinois in 1925. Mrs. Ellis had attended public schools of St. Louis, Mo. She received an LL.B. degree from John Marshall Law School of Chicago in 1925. She has been employed by the Municipal Court of Chicago where she served for several years in the Court of Domestic Relations. She is now engaged in the general practice of law. Mrs. Ellis has been a candidate on the Republican ticket for membership in the State Legislature. She is the legal advisor of the National Association of Colored Women's Clubs, is a member of the Cook County Bar Association; has held office in the National Bar Association; is a member of the Professional Women's Club and other organizations.

Mrs. Edith Spurlock Sampson was admitted to practice in the State of Illinois in 1927. She received her LL.B. degree from the John Marshall Law School of Chicago in 1925 and was the first woman ever to have an LL.M. degree conferred upon her by Loyola University. She received her LL.M. in 1927. In 1934 she was admitted to practice before the U.S. Supreme Court. Previously she had attended the Meadville Unitarian School, the New York School of Social Work and recently has been enrolled in the classes of the University of Chicago. She has been engaged in the field of Social Work and is at present a member of the staff of the Cook County Juvenile Court. Her practice of law is limited to such matters as do not interfere with her duties at the Juvenile Court. She is vice-president of the Cook County Bar Association; president of the Professional Women's Club; member of the American Association of Social Workers; the Democratic Lawyers Club and other civic organizations.

Mrs. George Pitts [Sophia Boaz Pitts] was in 1923 admitted to practice law in the State of Illinois. Mrs. Pitts is a graduate of Fisk University and later attended Northwestern University and the University of Chicago. She received her legal training at Kent College of Law in Chicago. Mrs. Pitts is a well known social worker and at one time was a member of the staff of the Juvenile Court. She is at present engaged in the general practice of law and takes an active part in Democratic politics. She is a member of the Cook County Bar Association, the Professional Women's Club, the Fisk Club, is secretary of the Illinois Children's Home, an Aid Society Committee and is affiliated with numerous other organizations.

Miss Beulah Wheeler is a [1924] graduate of Iowa University where she received her legal training. She has been admitted to practice in the courts of Kansas and Illinois. For three years before coming to Chicago she practiced law in Leavenworth, Kansas. She now conducts a business in Chicago.

Mrs. Clysses Goodall [Barbara Goodall] was admitted to practice in the State of Illinois in 1930. She had attended school in Texas and later received her legal education at the Chicago Law School where she received her degree. Mrs. Goodall is at present engaged in the general practice of law and is affiliated with numerous civic and social organizations.

Mrs. Ruth Brigerman, was admitted to practice law in the State of Illinois in 1931. She received her legal education at The Chicago Law School from which institution she received a degree. At the present time she is engaged in social work.

The women mentioned in the foregoing review constitute the majority of those colored women who have been licensed to practice law and no doubt there are others whose names have not been included. The writer has attempted to secure information about these others but has been unsuccessful.

Women in the Law

Ollie May Cooper

(1961)

Notwithstanding the victory of women in their fight of emancipation and the enticements and advantages of a career in law, the number of women active in the profession is still unusually small. In 1958 the American Bar Association estimated that of a total of 252,320 lawyers in the United States only 6,350 were women. And in 1960 out of a total of 40,381 students enrolled in 32 American law schools approved by the American Bar Association, only 1,429 of these students were women.

The skepticism with which women have viewed a career in law is not altogether impossible to understand. Despite emancipation, women encountered what might be termed a natural resistance from the men in the profession, based in large measure on the myth of women's inferiority. This attitude was reflected in the admission policies of law schools, many of which did not accept women as students.

Times have changed. Men still joke about women in the profession, but in reality appreciate their worth and welcome them as equals. Law school admission policies no longer discriminate against women.

Howard University School of Law has never excluded women and on the contrary has encouraged their enrollment. In keeping with the university policy against discrimination on the basis of sex, race or religion, Howard was the first law school in the District of Columbia to accept women as students. In fact, Charlotte E. Ray, who is believed to be the first woman ever to be graduated from a university law school, received her degree from Howard in 1872.

Emma M. Gillette [who is white] graduated in 1882 and later was co-founder of the Washington College of Law, now the Washington College of Law of the American University in Washington. Since its founding Howard has had

Washington Afro-American, July 29, 1961, at 6 (Supp.).

a much higher enrollment of women students than most other American law schools. Not only have women attended Howard, but many have achieved the highest scholastic honors and have often been the ranking students in their class.

Have women succeeded as lawyers in professional life? They certainly have. Women trained in the law have distinguished themselves in many fields. Only by way of example one may mention such figures as Sadie T. M. Alexander of Philadelphia who has achieved success as a businesswoman, practicing lawyer and public official; Edith Spurlock Sampson of Chicago, who has served as United States alternate delegate to the United Nations; Florence Allen, who is a federal judge; Jane M. Bolin who is a judge in New York City; and Vel Phillips, who is Democratic committeewoman from Wisconsin.

And what of the women who have recently graduated from Howard Law School? Almost all have embarked upon successful careers in law or law-related fields, in private practice and in government service. High positions even in state government have been filled by women graduates of Howard. The offices of tax assessor of the Virgin Islands, deputy attorney-general of California, assistant attorney general of Missouri either are or have been held by Howard women. Perhaps one of the most encouraging examples of opportunity for young women lawyers is Charlye Farris, a 1953 graduate who was appointed, approximately one year after her graduation, to serve as a county judge in Texas during the absence of the regular judge. Miss Farris was the first colored woman to serve as a judge in the State of Texas. Other recent Howard Law School women graduates are presently staff lawyers in the Department of Justice, the Civil Rights Commission, General Services Administration, Federal Housing Administration and other federal agencies.

No longer should women hesitate to seek a career in the law. Opportunities for colored women in the law are increasing rapidly as the ever widening and brightening horizons for the colored people appear.

A career in the law gives great promise to young women graduating from college, for economic advancement as well as for the achievement of honor and respect in the community.

Forty-five Years a Woman Lawyer

Sadie Tanner Mossell Alexander

(1988)

*F*ORTY-FIVE YEARS AGO ON JUNE 15th, 1927, I graduated from the Law School of the University of Pennsylvania. How well I recall some of my classmates observing, when reading the graduation program, that I had three earned degrees, shouting: "What degree will Sadie get next?" And the response coming loud and clear: "Mother! Mother!" I was not so fortunate as to have their anticipation become an early realization, but grateful that it did come four times thereafter.

In September, 1927, I was notified that I had passed the Pennsylvania Bar, and at my husband's suggestion arranged first to be admitted to the Orphans' Court. However, I made a serious error in deciding to wear a hat. As I stepped to the Bar of the Court, a tipstaff in a loud voice ordered me to "remove that hat." I was humiliated. There I stood, the only woman, with hat in hand. What an introduction to the Philadelphia Bar!

My husband had a large, active practice and needed my services. It never occurred to him or me that I would not join his staff. All of his associates and partners were graduates from either Yale or Harvard. One of his most capable partners, however, objected to my ever being employed and plainly stated: "I can not work with a woman." My husband who had no prejudices based upon sex in particular, nor otherwise, gave this partner the privilege of severing his relationship with the firm or accepting me as an employee, who would, if qualified, become a firm member. The partner remained. Furthermore, as the months passed he began asking me questions about variations in Pennsylvania law and requesting my opinion on a case. I knew I was not going to be the cause of breaking the partnership.

I did not comprehend when I was admitted to the Orphans' Court before

51 SHINGLE 20 (Winter 1988), magazine later renamed as PHILADELPHIA LAWYER.

admission to the other courts, the reason my husband had rushed this admission. However, I soon realized that none of the men liked this practice. It required bookkeeping, not drama and histrionics. There were no jury trials in cases before the Orphans' Court. In 1927, not even a Will contest was tried before a jury.

I also found a backlog of estates, requiring immediate and full attention. I had a most exceptional opportunity afforded me when Judge Thompson of the Orphans' Court called me to his office and stated: "You have a large volume of this work. I want you to learn to do it so well that when a judge sees your name on a backer he will know your pleading is in proper form. Therefore, I have arranged that all your petitions be referred to me. Mr. O'Brien, my tipstaff, will call you every Friday when the conference with the judges has ended and tell you what hour to come to my chambers so that I can discuss your pleadings with you." This magnanimous offer I gratefully accepted. For at least four months, I had the privilege, once a week, of personal tutoring by a master in Orphans' Court law and practice. At the last Friday conference we had, Judge Thompson said: "I'm satisfied that you are ready to go it on your own, but don't fail to come back if you need me." I hope that the character of my work in the courts has been such as fully to indicate the depth of my appreciation of Judge Thompson's concern for me and unselfish contribution to my career as a lawyer.

Only a few months after my admission to the Philadelphia Bar, I was appointed an Assistant City Solicitor, an event of such unusual occurrence in 1927, that it was front page news. There had only been one woman lawyer previously employed by the City Solicitors' office, and the then Hazel Hill Brown, Esquire, was the first and only woman Assistant District Attorney assigned to the now Family Court Division, where she has capably served as a Judge since April 15, 1952. The women lawyers at the Philadelphia Bar were extremely limited in numbers and were in general working as research assistants, brief writers in law firms or banks or for the Attorney General's office.

I considered myself most fortunate to have Orphans' Court cases assigned to me by my husband's firm, in which I was privileged to argue appeals not only before the full Orphans' Court bench but the State Supreme Court and the United States District Court.[1] This was indeed unusual. Women lawyers in 1927, and for years thereafter, prepared inventories, inheritance tax returns accounts, petitions for distribution and presented the same to the auditing judge. Except for about two other women and myself in private practice, I know of not one who was granted the privilege to argue her case before the full Bench or an appellate court, a privilege then reserved to male members of the firm.

However, despite substantial progress since I first started in practice, we still have among the members of the Bar a limited number of males who can-

1. *See, e.g.,* Coley's Estate, 304 Pa. 193, 155 A. 488 (1931).

not accept a woman as an opponent. As soon as they ascertain a woman practitioner represents their opponent, they begin laying roadblocks, such as absolutely unnecessary interrogations, preliminary objections, depositions, *et cetera, et cetera,* all of which information opposing counsel is willing to give, substantiated by photocopies of the evidence. I recall telling a male opponent in an equity hearing for a preliminary injunction who when his motion was refused, followed me into the corridor, and actually cursed me. My reply was: "I should give you my skirt and you give me your pants." My hope is that it is evident today that we have the same staying power as our male legal counterparts and that pants or skirts are both irrelevant.

There is so much more to tell . . . The most attractive part of City Hall to me today is the presence of four women judges, appointed to the Common Pleas bench in January 1972, by Governor Milton Shapp. Each one of them is a beautiful woman, well trained, experienced in the practice of law and a welcome addition to a previously all male Common Pleas Court. Judge Hazel H. Brown and Judge Juanita Kidd Stout [black women] have established enviable records which sets a standard for the judiciary. I dare predict that our four recent women appointees will set a standard their male colleagues will find it difficult to equal.

Jet-Propelled into the Law

Mahala Ashley Dickerson

(1995)

I WAS JET-PROPELLED INTO LAW SCHOOL. I had no legal women role models in Montgomery, Alabama, where I was born in 1912. For me, the nearest persons to role models would have been Abraham Lincoln and Clarence Darrow. No particular person encouraged me to become a lawyer, and since the field of law was rather dismal at the time, there were many who thought I made a bad choice. I was graduated *cum laude* from Fisk University in 1935, and was awarded my Phi Beta Kappa key fifty years later as this group did not recognize black colleges at the time I graduated. I also was graduated *cum laude* from the Howard University School of Law in 1948.

My greatest stimulus in law school came from Professors James Madison Nabrit Jr., James Wesley Bussey, Spottswood W. Robinson III, Howard Jenkins Jr., and George E. C. Hayes, who were all black.

Female students were treated with disdain if they were higher achievers and tolerated if they were sweet and mediocre. Sherman W. Smith, James L. Calhoun, and George N. Hilburn were some of my favorite study buddies. Juanita Kidd Stout, who left after two years at Howard, and I did most of our studying together.

Some of the male students did not show the proper respect in my opinion to Professor Jane C. Marshall Lucas. Professor Lucas was a law instructor during my last two years at the Law School. She is probably the first full-time woman law teacher at Howard University. She held the rank of instructor. If my memory serves me correctly, Lucas taught me a course then called Bills and Notes. She tried to organize the females together and I recall her attempts to organize the "Portia Club," a law club for women students. Miss Ollie May Cooper, a black woman lawyer, was always willing to give us advice as to the kinds of problems we would encounter as young attorneys.

An original submission to this volume.

During the time when I was in law school certain landmark cases were decided, such as Hurd et al. v. Hodge et al., Urciolo et al. v. Same,[1] dealing with restrictive covenants, Morgan v. Commonwealth of Virginia,[2] dealing with segregation in interstate travel, and Sipuel v. Board of Regents of the State of Oklahoma,[3] dealing with segregation in higher education. Thurgood Marshall and other attorneys arguing the cases would try them out on the law students at Howard. Such arguments were called "dry runs." Thurgood Marshall and other great civil rights lawyers about to argue cases before the U.S. Supreme Court would allow the students to play devil's advocate and critique their proposed arguments aimed at various justices then sitting on the Court. It also was inspiring to be able to visit the Supreme Court and to study at the Library of Congress.

I did not think it was even noteworthy that I became the first black woman attorney in the state of Alabama in 1948, with the able assistance of my mentor Arthur Davis Shores, one of two black lawyers in the state of Alabama. I was saddened by the fact that I was forced to leave my native state to obtain an education elsewhere, which cost me and my family more financially and diminished my contacts with classmates, who would become the future power brokers of Alabama.

As a woman lawyer, I was well received by the black population of Alabama. The white lawyers were mostly courteous. On my first appearance in court, I was ordered to the back of the courtroom by an armed sheriff, but left the courtroom instead of going to the back of this segregated hall of justice. Two white female attorneys took up the matter and introduced me to the sheriff and informed him that I was licensed to practice in the courts of Alabama. He later apologized. The judge whose courtroom I had been in came to my office, leaving apologies for what had happened with my brother-in-law, Dr. A. C. Dungee, whose office adjoined mine, but the courthouse seating remained segregated, although I was not asked to sit in the back anymore.

I had many clients but took another plunge into marriage and moved to Indianapolis after three years of practicing in Alabama. My second marriage was to an established black attorney in Indianapolis, Frank R. Beckwith, with whom I practiced for a year. Thereafter, I opened my own office. I was the first black female to practice in the city of Indianapolis and the second one to practice in the state of Indiana. In 1958, after a visit to Alaska, I decided to remain in the state and homestead. In 1959, I became the first black attorney in the state of Alaska. It was challenging and great fun and continues to be.

Many honors have been bestowed upon me and sometimes I wonder why.

---

1. 162 F.2d 233 (D.C. Cir. 1947).

2. 328 U.S. 373 (1946).

3. 332 U.S. 631 (1948).

My assignment as first black president of the National Association of Women Lawyers in 1982 was quite an arduous one. I felt my greatest accomplishment there was the fact that I had tried for many years of membership to convince them not to retaliate against the males for having kept women out of the mainstream of the American Bar Association. The year that I became president was the year we took in our first male attorneys.

In July, 1994, I was thrilled to be invited to Perdido Beach as the convocation speaker for the Alabama Bar Association. Most of the members of the Bar were minors at the time that I was practicing in Alabama. One retiring judge, age 59, told me how his lawyer father had brought him to juvenile court once, specifically to hear me argue a case. When asked which luncheon I wished to attend at the Alabama Bar Association's annual meeting, I selected the University of Alabama luncheon as I felt in a way that should have been my alma mater.

I have never regretted choosing the law. I have had a long, busy, fulfilling 46 years of practice and I will let nature take care of my retirement. I still enjoy what I do so much that I could not think of anything else to replace it. I have described myself as attorney for the hopeless, borrowing the title from a book I once read on the life of Clarence Darrow in which he was described as "Attorney for the Damned." The law is an excellent field for women. More and more women are entering the profession and doing quite well at it.

I had much help and encouragement from friends, family, and strangers. I merely did what I was jet-propelled to do. I have been greatly humbled by receiving such honors as Woman of the Year from Zeta Phi Beta back in Alabama in 1950, Mother of the Year from the Federation of Colored Women's Clubs in Anchorage in 1968, NAACP Freedom Award in 1982 in Anchorage, the B'hai Service to Humanity Award in 1986, the Distinguished Citizens Award from the Kappa Alpha Psi Fraternity in 1992, and an Honorary Doctor of Laws degree from the University of Alaska in 1994. I have advised friends and family that there will be no need for a memorial service as I have been given my honors while alive.

I have one appendage. I regretted Thurgood Marshall's death and wish that we would have had a less conservative justice than Clarence Thomas appointed to replace him. One day, another person of Thurgood Marshall's caliber, perhaps a black woman, will grace the Court.

Sheer Determination Brought
Me Through

GLENDORA MCILWAIN PUTNAM

(1994)

*W*HAT INSPIRED ME TO GO TO LAW SCHOOL? . . . I selected Boston University because it was near home and I could commute to it. In addition, it was accredited and admitted women, as Harvard did not at that time. Since I did not know whether I would stay in Massachusetts, I wanted to go to an accredited law school. There was one other black woman there who was in my class. I have forgotten her maiden name, but she became Victoria Harris, having married right after graduation . . .

I had a dismal experience at Boston University principally because they turned the law school into a warehouse. I entered in 1945 right at the end of World War II. [Soldiers returning from the war] were using the GI Bill for graduate school. Boston University let them in in droves and flunked them out in droves using true/false exams. It was a very stressful time. It was nothing to be in a class of 200 students. They lost a lot of good people and passed a lot of duds. Good true/false test takers could make it; others could not. It was not an enjoyable educational experience. So, we mostly made lawyers out of ourselves. Sheer determination brought me through.

I was admitted to the bar in Massachusetts only, in 1949. Getting started was very difficult. I think being a woman was the biggest barrier. I never got beyond that barrier to test the race barrier but from what black men were facing I suspect I would have fared no better. Once they discovered I could not type, they made clear that that was what women were hired to do.

My first real job was with the father of a law school classmate. I was responsible for supplementary process work, which I hated. I went to law school to help people, not to take away the jalopy some poor guy needed to get to work

---

An original submission to this volume.

to earn the money to pay the bill we were trying to collect. My boss and I did not hit it off because he said I was too soft.

Sad to say, I had no male or female lawyer role models before I went to law school. I would say that my first female role model was Constance Baker Motley, but that did not come until the mid-1950s when I began attending NAACP Legal Defense Fund Legal Institutes and the NAACP national conventions. There I found my role models in Thurgood Marshall and the attorneys from across the country working with them. They taught me so much about making the law a tool for civil rights advancement . . .

Now, for my tenure as an Assistant Attorney General of Massachusetts. Edward Brooke was the first to appoint me to that position and I was the first black woman attorney to occupy the post. Edward Brooke and I were classmates at Boston University Law School and kept up with each other. I worked in all his campaigns, two for state representative and one for secretary of state before he ran for Attorney General and won. We had worked on legal redress issues for the NAACP so he knew my interest. He had a civil rights division in the Attorney General's office and offered me the opportunity of my life, to work on the issues I went to law school to tackle. I did not become chief right away, but sometime into our tenure he asked me to head the division.

There had been women in other administrations, but only one in each administration. Brooke gave many women the experience during his tenure as Attorney General,[1] including one other black female attorney.

Most of the work I did, I did as counsel to the Massachusetts Commission Against Discrimination. They had no attorneys at that time, so the Attorney General had to represent them throughout the division. I did their litigation, drafted legislation to strengthen the laws, drafted opinions, counseled hearing officers, assisted with strategy, and gave general legal advice.

Then, I was asked by the Governor to chair the Commission and was charged with having to take the advice I had been giving . . . In 1977 I joined the Massachusetts Housing Finance Agency as its Equal Opportunity Officer where I could put all my experiences together to make the laws, case decisions, and regulations work. I retired from there in 1988 when I decided to spend full time completing my second term as national president of the YWCA of the USA.[2]

---

1. Brooke was elected to the U.S. Senate from Massachusetts in 1966.
2. *Retiree Putnam's Calling was Civil Rights,* MASS. LAWYERS WKLY, Feb. 18, 1991, at 29.

Forty Years a Lawyer

Veva Izelle Young

(1990)

*A*FTER STUDYING ETHICS AND RELIGION, I felt there was a kinship between the law of God and the law of man. My love for the law was further heightened by the courses in government I had taken in undergraduate school, where I became familiar with U.S. Supreme Court decisions, particularly in the field of constitutional law.

I always wanted to attend Howard University, but our finances did not allow it. There were three Youngs in college at the time. Because of segregation, Tennessee, my home state, did not allow us to attend the professional schools in our state, so I moved to Washington, D.C., where I worked in the day and attended the law school at night in 1944. Sometime during that period, my state passed legislation to pay tuition of nonwhites who wanted to attend professional schools out of state. So the state of Tennessee paid my tuition for the next two years, allowing me to graduate in the law class of 1947.

For the first year or so [of my law school days], there were not many distractions as all the boys were in the army, so there was not much to do but study, which was a full-time job. We paid the regular student activity fee, but the undergraduates did not want us to participate fully in the political process, especially "voting." But we managed to have fun on the weekends when we partied and studied.

Some of the professors knew how to impart their knowledge of a subject to the students. Among them were Professors William Henry Hastie, George E. C. Hayes, and Howard Jenkins Jr. I do not think that I had any favorites; however, I felt that some of the professors really knew the subject matter, but did not know how to impart it to others. My biggest disappointment was in criminal law.

I have always had a private practice. Looking back over forty years, I would

---

An original submission to this volume.

now advise all law school graduates to get a government job for about five years. I understand the experience is invaluable, while a private practice is somewhat circumscribed. I was fortunate that in 1948 I went with a law firm that did work for four black corporations, i.e., Illinois/Service Federal Savings and Loan Association, Unity Mutual Life Insurance Company, Metropolitan Mutual Assurance Company, and Victory Life Insurance Company. Our firm delivered good legal services. In the early 1980s, Ford Motor Company asked us to handle its Workman's Compensation work, but we had to turn it down. We could not get a black lawyer who was versed in compensation laws to come into the office . . .

Most of my classmates and women who were in law school took jobs while building a practice: Frankie Muse Freemen became a city attorney in St. Louis, and then was appointed to the U.S. Civil Rights Commission. Charlotte Pinkett, Josephine Anderson, Mahala Beckwith (Mahala Ashley Dickerson), and Mabel Dole Haden became teachers.[1] Mabel Dole Haden presently handles personal injury work.

Most of the women lawyers in Chicago, black and white, take jobs while building a practice. Most of the women judges had jobs in the city, state, or federal government where they became known to the political powers who slated them for judgeships. The rest of us are unsung and unknown unless we get a high profile case and get on television. This is also true of many white males who are judges. Their training ground is the city Corporation Counsels Office, states' attorneys office and the U.S. Attorney's Office.

In the past ten years, the climate has changed. Many of the large white firms are hiring black men and women, and the private practitioners are getting some of the city and state business because of black politicians. In Chicago, most of the black women lawyers with white firms practice motions court law, corporation law, and domestic relations law. Two or three of the black women lawyers are now gaining a foothold in criminal law, and there are about six administrative law judges.

Today, far too many women are looking for security and do not know the thrill of working hard to keep an office open.

---

1. All of these women became lawyers.

Lawyers Are Leaders in the Community

Jean Murrell Capers

(1994)

I AM EIGHTY-THREE years of age!
I retired from the Bench in 1986 simply because I was too old (seventy-three years) to stay there and I was ill, also. Ohio has the constitutional limit of seventy years for its judges since all are elected to a term of six years. One can continue, after retirement, to return as a Visiting Judge but I was too ill; the study of the law had changed so radically since I had been a student thus the philosophy of the law of the "lawyers" who came before me was somewhat of a source of irritation because of the lack of preparation of too many of them.

Because I had worked ever since I was seventeen years of age, I had to be involved in the law in a way that demanded response from me—not on my terms but to meet a deadline—and so, I returned to the very limited practice of the law: probate, family, and juvenile. I do not do any trial work since it is too stressful for my age. I shall retire, fully, from the law in September, 1995, having completed fifty years in the law as of July 17, 1995.

I would love to pen my reasons for entering the study of law since I taught school before deciding to go to law school. I graduated from Cleveland Law School because it was a night law school. I had to work during the day. My reasons for going to law school were far different from the reasons students attend law school today. Today, students are going to law school to get a *job*. I went to law school in order to be of broader service to the *people* since all of their ills were founded in the law.

I have been a member of the National Bar Association (NBA) since I graduated and passed the Bar of Ohio in 1945 and, of course, later became a Life Member. It was during the annual NBA meeting where I met Charles Hamilton Houston, William Henry Hastie, Sadie and Raymond Pace Alexander and Euclid

---

An original submission to this volume.

Taylor . . . I also joined the National Council of Negro Women, where I met five outstanding black woman lawyers: Georgia Jones Ellis, the first Negro woman assistant Corporation Counsel of Chicago; Edith Spurlock Sampson; Cora Brown from Detroit, a State Senator; H. Elsie Austin, Ohio's first Negro female Assistant Attorney General (1936); and Leona Pouncey Thurman, of Kansas City, Missouri.

We would not have been the first city of any size to have had a Negro mayor had it not been for me. It was my idea to draft a Negro for mayor of Cleveland, Ohio. Carl Stokes was elected as a result of having been *drafted,* not having presented himself for a candidate. He did not know anything about the effort that was being put forth for his nomination since he was not told. I called together ten people, most of whom had no experience in political organization work; taught them what a draft was; showed them how a Negro could not win running one-on-one with a candidate but would have an excellent chance . . . if he were the third candidate in the race . . . Stokes had been in the General Assembly for six months when we selected him. I wrote the material for the draft petition. Had I not been a lawyer, I couldn't have done this. Lawyers must be the leaders in the community; a leader cannot lead from behind.

Law Teacher, Lawyer and Judge

MARGARET AUSTIN HAYWOOD

(1993)

I TAUGHT AT THE ROBERT H. TERRELL Law School for five years before it closed around 1951–52. My husband was a member of my class that I was teaching—that is, he became my husband afterwards. After he graduated, he was a government employee, he left his job with the government, and we had a partnership with the law practice. That lasted thirteen years. Just coincidentally, or incidentally, that ended because my husband somehow couldn't adjust to the idea that I was making more money. Which is only natural—and I couldn't convince him that I didn't regard it as my money—it was our money—we can forget that issue and just concentrate on the facts. Anyway, that was something we were never able to overcome.

I taught Wills and Administration. [When Professor] Augustus W. Gray . . . became ill, he asked me to take over his class. I taught Personal Property—I had another excellent [black professor] in [Real] Property—Philip W. Thomas. I also taught Ethics [and Insurance]. Louis R. Mehlinger, who died in the last few years, at something over a hundred years old, was one of my favorite teachers, and I happened to be one of his favorite students. I guess because I was working then in a law office, I could always recite the jurat or an affirmation, so I sort of became his star pupil . . .

I have always been very strict about the matter of ethics. I remember an incident about a lawyer of my acquaintance; he had a secretary and he paid her an amount of money that was less than what would be a salary, because he allowed her to take in typing and use equipment in the office, charge and retain the money she got for that, and she was supposed to make the rest of her salary. I guess he was struggling—there were times when she didn't get paid her salary on Saturday, when she was supposed to be paid. There would be this terrible

---

Hon. Margaret A. Haywood, 27 NEW ENGLAND LAW REVIEW 613 (1993).

conflict because she would be sitting in his office on Saturday, waiting for him to come back, and he wouldn't be coming because he didn't have her money. Something about the ethics came up in a discussion about that between me and another lawyer. He said, "The trouble with you is that you're too ethical." And I said, "What's too—how can you be too ethical? You're either ethical or unethical."

My father was a public accountant. I didn't have to worry about finding office space when I left Charles Houston's firm. I decided to open my law office in the same office where my father had accounting services. Because my father was not a lawyer, he couldn't be a partner with me, so I took over the ownership of the accounting service, and made him manager of that. From then on, it was Austin Haywood Audit Service that was being operated by my father, and a law practice by myself. I was also teaching then at Terrell Law School.

I practiced mostly in the District. I've had maybe a case, now and then, in nearby Virginia, maybe a case, now and then, in the state of Maryland. I was admitted on motion to the [U.S.] District Court for the District of Maryland, but had only one case there. I did not feel that I could stretch myself to three jurisdictions. There are a lot of lawyers who do maybe two jurisdictions. But I didn't seek to establish any practice, and was not admitted to any Bars, outside the District of Columbia . . .

I am never going to be quite sure how I got to be a judge. Well, that's very interesting. I did apply for the position at the Juvenile Court. Marjorie McKenzie Lawson had been appointed.[1] My objective was to be the first Negro woman judge in the District of Columbia. When Marjorie Lawson got that job, I wasn't going to be the first, and I wasn't particularly interested. I thoroughly enjoyed the practice. I had a general practice, I had a lot of family practice, I had a lot of probate work. Although I knew better, my clients thought I was the only lawyer in Washington—and the best. So, I was having a wonderful time.

But apparently there were others interested in my becoming a judge, and efforts were made on my behalf. At the time, we didn't have a commission that nominates to the President as we have now. The [U.S.] Attorney General was the person who made the recommendation to the President. Apparently the Attorney General was informed who I was and what I was doing. He sent my name to the President. The Women's Bar Association, at a point before he sent the nomination, sent a committee to sit down with him and discuss me, which I'm

---

1. Lawson was a 1939 law graduate of the Robert H. Terrell Law School. In 1962, President John F. Kennedy nominated and the U.S. Senate confirmed Lawson to serve a ten year term on the newly organized Juvenile Court of the District of Columbia. *See* 108 Cong. Rec. 20092 (1962); *Chief Judge Morris Miller and Judge Lawson Sworn In*, 90 The DAILY WASH. LAW REP. 1659, Oct. 19, 1962 (also includes biographical information). Judge Lawson is the first black woman nominated by a president for a judicial post requiring confirmation by the U.S. Senate. She served in this post for three years.

sure was also very helpful. I think that the people who made a direct approach to the Attorney General were really supporting my getting appointed. The reason I say—it had to be that people wanted me, because the policy was then unspoken, but it seemed that people who contributed to the political party got the appointments. I was too poor, I didn't do that much contributing, so I'm sure it wasn't my money . . . I was a member of the Executive Council for the United Church of Christ, which had meetings of the Executive Council twice a year. In an April meeting, in New York City, I got a call from someone saying my name was in the paper as having been one of sixteen sent to the President. After that, the process of getting ready for confirmation hearings—submitting all the financial data and a copy of every speech [that I had] ever made, [and an] interview with the FBI . . .

Interestingly enough, some people don't know it, but before you get to the stage of that public hearing, you have already taken an oath, and said all the things that they want to know. When they have that public hearing, that's a total waste of money, as far as I'm concerned, because they already know everything about you. They already know what you have to say. You've said it under oath, so you're already vulnerable to any misstatements. Which is why I don't understand the crucifixion of Clarence Thomas, although it was pretty clear in that there were some things that were said publicly. It seems that the FBI had not been told some of those things that were testified to. But that's beside the point. Anyway, in my case, that process went on from April to July. The hearings were in June, and I actually was confirmed about June 30th, and sworn in on the 21st of July of 1972. . . .

Some Recollections of My Career

Constance Baker Motley

(1988)

I WANT TO THANK YOU FOR coming out to see this "all girls show." You know we're running against heavy competition. There is the antiques show next door, I gather, and then there is that "all male show"[1] out of Washington.

I trust that you have noted that all of the speakers who have preceded me have one constitutional gripe, so to speak, but I have two. I am supposed to tell you about some of my personal experiences over the last forty years as a black and a woman in the legal profession but let me note first that during that period I have spent most of my time trying to decide who is in the good guy camp and who is in the bad guy camp. As a result, my view of the world is that men fall into two categories, the good guys and the bad guys.

Now the one thing that most people have been curious about regarding my career and have always asked me about is, how I happened to study law. What made me decide to become a lawyer? That's a difficult question really because it is a very complicated question. But let me try to simplify it again for you. Let me say that my becoming a lawyer was the result of the commitment of one of the good guys. When I graduated from New Haven High School in 1939—those of you who are as old as I am remember that this Nation was trying to pull itself out of a depression and there was not much by way of opportunity for black people.

I became active in local community affairs and began attending adult meetings. As you see, I am very tall and at age fifteen I could pass for twenty. At age fifteen, I was president of the New Haven Youth Council and secretary of the New Haven Adult Council. I appeared at a meeting one night at a community center which had been built in New Haven for black people by a man whose

J. Law and Society 35 (1988).

1. Iran-Contra Affair Hearings.

name was Clarence Blakeslee. Mr. Blakeslee was a very successful businessman and one of the things he did with his money was to aid black people and others to secure an education. He was concerned that the community house which he had built was not being used by the black people in New Haven. So he called a meeting to try to find out what could be done to get black people to participate in this facility that he had built for them. When I appeared at the meeting, I had graduated from high school about a year before. I said that I thought the problem was that the board of directors of the community center did not have any black people on it and therefore black people were not really concerned. All the leading black people in the town who were there were very annoyed with me for having brought up this very delicate subject at this public meeting. Mr. Blakeslee was not. (You have to remember that this was the Fall of 1940.) The next day he asked the director of the community center to have me come to his office to see him. I went there and Mr. Blakeslee said to me "How come you're not in college?" He said "I looked up your high school record and I see that you graduated with honors." I said "Well, Mr. Blakeslee, I don't have money to go to college." He said "Well, I'd be glad to pay for your college education, what would you like to do?" I said to him, "I'd like to study law." He said to me, "Well I don't know much about women and law but if that's what you want to do, I'm ready to pay for it."

I went home and told my parents this story. They didn't much believe it. But they didn't oppose it. They had never encouraged me to become a lawyer. That was not in their dreams for me. They thought I should be a hairdresser. I even thought I should be an interior decorator when I was in the eighth grade. But anyway, I went off to college in February 1941. I graduated from New York University in October 1943 with a bachelor's degree in economics. Thereafter, I was admitted to Columbia Law School. When I got there in February 1944, it was against the background of the fact that the dean of the law school had earlier voted against the admission of women to the law school. In that atmosphere the few women that were there nevertheless survived and graduated. When I graduated in 1946, you would not have been able to find a single person ready to bet twenty-five cents that I would be successful in the legal profession. I didn't believe it either. But the problem with us was that we could not foresee then, as we cannot foresee now, that post-war America would be dramatically changed by two revolutions which would carry blacks and women into the mainstream of American life.

Just before I graduated from Columbia Law School, I was fortunate enough to get a job as a law clerk on the staff of the NAACP Legal Defense and Educational Fund. The chief counsel was Thurgood Marshall. And there was another one of the good guys, because if it had not been for Thurgood Marshall's liberal view of how women probably ought to have the same chance as men to become lawyers, I probably would not be standing here today telling you about my career. Having joined that staff in 1945, I was on the ground floor of the civil rights revolution as it has come to be known. Because we were a small staff and it was not very fashionable in those days to be working on civil rights, I got an opportunity that few lawyers graduating from Columbia Law School with me have had an opportunity to do and that is actually to try major cases, take appeals to courts of appeal, and to argue in the United States Supreme Court.

In those very early days our work entailed creating the legal theories on which we would have to win our cases. We became legal craftsmen in that respect. As you know, our early work in civil rights involved segregation in education which culminated in the *Brown*[2] decision in 1954.

During the course of my work with the NAACP Legal Defense and Educational Fund, I traveled around the country trying school desegregation cases and other kinds of desegregation cases. One of the early cases I appeared in as a trial lawyer was a case in Mississippi involving the equalization of black teachers' salaries in 1949.[3] I remember that case very well because the local newspaper had a big story that day when the trial began to the effect that there were two Negro lawyers from New York who were going to try the case and one of them was a woman. The courthouse was packed; not only because this was the first case in this century in which blacks in Mississippi sought to attack the establishment and to try to end segregation but because, as the local newspaper said, here was this Negro woman lawyer from New York.

Among others, I represented James Meredith in his long fight to enter the University of Mississippi,[4] Charlayne Hunter and Hamilton Holmes in their fight to enter the University of Georgia[5] and many other cases of that kind. One of the things I remember about my career in the 1950s and early 1960s is being the only woman in the courtroom. I think on one occasion in the Fifth Circuit there was a woman, a patent lawyer, an elderly woman who argued a case. In the period 1949 to 1964, I tried school desegregation and other cases in eleven southern states and the District of Columbia and in that time I saw only one woman argue a case in the Fifth Circuit.

As I've indicated, the opportunity which I got to actually try cases, to argue appeals, and to argue cases in the United States Supreme Court led to my future career. In 1964, I was elected to the New York State Senate . . . I was the first black woman to sit in the New York State Senate. There was one woman who preceded me and was there for a brief period of time, a white woman, but I was the first black woman in the New York State Senate. My stay there was very brief, February 1964 to February 1965, when I was elected president of the Bor-

---

2. Brown v. Bd. of Educ., 347 U.S. 483 (1954).
3. Bates v. Batte, 187 F.2d 142 (5th Cir. 1951), *cert. den.* 342 U.S. 815 (1951).
4. Meredith v. Fair, 202 F. Supp. 224 (S.D. Miss. 1962), *rev'd*, 305 F.2d 343 (5th Cir. 1962).
5. Holmes v. Danner, 191 F. Supp. 394 (M.D. Ga. 1961). *See also* Charlayne Hunter-Gault, *The Lives They Lived: Hamilton E. Holmes,* N.Y. Times, Dec. 31, 1995, at 24.

ough of Manhattan. I remember that at our farewell dinner in the Senate, which they had every year, one of my colleagues came over to me and said, "How have you enjoyed your stay here in the Senate?" I said, "Oh, very well." And he said, "You remember me don't you, you know my name?" I said, "Not really." He said, "How come?" He said, "I spoke to you before." I said, "That's because all you guys look alike to me." There were only two black males in the New York State Senate at that time, both of whom became New York State Supreme Court Justices, one in Brooklyn and one in the Bronx.

Well, as I said, shortly after that I was elected president of the Borough of Manhattan. In that position I was the only woman on the New York City Board of Estimate. Now that's a peculiar New York City institution and don't ask me to explain it but the long and short of it is that until last year we have not had another woman to be president of any borough in the City of New York.[6]

In 1966, as a result of my work in the civil rights field, I was appointed to the United States District Court for the Southern District of New York by President Johnson—the first woman and the first black. Thurgood Marshall had been appointed in 1961 to serve on the Court of Appeals for the Second Circuit.

I remember after being appointed going out to Berkeley, California to attend a school for new federal judges. At that meeting the chairman of the group, who was a federal judge, whose name I have forgotten—it's just as well—he introduced each new judge at the meeting. In doing so, he told those assembled about how great each new judge was, how each had distinguished himself in the law. When it came to introducing me, he said simply that I had been on the Board of United Church Women, and I had been on the Board of the YWCA, and that was it. Former Supreme Court Justice Tom Clark, who was co-chairman of the meeting, grabbed the microphone and said, "Just a minute Mr. Chairman, I would like to say something about Mrs. Motley.[7] She has appeared in our court and argued, I don't know, twenty cases." I said, "No, it's only ten." But anyway after that little session we were having lunch together and he said to me that he had been earlier that day in the locker room after he had a game of golf with some of the other men and he overheard the conversation in the locker room and this had to do with the appointment of Shirley Hufstedler to the Ninth Circuit. And he said to me these men were just running this poor woman down. He said "You know what I said to them, I said do any of you know this woman?" And, he said, "Of course none of them did."

When I was appointed in 1966 there were only four other women serving on the federal bench. One of these was Sarah Hughes in Texas, the other was Burnita Matthews in the District of Columbia, the other was Florence Allen who

---

6. New York City as you know is composed of five boroughs: Manhattan or New York County, Kings County (Brooklyn), Bronx County, Queens County, and Richmond County (Staten Island).

7. He called me Mrs. Motley because that is how he addressed me when I argued ten cases before the United States Supreme Court while he was there.

was a Court of Appeals judge on the Sixth Circuit, and the other was Mary Donlon who was on the Customs Court. I was the fifth woman appointed. There was tremendous opposition to my appointment, not only from southern Senators but from other federal judges, but I finally made it through the Senate. I was nominated January 25, 1966 but not confirmed until August 1966, thanks to Senator Eastland of Mississippi. I have managed to survive twenty years and four months as the chief judge of our court. I am now a senior judge and I hope to continue in that position for some time to come.

We now have, I understand, about sixty women on the federal bench, most of whom were appointed by President Carter when he was President some time ago. What I think we really need now is an affirmative action program for women. We are always ruling on somebody else's affirmative action program, but I think that the reality is that although women have made tremendous progress in the legal profession there is not going to be much change without an affirmative action program in the federal courts.

I am personally pleased by the amount of progress which we have seen in the last twenty years. I remember when I first went on the bench in New York women were not hired in the U.S. Attorney's Office on the criminal side. They were limited to the civil side and then I think there were only a couple of women at that time. Now it seems to me every time I look up I see another little girl who is going to try a great big Mafia case that some said could not be done by a woman twenty years ago. I think I have license to say *little girl*, but I know a judge who got in trouble for that in a New York State court. It is true that there has been a tremendous change and I expect that, as some have indicated, it is going to be largely a woman's profession in the next century. I think if we are going to see any real change in the federal bench soon we are going to have to get after the United States Senators and the President, who appoint federal judges, to get them involved in some kind of affirmative action. . . .

The Power of Black Women

The power of black women is unmeasured and untold. That power has its origin in slavery: it is the power of self defense, personal survival, and defense of family, sometimes using the law as a means to achieve this end. As her stories are unearthed, explained, and asserted in a legal framework, it is indisputable that the black woman has been a potent force throughout her sojourn in America. In part 2 we learn more about how black women lawyers wield their power and confront the legal culture that subordinates them.

We learn from these writings that black women lawyers have used the Constitution and the political process to wield power and to redefine their legal, socioeconomic status in America. To enhance their political strengths and influence, black women have often combined with white women, and vice versa, as common allies to challenge gender- and race-based bias. However, because black women have not always been invited as equal partners in the broader movement to liberate women, they have wielded their power and articulated their interests through black women's organizations.

Women Lawyers Must Balk Both Color and Sex Bias

Ruth Whitehead Whaley

(1949)

THERE IS STILL CONSIDERABLE interest in the situation of a Negro woman who is a lawyer.

Obviously, she must have the educational training required of all lawyers, must pass the same Bar examination for a license to practice law. As a Negro, she is subject to all the illogical inequalities which inevitably accompany the lack of full integration of Negroes into our American life.

But interest really centers around the questions (1) what more if anything does "being a lawyer" require of a Negro woman than it does of any other person who is a lawyer, (2) is it more difficult for her, (3) can she work at her profession with no greater handicaps than those suffered by a Negro man? . . .

More is required of a Negro woman who is a lawyer by her colleagues, the courts and the community. This performance "over and beyond the call of duty" is not generally a conscious requirement on their part. It is the penalty usually exacted from a minority or from pioneers, and Negro women, [who] are a minority among lawyers. History may well record as a pioneer every Negro woman who in the year, 1949, is a lawyer.

In the public mind, lawyers are divided thus: (1) Men—(a) White—Negro; (2) Women—(b) White—Negro. She is the last in this divisive thinking to enter the field, her number is still comparatively few. In 1930, there were about 25 Negro women in the United States who were lawyers. New York City and Chicago have the largest number. There are 12–15 in New York City. Less than one-half of them are engaged in active practice. Today, there are less than 150 in the entire United States, of whom less than 100 actually practice law. It is of this latter small group I write . . .

All women who are lawyers must meet the competition of their male col-

---

THE NEW YORK AGE, Oct. 29, 1949, at 27.

leagues and occasionally one forgets to be gallant in his thinking and the overlooked errors of a male colleague become the colossal blunders of the woman.

Because the Court has for these centuries been a male precinct, no woman
can afford the usual deficiencies in performance else she is likely to receive its
silent contempt for its patronizing forbearance. Negro women are more easily
identified, they are less in number and more recent invaders.

The community accepts her adventurous role but scrutinizes closely
whether she is making her normal contribution to it as a woman. In addition,
she receives more calls for community service than her male colleagues because
her number is few, and where courtesy or need seems to call for the name and
presence of a woman and also a representative of the legal profession, this need
is ofttimes combined by naming the woman who is a lawyer.

Her clients have a tendency to accept her on a more highly individualized
basis than even the usual selective method between attorney and client, but once
she has served them satisfactorily, they are bound to her by "hoops of steel" and
whatever their prior or general opinion of women as lawyers, her clients are sure
that "she," their lawyer is "an exception." (This thinking is generally incident to
minority representation.)

Among Negro women who are lawyers as is true of white women, the majority have not ventured into the active practice of the law or if they did, have
not remained long. They are to be found in various governmental positions in
the fields of social work and teaching with a scattering representation in business and other vocations.

Their leadership and general participation is impressed upon political and
civic groups.

Women generally suffer from lack of the numerous opportunities for ca-
sual meetings with potential clients which their male colleagues enjoy, therefore,
their public meetings are a necessity and because she has not yet ceased to be
Exhibit A. The Negro woman has opportunity for and abundance of [such
meetings], which if wisely used and fairly distributed over the various areas of
community life are rewarding to her as an individual and as a lawyer. That their
use and her service therein given may deprive her of much of her leisure time
and compel her to drink deeply but quickly of home joys and many feminine
interests is a part of the price she pays for having selected a field so broad and
exacting, but so fertile in service and attendant satisfaction, so generous with its
favors of distinction.

Despite her recent arrival (in 1920 there were 4) and her comparatively few
numbers (in 1940 there were over 175,000 lawyers in the United States, for whom
about 1,500 were Negro and less than 75 Negro women) the Negro woman has
deported herself with excellence not only in actual practice and court work, but
in assimilating quickly into public service as a lawyer. They are now represented
on the Bench in the City, County and State Attorneys' Offices, and despite the

normal handicaps incident to minorities and pioneers, they should no longer be "on trial."

After over 20 years in active practice in New York City, my own devotion to the law has not wavered. My admiration is undimmed and there is no sweeter music to my ears than "Hear ye, Hear ye, His Honor the Justice of the Court— all persons have business of the Court draw near, give your attention and ye shall be heard."

This is Democracy's battle cry.

Constitutional Law and Black Women

Pauli Murray

(1970)

*T*HE SUBJECT OF BLACK WOMEN and the law is of particular interest today because of the contemporary movement of women's rights and the controversy over the relationship of Black women to this movement . . . It is . . . my in-
tention to . . . examine some of the parallels between discrimination because of
race and discrimination because of sex in order that we may gain some insight
into the legal status of women generally and how this affects the rights of Black
women.

Historically, in the United States there have been striking similarities between the status of Blacks and the status of women and the discrimination suffered by both groups. In the first place, legal classifications in each case have been
based upon fixed, immutable biological characteristics. In the case of Blacks, it
was skin pigment and other visible differences; in the case of women, it was the
biological difference of sex. Race and sex differ from temporary characteristics
such as age, alienage, or even religion. An individual is locked into the classification by birth and can never escape. The racial or sexual identity is public, visible and involuntary and the stereotypes and prejudices that attach to these
characteristics are continuously stimulated, thus perpetuating discrimination
and making it more difficult to eradicate.

Secondly, the assumptions upon which legal distinctions have been made
on the basis of both race and sex have often been the same. That the innate differences between the proscribed group and the dominant society (in the one
case White society, in the other, males) justify differential treatment. And in each
case the underlying assumption was the inherent inferiority of the group discriminated against. For example, a strong argument against according Negroes

AFRO-AMERICAN SERIES, NO. 1, AFRO-AMERICAN STUDIES PROGRAM, Boston University 33 (1970).

the rights of citizenship was that they were intellectually inferior to Whites. This assertion rested upon the "scientific" finding that Blacks on the average had a smaller brain than Whites. Similarly, it was argued that women had a smaller brain than men and therefore lacked the mental capacity to exercise properly the right to vote.

Thirdly, the types of discrimination against both groups have been similar. In fact, some historians note that the subordinate legal and social status of women served as a model for the American Slave Codes. The traditional treatment of a woman as a husband's property and subject to his corporal punishment as well as other restrictions upon her freedom formed precedents for the later treatment of slaves. In the Middle Ages, women were held incompetent to testify in the canonical courts. Women were also the most frequent victims of burning at the stake, a barbaric punishment that foreshadowed lynching. Legal disabilities imposed upon slaves (and often free Blacks)—lack of voting rights, denial of the right to serve on juries or hold public office, incapacity to give testimony in court actions in which a White person was a party—all these women suffered at one time or another during their history. The similarities between the position of slaves and women were so obvious that pro-slavery writers before the Civil War sought to justify slavery by pointing out its close analogy to the position of women and children. As late as 1944, a justice of the North Carolina Supreme Court reviewing the historical position of women noted "the barbarous view of the inferiority of women which manifested itself in civil and political oppression so akin to slavery that we can find no adequate word to describe her present status with men except emancipation."[1]

The results of the discrimination against both groups have also been similar. Legal disabilities have contributed to social disabilities. Discrimination by law has reinforced private discrimination and produced a powerlessness in both Blacks and women. Both groups have suffered discrimination particularly in employment and in education, and if they have not been wholly excluded have been highly under-represented in the decision making processes that affect their lives. Note also that the legislators who make the laws, the judges who interpret and apply the laws, which have perpetuated the inequality of both Blacks and women, have been the same social class—White males.

It is not surprising, therefore, that women Abolitionists of the early 19th Century became the pioneers in the struggle for women's rights. They saw the analogy between their own subordination and that of the slaves. American law, inherited from the common law of England, was particularly harsh against married women. Although softened somewhat by principles of equity, it nevertheless contained features that made the lot of a married woman an unenviable one. When a woman married, she was said to suffer a kind of "civil death." Accord-

---

1. State v. Emery, 224 N.C. 581, 596, 31 S.E.2d 858, 868 (1944) (Seawell, J., dissenting).

ing to the law, the husband and wife were now fused into a single being and the husband was the head. The wife lost control over her earnings, her separate property and the custody of her children. Women were often classified in the law with "children and imbeciles."

About the middle of the 19th Century, the states began to adopt "Married Women's Acts," which, little by little, removed some of these legal disabilities. However, even today in various states are found vestiges of this unequal, inferior common law position of women. For example, . . . [o]nly six states permit a woman to establish a separate domicile from her husband for all purposes, although a few states permit her to do so for certain activities, such as voting.

Another legal disability, or considered so by many women, is the change of name upon marriage. It is symbolic of the loss of a woman's separate identity. Some women have used their maiden names as professional names after marriage. The law is not entirely settled in this area, but there are court decisions denying a woman the right to use her maiden name to vote, or for her automobile registration, or even where she is an artist and has built a professional reputation under her maiden name. Some states require a woman to go through a legal process in order to retain her maiden name.

In many states, both the age of attaining majority and the age of the right to marry without parental consent differ as to the two sexes. Normally, it is lower for the female than for the male. On the surface, this would seem to be advantageous to women in that the female is regarded as being more mature than the male. However, this is not the reason for the difference. As Professor Leo Kanowitz has pointed out in *Women and the Law*,[2] the underlying social attitude supporting the difference in ages is that a woman's chief function is to marry at an earlier age. A man, however, is expected to prepare for greater things and in the judgment of the legislature, must delay his marriage until a later time.

The law traditionally has given a husband a right of action to sue for the loss of his wife's consortium. For example, if the wife is injured in an automobile accident, the husband has a right to sue not only for her personal and bodily injury but also for the loss of his wife's "wifely relationship," the sexual relationship and his right to all that his marital relationship implies. Historically women have not had a reciprocal right to sue for the loss of the husband's consortium. This issue is now being fought out in the courts, who are taking a different view. However, the fact that women must litigate this issue underlines their inferior status under the law.

About eleven states still impose certain restrictions upon the married woman's capacity to enter into contractual relations. A few states do not allow a woman to dispose of her real property unless her husband joins in the con-

---

2. LEO KANOWITZ, WOMEN AND THE LAW: THE UNFINISHED REVOLUTION 5 (Albuquerque, University of New Mexico Press 1969).

veyance. In some states a woman cannot co-sign a note for a third party unless her husband joins in the co-signing. Perhaps an even more blatant discrimination is found in the laws of some states which do not allow a married woman to enter into an independent business enterprise without making an application to the court, and even then sometimes the husband must give consent.

A number of states apply differential punishment to men and women for the same offense under criminal law. For example, a man commits an offense and is sentenced to two years under a law that imposes a maximum of five years. A woman convicted of the same offense may be required under the law to be sentenced to a women's reformatory for an indefinite term, which might mean the entire five years. The theory behind this is that women's reformatories are experiments in social corrections and they enjoy a special status. The ultimate result, however, is that a woman is given a more severe sentence.

The most widespread legal distinctions based on sex and that have caused the greatest controversy in recent years are the state "Labor Protective" laws applicable to women only. These laws fall roughly into two classes. One class confers a benefit upon women, such as minimum wage laws, or requirements of rest periods for women workers, or requiring lounges or seats for working women. Often these benefits have been extended to male workers by employer action or by administrative or judicial decisions.

The second class of laws are those that act as restrictions upon women's employment opportunities. These include laws that exclude women from certain occupations such as mining or bartending, laws that prohibit women from night work in certain jobs, weight lifting restrictions, and maximum hour laws, which prohibit the employment of a woman longer than eight hours in any single day or more than forty-eight hours in a week. These laws, which were originally enacted to insure health standards for women at a time when they were the victims of sweatshop conditions, were not organized in trade unions and lacked the power to vote. They were upheld by the United States Supreme Court at a time when that Court declared similar legislation applicable to male workers unconstitutional as unwarranted interference with the liberty of the worker to enter into contract. Ultimately, however, due to changes in technology and in the economic role of women, these laws have resulted in more discrimination than protection. For example, a woman having the requisite seniority and skills bids for a job in the plant, which for her would be a promotion with more pay. The employer tells her, "I can't hire you for this job because it requires overtime work and the state law does not allow me to work you overtime." So the promotion goes to a man with less skill and less seniority than the woman worker. Similarly, state laws or labor regulations require that no woman shall be employed on a job which involves lifting more than a specific weight: these regulations vary from "over 15" to "more than 50" pounds. Some women have pointed out that if such regulations were applied throughout society, not just in employment, no grocery bags would be lifted by women, no children would be carried by their mothers, and some women would even be prohibited from lifting their handbags!

Like Blacks, women have traditionally suffered educational inequalities, particularly in higher education. Sex discrimination is practiced not only by private institutions but also by state-supported institutions and by colleges and universities, which receive substantial federal aid. It is fairly well documented that many institutions of higher education require higher admissions standards of female students than of male students and also apply female quotas. In certain professional schools, notably medical institutions, there has been widespread application of the so-called "equal rejection" theory. For example, fifty men and ten women apply to the same medical school. Twenty-five men and five women are accepted. The medical school admissions officials insist there is no sex discrimination because an equal proportion of each group of applicants has been accepted. They ignore the possibility that the five women who have been rejected may be more highly qualified than some of the twenty-five men who are accepted. The result of this policy is that although medical studies indicate there is an urgent need for physicians in many fields today, for many years the percentage of women students admitted to medical schools has been kept at the low figure of 6% to 9%.

These illustrations indicate that the forms of legal discrimination on the basis of sex are quite similar to those on the basis of race. The constitutional position of women has followed a pattern not unlike that of Blacks. Those of you who are familiar with the history of the Fourteenth Amendment are aware of the fact that for many decades after the Civil War, that Amendment was narrowly interpreted so that it failed to achieve for Blacks those rights of citizenship that its framers had envisioned. You will recall that in 1873, the Supreme Court decided the *Slaughter-House Cases*,[3] which practically made a dead letter of the clause in the Fourteenth Amendment that provides that no State shall abridge the privileges and immunities of citizens of the United States. The Court held that this clause applied only to federal rights, rights that arise out of the federal Constitution. This had the effect of not only narrowing the area of protection of the civil rights of Blacks but those of women as well. In the same year, the Court decided the case of *Bradwell v. Illinois*.[4] Myra Bradwell was denied the right to practice law in the State of Illinois. The state court held that as a married woman restrictions on her ability to enter into contractual agreements would be embarrassing to her clients. Mrs. Bradwell appealed to the Supreme Court under the privileges and immunities of the Fourteenth Amendment. That Court denied her appeal on the ground that the right to practice law was

---

3. 83 U.S. (16 Wall.) 36 (1872).
4. 83 U.S. (16 Wall.) 130 (1872).

not a privilege or immunity of citizens of the United States and the regulation of admission to the bar was within the police power of the state . . .

As late as 1896, the same year in which the Supreme Court promulgated the "separate but equal" racial doctrine in *Plessy v. Ferguson*,[5] the court refused to overrule a Virginia court holding which barred a woman attorney from the practice of law in that state. That case was used as a precedent to uphold a Maryland law which limited the practice of law to White males. A Black man challenged this law but the Maryland court quoted the *Bradwell* case and the 1869 case holding that the regulation of the legal profession was within the power of the state. Thus, you can see how the courts have used one type of discrimination to reinforce others.

In 1908, the famous case of *Muller v. Oregon*[6] upheld the power of a state to pass maximum-hours legislation applicable to women only. The Court justified differential legislation for women by pointing out that there were significant biological and psychological differences between men and women, that woman was dependent upon the male and needed his protection and that therefore sex was a reasonable basis for classification. This ruling proved as destructive to the rights of women as the "separate but equal" doctrine to the rights of Blacks. Later courts relied upon the *Muller* case to uphold the exclusion of women from jury service, from state educational institutions, and differential treatment in other cases . . .

Let me suggest that this is not a static situation, and under the pressure of women the law is beginning to change. A landmark decision in 1966 by a three-judge federal court in Alabama held in *White v. Crook*[7] that the laws of Alabama, which wholly excluded women from jury service, were unconstitutional and that the Fourteenth Amendment protects against sex discrimination as well as race discrimination. This case has particular significance for Black women. You will recall that during the civil rights struggle in Alabama in 1965, Mrs. Viola Liuzzo and Jonathan M. Daniels, a young seminarian from New Hampshire, were murdered in Lowndes County. Their accused murderers were later acquitted. Analysis of the situation showed that the all-White, all-male juries that resulted in these acquittals were drawn from jury lists that represented only 7% of [the] population of the county. Although Blacks, male and female, heavily outnumbered Whites in Lowndes County, Black males were excluded from jury service by administrative practices and *all* females were excluded under the Constitution and laws of Alabama. A Black woman, Gardenia White, was one of the plaintiffs in the court action that challenged the validity of these practices. Thus, Mrs. White won jury service rights not only for herself but for all the women of

---

5. 163 U.S. 537 (1896).

6. 208 U.S. 412 (1908).

7. 251 F. Supp. 401 (N.D. Ala. 1966).

Alabama, Black and White. After this case Mississippi and South Carolina finally removed their bars against women serving on juries. It was not until 1967 that the last bar against jury service for women was removed in the United States . . .

In 1971, the Supreme Court of California held unconstitutional a California statute that prohibited women from working as barmaids in taverns. For the first time in the history of judicial decisions, an American court made the connection between race discrimination and sex discrimination by declaring that sex classifications, like racial classifications, should be treated as "constitutionally suspect." This means that the state bears a heavier burden of justification of the law involved than in other legal distinctions and must show an overriding state interest that compels the discrimination. The California court declared:

> Sex, like race and lineage, is an immutable trait, a status into which the class members are locked by accident of birth. What differentiates sex from nonsuspect statuses, such as intelligence or physical disability, and aligns it with recognized suspect classifications is that the characteristic frequently bears no relationship with the ability to perform or contribute to society. The result is that the whole class is relegated to an inferior legal status without regard to the characteristics and capabilities of its individual members.[8]

Against this background we must view the status of the Black woman under the law. We must bear in mind her position is affected not merely by her relationship to a Black male but also by the position of women generally in the total society. Because she has suffered the dual handicap of disabilities because of race and sex she occupies the lowest socio-economic status of any group in society. Her degraded position began, of course, with the slavery experience. The brutal invasion of the personal dignity and privacy of the Black woman during slavery can hardly be compared with that of any other group. The slave woman was equated to a "brood mare" in the law and her children were referred to as "increase" in the same manner as reference to the increase of cattle and other animal stock. The forcible rape of a female slave by a person other than her master was not considered a crime but only a trespass upon and injury to the property of her master for which the master could sue for damages. The rapist was not brought before a criminal court. Rape by the master was prerogative of ownership. Angela Davis in *The Black Scholar*, December 1971, makes the intriguing argument that the rape of a Black woman was more than sexual gratification by the master. She asserts that it was another technique in degrading the woman and stifling slave resistance because there is considerable evidence that slave women physically resisted the sexual advances of their masters.[9]

---

8. Sail'er Inn, Inc. v. Kirby, 5 Cal. 3d 1, 18, 485 P.2d 529, 540 (1971) (notes omitted).

9. Angela Davis, *The Black Woman's Role in the Community of Slaves*, 3 BLACK SCHOLAR 2–3 (Dec. 1971).

I suggest that Black women and Black men suffered a rough equality of degradation in slavery. Much has been said about the psychological and often literal castration of the Black male, the denial of his manhood as measured by the distance between his status and that of the dominant White male in society. What is often overlooked is the distance between the degraded Black female and the exalted stereotype of her White counterpart, the Southern lady. She was robbed of an acceptable self-image of womanhood as the Black male was robbed of an acceptable view of his manhood.

This heritage of low status has continued into the present . . . Given these facts, it seems clear that Black women face special social and economic hazards the elimination of which depends upon not merely uprooting racism from our social institutions but sexism as well. Thus Black women have an important stake in the present movement to make the guarantee of equal rights without regard to sex part of the fundamental law of the land.

Women Must Wield Their Power
for the Sake of Justice

Patricia Roberts Harris

(1979)

*T*HE GROWTH OF THE WOMEN'S CAUCUS over the last eight years occurred during some very trying times in this nation's history. The involvement in Southeast Asia, the scandal of Watergate, and the development of a new "Me Decade" has resulted in an era of almost unrelieved public cynicism about the political process.

The Caucus has weathered well this dark and stormy period. Its purpose from the outset has remained clear: to secure equality under the law for all women and to win equal representation for women in government.

We have rallied behind those two goals and we have now reached a point where our voice is being heard and our political power respected. Our voice is heard in state houses and city halls throughout the land. The percentage of women elected to state legislatures has doubled in the last ten years. More than 700 women now serve as mayors of their communities.

This convention affords us the opportunity to review our accomplishments and to define more fully our goals and strategies for the 1980s.

In terms of accomplishments, I am proud that the Carter administration has broken new ground in recognizing and utilizing the talents of women. The statistics bear me out: women are now visible in more top federal government positions than in any other time in the history of American government. Twenty-one percent of political appointees of the administration are women. This contrasts with the previous administration's then all-time high figure of 12.9 percent. This increase has not been by chance, but by design.

Of the five women who have served as cabinet members in the history of our nation, two were appointed by President Carter. President Carter named the

---

Remarks before the Women's Political Caucus Convention, Cincinnati, Ohio, July 14, 1979. In 1979, the author was Secretary of Housing and Urban Development.

first seven women ever to serve as general counsels of departments. Twelve of the 18 women in federal judgeships were appointed by the president. The administration also pushed through the Civil Service Reform Act. We expect this legislation to help increase the number of women in supervisory and managerial jobs.

In my own department, there has been a dramatic increase over the last two years in the number of women working in managerial positions. Forty-nine percent of all appointed positions at HUD are now held by women, and nearly half of those are at the professional level. This increase in the employment ranks has had a notable effect on our policy and program development. We have found that having women at the top and in the middle makes a real difference.

In the program areas of the Department of Housing and Urban Development, [HUD] is becoming increasingly sensitive to the fact that housing is a "women's issue." The overwhelming majority of HUD's constituency in the public housing and housing assistance programs are women. Because so high a percentage of our senior citizens are women, our housing programs for the elderly have a large female constituency. This has long been the case, but we women who are in charge are requiring our programs to reflect these realities.

HUD is engaging in major initiatives specifically designed to help women and their housing needs. For example, the Women and Mortgage Credit Project is a two-year program which will provide technical assistance to women on the advantages and disadvantages of home ownership and on the process of purchasing a home.

HUD is spreading the word that women are an untapped market for the mortgage lending industry. HUD's message to the lending institutions is simple: women are good credit.

In addition, HUD is responding to the terrifying increase of violence occurring in American homes. As a result of the efforts of HUD's newly created Women's Policy and Program Office, shelters for battered women are now eligible for Community Development Block Grant Funds.

To date, HUD has funded approximately 20 battered women's shelters. We would like to triple that number in the coming fiscal year. More significantly, a government-wide effort to combat this problem has been initiated, and the president has established an Interdepartmental Committee on Domestic Violence. Economic independence—which is vital to the mental and physical well-being of all women—is especially important to those who are victims of domestic violence. We must work not only to provide temporary shelter for such women, but also to assure that they can lead full, independent lives.

Clearly we women are beginning to gain some victories, and more of our needs are being considered. But we are not deceived. Our goal of full equality is still well ahead of us. As of today, thirty-five states have responded to our call and have ratified the Equal Rights Amendment. Last spring, both the House and the Senate felt our power and granted an extension to the ratification of the ERA. We are heading down the home stretch in the drive for ratification. We need to win three states by 1983, and we women of the Carter administration, and the men, stand shoulder to shoulder with you in a massive effort to win ratification. And win we shall!

We women still have far to go in the labor market before we reach equality with men. Despite significant individual achievement, as a group, we are marching backward from equality with men. In 1955, the median income of full-time working women was 63.9 percent of that of men. That number has *dropped* five points, and full-time working women now earn only 58.9 percent of that of men.

One of my witty colleagues once said that we would not have equality of men and women until mediocre women were as likely to be chosen for a job as are mediocre men. Today our problem isn't equality in mediocrity. Our problem still is that a woman with qualifications superior to those of a male is very likely to earn less. For those who say women have it made, I want them to explain the alarming fact that in this country a male high school drop-out earns more than a female college graduate. More specifically, he earns, on the average, $1,604 more per year . . . more!

Notwithstanding the Equal Pay Act, and with only a few exceptions, women's salaries are lower than those of men with comparable training and experience at every age, every academic degree level, in every field and with every type of employer.

Black women today are near income levels of White women. But those of you who are White who like to think that Black women are getting something you are not, I will remind you that those data showing the gap between the income of Black and White women is narrowing only mean that we Black women have climbed into the barrel with you, and we are together, I repeat, together, at the bottom of the barrel. Women as a whole, White and Black, are earning a lower percentage of male income than we did twenty-five years ago.

Of course, this is largely due to occupational segregation. Nearly 80 percent of all working women are still employed in the traditional clerical, sales, service, or light factory jobs. Women still only represent 9 percent of the lawyers, 11 percent of the doctors, and 6 percent of the top managers and administrators in this nation. Many of us in these fields have only recently entered . . .

For many women in this country today, mere survival is a major achievement. Nearly half of the female heads of households support themselves and their children on $6,000 or less a year. They live in older homes with leaking roofs and sagging ceilings . . . Women's housing options are limited. The mortgage market discriminates against women, and landlords discriminate against tenants with children. Poverty is increasingly becoming a female problem. We women, regardless of race, are at the bottom of the economic barrel. We can hope that those prejudices will be overcome once significant numbers of women are in positions of authority and responsibility and so-called male virtues are no longer viewed as women's vices.

We all know of the double standard. If the boss is a he, he is called assertive for the same behavior that earns women the adjective pushy. He is meticulous, she is picky. He is persistent, she doesn't know when to quit. He exercises authority, she is tyrannical. He is firm, she is abrasive . . .

I eagerly anticipate a time when we women are not judged by the exception because of our gender, but only because of our exceptional individuality. I look forward instead to a time when we are no longer the exception to the rule, but when we are the rule . . .

When we say that conscience brought us into the [women's] movement, can we justify political expediency in order to maintain political position, or must we make our contributions to a rebirth of strong ethical commitment, even if we lose political advantage? We must all continue to think about it . . .

Women in authority must not seek solely to protect their positions or to preserve their power. We must risk our positions and wield our power for justice's sake. We women must not solely infiltrate the system, learn the ropes, and then support present practices, no matter how wrongheaded. We must rededicate and redirect government to serve the people of this nation. I know this is not easy. We will be ridiculed and parodied, because if our cause is right and cannot be destroyed, those who oppose our cause, will seek to destroy our credibility. Nonetheless, we women must transform the system, not conform to it . . .

I look forward to the time when there are as many women in the Cabinet as there are men; when the gentlewomen of the House number in the hundreds, and a woman senator is not an anomaly.

But I don't stop with where we are: although the state houses across the country know they are no longer open only to the woman who is the governor's wife, there is a White House that must one day have a woman in the Oval Office.

I want to hear the Speaker of the House addressed as Madam Speaker, and I want to listen as she introduces Madam President to the Congress assembled for the State of the Union. I want Madam President to look down from the podium at the women of the Supreme Court who will be indicative of the significant number of women judges throughout the federal and state judicial systems . . .

The success of the women's movement today is largely due to our ability to maintain the kind of vision which the country as a whole has seemed to lose; a vision of the kind of world in which we want to live: a world of equality for all. . . .

The Power of Black Women
to Tell Their Stories

ANITA FAYE HILL

(1992)

I WANT TO SHARE WITH YOU some of the stories of African-American women. I choose these stories out of many that I could bring to you, not simply because I relate closely to the main characters in terms of race and gender, but also because they illustrate the impact of the intersection of race and gender for African-American women and other women of color. These stories contain valuable lessons about the power of racism and sexism in this country and the struggle against it, and even more importantly, about the power of individuals to resist the subordination and oppression that are both institutionalized and acculturalized in our society. Finally, and even tragically, the stories indicate how the law and society answer, ignore, and in some cases silence the individuals who decry disempowerment based on race and gender.

I am going to begin the story from slavery. Stories of abuse and subordination of female slaves and African-American women during the era following slavery have been chronicled, but not widely told. Yet historical anecdotal evidence exists that suggests that the abuse was widespread. Perhaps no more compelling story exists than the story of Celia, a slave. In 1858, at the age of nineteen, Celia was hanged by the state of Missouri for the murder of her abusive owner. Her tragedy began when she was purchased by her abuser at the age of fourteen. Over the next five years, she was forced to submit to his sexual advances and even bore two children by him. In an attempt to defend herself from his advances, she killed him, and though the state allowed a woman to use deadly force to protect herself from rape, the court denied this defense to Celia.[1]

In limiting such a right to white women, the court concluded that if Celia's

---

An original submission to this volume.

1. *See* MELTON A. MCLAURIN, CELIA A SLAVE: A TRUE STORY OF VIOLENCE AND RETRIBUTION IN ANTEBELLUM MISSOURI (Athens, University of Georgia 1991).

owner was in the habit of visiting her cabin for purposes of sex and went there on the night of his death for that or any other purpose, Celia had no choice but to accept his advances. Thus, as property, Celia's right to control her economic destiny, as well as her right to protect her personal dignity, were denied. As a female who was the property of her owner, the denial of her personal dignity carried greater implications and risks than that even of her fellow male slaves.

This denial of her right to protect herself resulted in her death by hanging. What is more, Celia, as a slave, was prohibited from testifying at her own trial. Her story has been noted by Judge A. Leon Higginbotham Jr.,[2] an outstanding jurist, legal historian, and scholar, yet we will never have the benefit of interpreting Celia's own words as she was contemporaneously and, of course, for all of history, silenced.

The power of the ability of one to tell one's own story was lost in the slaveholding society. Slaves were forbidden to read and write, and penalties were imposed upon those who were found guilty of teaching basic reading and writing to slaves. Society disempowered Celia in a variety of ways too numerous to detail, but the final act of disempowerment was in forbidding her to speak on her own behalf because of her race and because of her social class.

Students of legal history, of course, are familiar with the *Plessy v. Ferguson*[3] case, and we are all aware of Rosa Parks and her refusal to abide by the Jim Crow rules that required that she stand on a bus while seats designated for whites remained vacant. Parks's courageous act was preceded, however, by a similar challenge brought by Ida B. Wells in Tennessee.

I want to compare the Celia story with the Wells story. While Celia's story is one of a rejection of personal oppression that could be expanded to a rejection of a system of slavery, Ida Wells's story is a story of a direct attack on systemic oppression. It is a direct attack on the segregation that was developing in the South after Reconstruction had ended.

What happened was that Wells refused to sit in a section of a train designated for people of African descent. Her protest did not end with the physical attack that she levied on the railroad official who forcibly removed her from the train. In fact, in her description she "sank her teeth into his arm" as he tried to remove her. She went on to challenge segregation in the court system in Tennessee and, in fact, won a jury verdict of $500 at the trial level. The headline of the local Memphis paper, the *Memphis Appeal,* rather flippantly read, "Darkie Damsel Wins Damages."

The Chesapeake & Ohio Railroad Company, of course, appealed to a

---

2. *See, e.g.,* A. Leon Higginbotham Jr. and Ann F. Jacobs, *The "Law Only As an Enemy": The Legitimization of Racial Powerlessness Through the Colonial and Antebellum Criminal Laws of Virginia,* 70 N.C.L. REV. 969, 1056 n.511 (1992); Neal Kumar Katyal, *Men Who Own Women: A Thirteenth Amendment Critique of Forced Prostitution,* 103 YALE L.J. 791, 799–800 n.55 (1993).

3. 163 U.S. 537 (1896).

higher court, and just as a safeguard, company officials offered Wells more money than the jury award that she was to get if she would just agree to drop the suit, not to contest the appeal. Wells, of course, rejected the offer, and the Supreme Court of Tennessee, realizing the significance of Wells's challenge to the system of apartheid that was developing in the South, denied the jury verdict and threw out the damage award.[4]

What was happening was that it was just simply easier for the court to deny Wells's right to sit where she chose to sit on a train, rather than to acknowledge the rights that could be inferred if hers were recognized. The court chose to withhold from African-Americans the power to redress wrongs against them, despite the promises of the Constitution. The court chose, instead, to retain that power in its legislature, which chose to discriminate against blacks.

Wells retained her power to speak about these and other inequities and did so as a journalist and advocate for the rights of African-Americans throughout her life. She was later described by this same Memphis newspaper in less flippant terms. However, the terms were so repulsive and vulgar that foreign papers refused to print the language.

So what you do have with these two stories is some sense of advancement. At least for Wells, she was able to speak on her own behalf in the suit. Nevertheless, she failed to prevail in the suit. The tragic parallel of these stories is that their significance to the parties and to others involved was limited because the law and society refused to acknowledge basic rights.

Yet one must surely ask—when you think about these stories, and when people speak about history, one has to ask—What do these stories of people of the past, of African-American women and men of the past and women in the past, have to do with what is going on today? Certainly the denials of the past, one would argue, were based on contemporaneous events that are in the past and which carry no influence today.

An example of a situation that occurred in 1989 is the case of Brooms v. Regal Tube Company.[5] In that case, the plaintiff complained of sexual and racial harassment directed at her by her supervisor. The harassment began with the use of racial slurs, or racial slurs coupled with sexual innuendo. It escalated from there. Eventually, the supervisor directly propositioned the plaintiff. She declined. In addition, while in his office, he showed her photocopies of racist pornographic pictures, as well as pornographic photos of interracial couples, and made sexual remarks about the talent of black women. At one point while in his office, the alleged assailant grabbed the plaintiff's arm and threatened to kill her if she moved.

She escaped, ran away, and fell down a flight of stairs. Brooms suffered

---

4. Chesapeake, Ohio & Southwestern R.R. Co. v. Wells, 85 Tenn. 613, 4 S.W. 5 (1887).
5. 881 F.2d 412 (7th Cir. 1989).

physical as well as psychiatric injury as a result of the behavior of her supervisor. In prevailing in her suit, she was awarded back pay that accumulated during the time she was away from her job because of the abuse. However, her claim for damages for her extensive physical and emotional injury were dismissed, and rightfully so, because the law, as established at the time, did not cover such injuries.

Brooms's case was one of the cases that was presented before the Senate as it considered the Civil Rights Act of 1990.[6] That statute would have allowed a court to award compensatory damages and punitive damages in such cases as Brooms's. The act was passed by Congress, but was vetoed by President George Bush.

Ultimately, the Civil Rights Act of 1991 was passed and signed into law by the president during a period of, shall I say, increasing public awareness of the problem of sexual harassment in the workplace.

Brooms's case, like numerous others before hers and probably some since,[7] represented a situation where wrongs went without remedy, yet ultimately what makes her case different from the Celia case, and even from the Wells case, was not only that she was able to tell her story, not that she prevailed, but what makes her case different is that society responded to encourage reform in the law, which will assist other women like Brooms.

Consider this story. It is the story of another woman, twenty-one years old, and it is a story about the rejection of myths that plague women who raise claims about sexual assault in modern society. The case has been dubbed "the Lacrosse rape case." The jury in that case acquitted three defendants of various charges of sexual assault.[8] It concluded that the gang assault of a twenty-one-year-old was, in fact, consensual. It reached this conclusion even though some of the defendants who had accepted plea bargain offers corroborated the complaining witnesses' story that the woman had been given several drinks that, without her knowledge, were laced with vodka. The defendants also corroborated the fact the young woman could hardly walk and had passed out during the encounter.[9]

In the face of this evidence, one male juror analyzed the witnesses' claim in this way: "Hell hath no fury like a woman scorned."

One certainly has to be careful in analyzing reactions to rape cases. We certainly do not want to go back to the era when black men were killed for ap-

---

6. See Civil Rights Act of 1990, 136 Cong. Rec. H6746, H6751 (1990); Civil Rights and Women's Equity in Employment Act of 1991, 137 Cong. Rec. H3876, H3903 (1991) (Brooms case mentioned).

7. *See, e.g.,* Richard C. Reuben, *Suing the Firm,* 81 A.B.A. J. 68, Dec. 1995 (Nancy O'Mara Ezold won a discrimination lawsuit against a major law firm but it was reversed on appeal).

8. Beth Holland, *Lawyer: St. John's Expelling 3; Despite Sex-Abuse Acquittal,* NEWSDAY, Aug. 27, 1991, at 8.

9. Peg Tyre, *Rape Accuser Was Likely Helpless,* NEWSDAY, July 9, 1991, at 4; Ilene Barth, *Why No Vigils at This Assault Trial?* NEWSDAY, June 10, 1991, at 68.

proaching white women. I firmly believe that in criminal proceedings, the rights of all accused must always be protected, with the burden on the state to make its case. Yet we must be careful that the myths and clichés based on those myths do not impose an added burden on women who seek redress for sexual assault and misconduct.

Are we willing to consider that the jury in the Brooms case might have operated under these myths? In that *New York* case, there is indication that race and ethnicity may have been factors, as well. The defendants were all white, the complaining witness was black. The defendants were all born and reared in the United States, the complaining witness was from Jamaica, and by some accounts spoke with a slight accent.

Leading scholars have concluded that the race of the parties in rape prosecutions is significant in predicting the outcome of rape cases, and, moreover, the juries are less likely to believe black women who complain of rape, whatever the race of the alleged assailant. While we cannot be sure what role the race of the parties played in the Brooms case, can we say with certainty that the result would have been the same if the races of the parties were reversed?

In the face of racism and sexism, it is easy to understand the typical response of society, to gauge its pervasiveness, to breathe a collective sigh, and to simply get on with the business of day-to-day living. But I propose a different, yet really a very modest, response. Suppose we look at each of these stories . . . and ask, "What if?" What if the court and the jury in the case of Celia listened to Celia's stories in her words? What if the law had not further denied her humanity by forbidding her to speak on her own behalf? Might the jury have come to terms with the ultimate debasement of slavery? Might the cases of Dred Scott and Celia not have been the first steps toward the nation's rejection of racial oppression?

What if the Supreme Court of Tennessee had taken seriously the claim of Ida B. Wells when she asserted that the Civil War amendments to the Constitution protected her from different treatment based on race? What if her suit against the Chesapeake & Ohio Railway, or if *Plessy,* later in his, had prevailed, creating the opportunity to end Jim Crowism before it took root and ravaged the South? Might she have saved the lives of many who were lynched and firebombed and whose dreams were destroyed by the devastation of segregation? Might she have saved the country the shame of living for centuries in slavery and for nearly a century more in a post-slavery state?

What might have happened if the jury in the Brooms case had seen the young woman who was the subject of this assault in this case and recalled that the three men were convicted of assault charges? What if they had seen her without the veil of cultural myths that shroud such claims? What if the jury had heard the expert testimony that explains victims' reactions to rape, rather than relying on cultural myths in interpreting whether the victim consented to the behavior? Might the case have paved the way for considering invaluable evidence in other sexual assault cases? . . .

There is significance in who tells a story—who gets to tell their story, who is listening, and how well. Certainly individuals must be able to tell about their experiences of oppression, and they must have the power to do so in their own words, but that is not enough. The burden, then, is on others, all of us, to hear, to listen. Courage should not be confined to those who speak out against oppression. Courage must be the guide for those who have the power to make change. We show courage when we are willing to speak on behalf of the powerless, to redress wrongs by our institutions, and to lead when leadership will not. One person's courage can begin the process of change, but it takes the courage of many to complete it.

Who gets to tell a story and how it is told is a question of power, both political and social.

The Black Woman: Who Represents Her?

Issie Lee Shelton Jenkins

(1980)

*I*N 1892, IN HER BOOK, *A Voice from the South,* Anna Julia Cooper, a former slave, and the second female school principal in Washington, D.C., wrote:

> A colored woman of today occupies . . . a unique position in this country . . . [T]he woman of today finds herself in the presence of responsibility which ramify through the profoundest and most varied interest of her country and her race . . . No plan for renovating society, no scheme for purifying politics, no reform in church or in state, no moral, social, or economic question, no movement upward or downward in the human plan is lost on her.[1]

Ms. Cooper saw the black woman . . . "at the gateway of [a] new era of American civilization," having the opportunity to wield her influence on the future social, economic, and moral achievements of the race, and to see the possibilities before it.[2] She was concerned that Black women be ready for this role. She wrote:

> What a responsibility then to have the sole management of the primal lights and shadows! Such is the colored woman's office. She must stamp weal or woe on the coming history of this people. May she see her opportunity and vindicate her high prerogative.[3]

Remarks before the 1980 Annual Meeting of Zeta Phi Beta Sorority.

1. ANNA J. COOPER, A VOICE FROM THE SOUTH 134, 142–43 (Xenia, Ohio, The Aldine Printing House 1892).

2. *Id.* at 143.

3. *Id.* at 145.

Though Anna Julia Cooper saw the Black woman's role as clear in 1892, historically, the Black woman has had an ambiguous role in American society. Because we are women, white society has considered us less of a threat than the Black man. Accordingly, white society allowed us, sometimes forcing us, into service in the white family; raising their children, nursing their sick, and running the white home. The Black woman's intimate contact with white people often made her the interpreter and intermediary of the white culture in the Black home. At the same time the Black woman was, and still is, working very closely with the Black man to keep the Black family together and assure the survival of the Black community. This dual role that the Black woman has played since slavery, is fraught with conflict, and has imposed great tensions on her.

W. E. B. Du Bois, in his book *The Souls of Black Folk,* described another conflict to which all Blacks are subject, including the Black woman. He wrote:

> [T]he Negro is a sort of seventh son, born with a veil, and gifted with second-sight in this American world,—a world which yields him no true self-consciousness, but only lets him see himself through the revelation of the other world. *It is a peculiar sensation, this double-consciousness, this sense of always looking at one's self through the eyes of others, of measuring one's self by the tape of a world that looks on in amused contempt and pity.* One ever feels his twoness,—an American, a Negro; two souls; two thoughts; two unreconciled strivings, two warring ideals in one dark body whose dogged strength alone keeps it from being torn asunder.[4]

Du Bois wrote this passage in 1903. Many years have passed, and many changes have occurred in our society with respect to Black conditions, but who among us here can say that she has never experienced this *double consciousness* . . . In modern times, the Black woman still must contend with this dual consciousness . . . Let me just note that while called by other names, this same concept has been written about by many Black historians, writers, and psychologists . . . Today this dualism has reached a new peak for the Black woman, because of the enormous pressure that the women's movement in general has placed on her. Joyce Ladner has written,

> Many Black women who have traditionally accepted the white models of femininity are now rejecting them for the same general reasons that I have proposed we should reject the white middle class life style. Black women in this society are the only ethnic or racial group which has had the opportunity to be women. By this I simply mean that much of the current fo-

---

4. W.E.B. Du Bois, The Souls of Black Folk 45 (New York, New American Library 1969) (emphasis added).

cus on being liberated from the constraints and protectiveness of the society which is proposed by women's liberation groups has never applied to Black women, and in that sense, we have always been "free," and able to develop as individuals even under the most harsh circumstances. This freedom, as well as the tremendous hardships from which Black women suffered, allowed for the development of a female personality that is rarely described in the scholarly journals for its obstinate strength and ability to survive. Neither is its peculiar humanistic character and quiet courage viewed as the epitome of what the American model of femininity should be.[5]

You and I know that the Black woman suffers from two handicaps in this country—that of being Black and of being female. This would seem to indicate that we ought to be very active in the women's liberation movements. Yet, the number of Black women active in the movement have been small, and even among some of those there is not total agreement with all of the goals of the movement. Some have said that it is difficult to find a truly total Black feminist. Why is this? Is it that the problems which the women's liberation movement attempts to address are less relevant to the Black woman? Are the problems of white middle class women, basically the leaders of the feminist movement, different from those of Black women? . . .

Whether you agree with her or not, it is clear that Black women tend to view their problems larger than those of the women's movement. One characteristic of the women's liberation movement appears to be a battle between the sexes—a struggle for equalization of power in interpersonal relationships. Some would say that this is the kind of battle that Black folk can ill afford to engage in. There are too many other battles to be fought. Black women have not traditionally perceived their enemy to be Black men, but rather to be the forces in our society which tends to prevent the attainment of equal opportunity for Black men, women and children . . .

Given the status of Blacks and of Black women in particular, I want to turn to my concern for representation of the interest of Black women. Clearly, with the variety of problems which we need to work toward solving we need our interest to be strongly and aggressively represented in those forums where creative solutions and changes can be initiated. I am talking about such forums as our respective state and local governing bodies, the congress, The White House, relevant conferences and conventions, federal agencies, and state agencies. We need representation that can obtain access to and provide input into policy-making which will affect the Black community.

---

5. JOYCE LADNER, TOMORROW'S TOMORROW: THE BLACK WOMAN 280 (Garden City, N.Y., Doubleday 1972).

Although we have made significant gains in securing Black elected and appointed officials at both the local and national levels, the relative proportions of Black representatives in legislatures and the congress is still very small, thereby limiting the voting influence of these representatives. The same is true with respect to Black officials. Their influence on policies of any administration, also is limited.

Thus, there is a major role to be played by Black women's organizations to bring their influence to bear on issues, and on officials and politicians who will make the policy and legislative decisions on matters involving employment, education, housing, urban development, and other issues which directly impact on Black women, and on the Black community.

The history of the Black women's organization movement is a long one. Black women organized at first at the local level. During the Civil War, local Black women organizations performed many daring rescue feats supplying relief to the Black regiments and to freedmen. Local women clubs sprang up in cities and they began to exchange information and delegates and to form loose federations.

However, it was not until 1896 that any viable national organization of Black women was formed. Students of history know that after the Civil War lynching of Black men increased. In 1895, European countries began to protest such conduct. Part of this protest resulted from the speaking campaign abroad conducted by Ida Wells Barnett, an Afro-American woman whose speaking tour of England, aroused a great debate in that country over lynching and was the basis for the formation of a British anti-lynching society. The south was offended by this campaign, and in a widely circulated statement by the president of the Missouri Press Association to British Society it was stated, "The Negroes in this country were wholly devoid of morality, the women were prostitutes and all were natural thieves and liars."

We are told that as a result of this response, Black club women were determined to fight back. This statement by the Missouri Press Association promoted the convening of the First National Conference of Colored Women, which led to the formation of the National Association of Colored Women in 1896.

We know that the Black sororities were formed in the early 1900's, with Zeta Phi Beta being founded in 1920. We are all aware of various church women's groups that were formed in the first half of the 1900's as well as professional organizations. In 1935, Mary Macleod Bethune founded the National Council of Negro Women, an umbrella organization made up of some 26 Black women's organizations, and representing over 3 million Black women.

Too little tribute has been given to the role that Black women's organizations have played in the life of the Black community, or to the larger role they have played in this country. In summary they have:

1) Provided local community services, welfare and charitable assistance;
2) Been instrumental in providing training programs and/or making training information available to the Black community;
3) Fostered and facilitated higher educational goals and opportunities for Black youth, both male and female, through scholarship assistance, stay in school programs, and through local remedial education assistance;
4) Promoted Black cultural programs and artists, fostering the development of cultural pride on the part of all Blacks;
5) Played a significant role in voter registration of Blacks, and encouraged utilization of the vote as an effective instrument of change in this country;
6) Encouraged and assisted in the development of home ownership programs affordable by all income levels, and worked for adequate housing for the poor;
7) Raised funds and collected funds for hunger programs and implemented systems for distribution of such funds and food;
8) Lobbied, both local and state legislatures, as well as congress for legislation promoting the rights of minorities and women, as well as for legislation which would improve the quality of life for all Americans;
9) Provided a mechanism for fellowship among Black women and for socializing and sharing common goals and objectives; and finally, but certainly not least,
10) Provided a mechanism through which Black women could develop and exercise leadership skills, which have in a number of instances been translated and utilized in services beyond the organization of the Black community . . .

My own observations are that as Black women we need to make a greater commitment to our Black organizations. *Believe me politicians and policymakers are influenced by the pressures brought by numbers.* Our organizations provide us a means of collectively exercising the influence of our total membership on those who exercise power in our system. For some of us, it is the only way to be heard effectively. Yet, we have to understand that it takes more than just an organization to be effective. It takes leadership, resources, and the ability to gain access to the right sources, as well as the ability to form coalitions around issues, or problems. The issues are becoming more sophisticated, the stakes are higher, the competing interests larger . . . To represent us well, our Black organizations must devise means of finding out what it is we want to do, how we the membership stand on an issue . . .

Anna Julia Cooper believed in 1896 that the opportunities for us, as Black women, to make significant impact on how our lives and the lives of Black people are fashioned is there. We must determine that we are going to continue to support our Black organizations, not just at the level of the past, but at an increased level. For those of us who may have been disenchanted because our leadership was not as active as we would like; or our programs are not ones we would choose, or for any other reason, we must not let this disenchantment turn us away from our organizations. If we believe in what we want, we must work within for change, while continuing our support.

PART 3

Legal Education, the Legal Academy, and the Legal Profession

In 1897, Lutie A. Lytle, a black woman, became the first woman in the nation to teach law in a chartered law school.[1] Unfortunately, no known statements to enlighten us about her experience and philosophy as a law teacher at Central Tennessee Law School in Nashville have been unearthed.

Until recently, there has been a dearth of black women entering American law schools. For example, in 1970 there were 446 black women lawyers and 11,664 white women lawyers in the nation. The 1990 census shows 11,006 black women lawyers and 161,044 white women lawyers.[2] Although women have faced significant obstacles in their efforts to enter white law schools, black women have fared much better in their admission to historically black law schools.

The first group of articles are by black women lawyers on their struggles to overcome racial and gender barriers in white and black law schools, including articles by the first black woman to establish a law school and the first black tenure-track law professor at a white law school. Pauli Murray's appeal to Harvard Law School to admit her to its graduate law program in 1944 is a core document leading to the admission of women who later entered Harvard's law school in 1950.[3] In addition, two accounts of efforts by black women to be admitted to the University of Michigan reveal disappointment by one black woman law student admitted in 1936, and triumph by another in 1944, the year that the University of Michigan graduated its first black woman.

A second group of articles are by black women on the legal profession. There

---

1. See J. CLAY SMITH JR., EMANCIPATION: THE MAKING OF THE BLACK LAWYER, 1844–1944, at 58 (Philadelphia, University of Pennsylvania Press 1993).

2. See Appendix C, *infra. See also* Richard Chused, *The Hiring and Retention of Minorities and Women on American Law School Faculties,* 137 U. PA. L. REV. 537 (1988).

3. See Foreword, ALUMNAE DIRECTORY, WOMEN AT HARVARD LAW SCHOOL: CELEBRATING 35: 1953–1988 (1988).

is a scarcity of statements and articles by black women lawyers on the legal profession because black women historically have not been included in policy-making roles in white bar groups. Since 1925, black women have had the greatest impact in historically black bar groups, as have black male lawyers. In recent years, as more black women have become active in the American Bar Association, they have also raised their voices urging that group, and other bar groups, to expand their programs and focus on issues relevant to black lawyers.

Pauli Murray's Appeal: For Admission to Harvard Law School

PAULI MURRAY

(1944)

I WISH TO MAKE FORMAL APPLICATION for a review of my application to enter Harvard University Law School for graduate work. The correspondence relating to this application to-date will be found in the files of Prof. T. R. Powell, Chairman of the Committee on Graduate Studies. These are my reasons and the justification for my request for a review:

(A) Personal Factors

(1) During my three years at Howard Law School, my training was much influenced by men of Harvard, whose records stand for themselves, to-wit, James A. Washington, Jr., Bernard Jefferson, William H. Hastie, Charles Houston and Leon A. Ransom. For three years I hoped I might be able to some day win the "Harvard Crimson for my academic gown" as I watched the Harvard men march in our faculty processions, both the men from the law school and the men from the other departments.

(2) There is a campus tradition, that Howard is a miniature edition in sepia of Harvard, and I have been caught between the tradition of Howard and the tradition of Harvard not to admit women.

(3) Very recent medical examination reveals me to be a functionally normal woman with perhaps a "male slant" on things, which may account for my insistence upon getting into Harvard.

Petition by Pauli Murray to Harvard University Graduate School for admission to Harvard Law School's Masters of Law Program, circa summer, 1944. Fifty-two years later ten black 1975 Harvard law graduates tell what it was like at the law school. Patricia J. Williams, *Notes from a Small World,* THE NEW YORKER, April 9 & May 6, 1996, at 87. Nearly fifty-five years later, Lani Guinier became the first black woman appointed with tenure as a professor at the Harvard Law School. Ethan Bronner, *Lani Guinier Joins Faculty of Law School at Harvard,* N.Y. TIMES, Jan. 24, 1998, at A12. No doubt, Professor Derrick Bell's protest to have a black woman on the faculty influenced this decision. Derrick Bell, *At Last, Harvard Sees the Light,* N.Y. TIMES, Jan. 29, 1998, at A27.

(4) At present the Howard man at Harvard is or was during the year 1943–44 Francisco Carniero, former Chief Justice of the Court of Peers, and an honor student throughout his career in Liberal Arts College. We had joint classes last year at law school and I was his rival. In some courses he topped me by two points, in a very difficult course I topped him by a number of points.

(5) I have stood "top man" in my class against keen competition for three years, and until the national newspaper publicity that "Pauli Murray had been awarded a Rosenwald Fellowship to do graduate study in labor law at Harvard University," I had a record which was potentially the highest record that had ever come through the Howard School of Law, and your records will affirm this. I was alternately congratulated and kidded by turns. Many people did not know of Harvard's regulation against women. Only Harvard men knew.

(6) Sometime during the fall of 1943, the rumor began on Howard Campus that Harvard had let down its bars against women, and that women were now free to go to the Law School. Not content with the rumors I wrote to the Secretary of the Harvard Law School, I think, and asked for a confirmation or denial of the rumors. A letter from the office of the Secretary, under date of January 5th, 1944, informed me: "Your letter of the fourth is received. The definite ruling of the Harvard Law School in regard to the admission of women is that the School is not open to women for registration." The letter was initialed M.M.

(7) On the same day I wrote the letter to Harvard I had filed my application with the Rosenwald Fund, and in the space listed for choice of school I wrote, "I should like to obtain my Master's Degree at Harvard University, in the event they have removed their bar against women students. If not, then I should like to work at Yale University or at any other University which has advanced in the field of Labor Law. I cannot state at this time under what authorities I should like to do my graduate work, since at present many of the authorizations in Labor Law are on leave from their universities and working for the United States Government." I was therefore surprised when the publicity came through; I was more than surprised; I was mortified; it was such an emotional shock that I almost went to pieces as the four C's on my examinations will indicate. Under the impact of this comedy of errors and the general strain of completing the three years work, some internal problems of our own school, and the sheer disappointment of it all, I could not review for my final exams and took them all without any preparation whatsoever. Any law school student will tell you what that means. For me it meant the loss of the most enviable record at Howard University School of Law. It was particularly important to gain this record in order to lessen the general prejudice which men have against women entering the legal profession. This loss was both a disappointment to me and a keen disappointment to those professors who had watched my career, helped to shape it, and hoped to send me out a "shining light" for the legal profession. It was a complete reversal from my freshman year record and showed no growth at all, but

rather retrogression. It also suggested instability, which is not a recommendation for a potential lawyer who must stand up against many emotional strains in the course of his career. The penalty for letting this thing "get me down" has been to stand here and take the silent disappointment of my professors instead of running away and forgetting the whole business.

(8) Having "taken all this punishment" my naturally aggressive temperament decided not to take it lying down, but to put up a clean fight to get into Harvard. Professor Powell's files will give you the complete story from this point.

(9) One humorous factor which should not be overlooked is that I toy with words. I held certificates or degrees from Hillside High, from Hunter College, from Howard University, and I used to kid everybody and say "When I get my degree from Harvard, I'll belong to the 4-H club." Silly, no doubt, but that's the way some of us help ourselves along, by finding something to laugh at.

(B) Social Factors

(1) I have met a number of women and have heard of many others who wished to attend Harvard and yet were refused. This fight is not mine, but that of women who feel they should have free access to the very best of legal education. Harvard still carries the reputation of being the No. 1 Law School where all No. 1 students want to go. It also carries with it prestige value, the school of presidents, prime ministers, judges, governors, etc. which women of intellectual talent desire equally with men.

(2) The traditions of the United States are being broken right and left—that is those traditions which stand in the way of progress. Howard has even broken a few. Last year we had our first woman president of Student Council, the most outstanding student this year and president of the 1944–45 Student Council is a woman and comes from Harvard's own state, Miss Ruth Powell, 33 Emerson Road, Milton, Mass. For the first time in more than 25 years, a downtown white restaurant served a group of Negro students without any commotion beyond the usual curiosity and dramatic incidents which attend any kind of group demonstration. The leader of this demonstration was again Miss Powell, of your state; the technique used was a realization of the philosophy of Thoreau from your state. The Law School of Howard University elected its first woman Chief Justice of the Court of Peers and woman president of the Senior Class.[1] These are minute "mirrorings" of what is going on in the larger community.

Along with this breaking of traditions, women are taking their places shoulder to shoulder with men in the prosecution of the present war. Miss Powell was a number 1 welder in the Boston shipyards last year. I alternated between victory garden farming, washing dishes in a restaurant and waiting tables to serve Red Cross women on their way overseas, Wacs, Waves, men in the army, navy and air corps who were either in New York on furlough or on their way to

---

1. Pauli Murray.

battle. My women colleagues this summer are working as welders, or riveters, or newspaper women, or in any job in which they can make a contribution to the labor force of the country.

Women are practicing before the Supreme Court, they have become judges and good lawyers, they are represented on the President's Cabinet and greater demand is being made for women lawyers in administrative positions as the men move into the armed forces. They are proving themselves worthy of the confidence and trust placed in them and many of them of stepping right into the jobs which their husbands have left behind. They are taking an intelligent view toward the political events at home and abroad, and statistics show they are in the majority of the voting population this year. A spot-check on memory would indicate there are only four important places they are not now holding— (1) As graduates of Harvard University, (2) as President of the United States, (3) as a member of the United States Supreme Court, and as (4) workers in the mines.

Although Harvard might lose in the sense of a loss of tradition, it might gain in the quality of the law school student personnel.

(3) The present war will cost the United States much in the sacrifice of young men, who, but for the war would be our future law-makers, judges, governors, and leaders in government. I understand the registration at Harvard Law School has been almost annihilated. Rumor has it that only 4 graduate students were there during the past year. The question is not whether Harvard may withstand the economic loss of a low registration; no one doubts the tremendous financial resources at Harvard's disposal. The question is rather, the great institutions of learning must close their doors because of lack of students and rob the future of a whole generation of professional people equipped to guide our country through the post-war period of readjustments, or whether because Harvard refuses to replace its men with women as other institutions are forced to do, it allows tradition to stand in the way of progress. I saw this need at Howard and have spent no little time urging and encouraging talented young women to enter law school. My own record has inspired at least a dozen women to study law, and some have even switched from sociology majors and other fields to political science. As members of a minority group, these women have seen the value of lawyers to implement public discussion of the problems we face, and to gain justice for our group before the courts of the nation.

(4) What will be some of the consequences of Harvard's failure to admit me? Perhaps none of them will really hurt Harvard, but they will tend to discredit the liberal tradition which Harvard has symbolized. First of all, the Negro press will blast this rejection to the nation. Your rejection will not stand on its merits, but in the mind of many people who do not know the facts the issue will be confused with the belief that Harvard is turning down a Negro: I know my folks and my newspaper men, having dabbled in publicity myself. Once be-

fore I was rejected by the University of North Carolina as an applicant for graduate work. I tried to learn from my mistakes in that application, and not to antagonize the policy-makers at Harvard. I believe with reason and discussion of my application on its merits, an agreement can be reached. Nor do I want to try and discredit Harvard, nor even threaten publicity. The fact is a number of representatives of the national Negro press and also a few white newspapermen know about this Harvard application already and think it fine newspaper material. I have held back any release because it seemed more like good sportsmanship to "play the game," asking Harvard for a thorough discussion of the whole matter by the proper persons, boards, committees, and whatnot, than to attempt any social pressure.

The second consequence is that even if you reject my application and I give up the fight, you will not be rid of applications and similar kinds of arguments on the part of young women. The young women down here at Howard are depending upon me to open the door to Harvard. They will follow with their own applications if my guess is correct—many of them want to go to Harvard as their fathers and brothers have done. When young white women get wind of it, they will begin renewing their efforts, and it may end up in a veritable pressure, since women are now demanding an "equal rights" constitutional amendment.

Already there is a great deal of discussion going on Howard campus as to the merits of my application. I've polled the Harvard men. They seem quite sympathetic.

This is as much as I care to say now. Would it be asking too much to let this appeal go up on its merits, and get an expression of opinion from the men of Harvard, as students, as alumni, as well as the proper administrative channels— the President of Harvard and the Board of Trustees?

Second Black Woman at University
of Michigan's Law School

LUCIA THEODOSIA THOMAS

(1994)

I WAS THE SECOND NEGRO WOMAN to enter the University of Michigan Law School. I was admitted to the University of Michigan Law School in 1936, but when I applied for admission to the law school they did not know that I was black. I was awarded the LaVerne Noyes scholarship. This was a scholarship that was set aside for veterans' children. My father was a captain in the U.S. Army and had fought in World War I. The admissions officer at the law school told me that since I had graduated from Xavier University, I had a good chance of being admitted. He assumed that I was white because Xavier was a Catholic university, and he did not know that blacks were Catholic, and that Xavier was a black university. The name of the admissions officer was a man named Paul A. Leidy, a native of Mississippi.

Leidy was also a member of the law faculty at Michigan from 1926 to 1952. When I arrived on the Ann Arbor campus in 1936, Professor Leidy told me that only one other black woman student, a woman from Detroit, had ever attended the law school, and that she left after three months. After Professor Leidy made this statement, I told him that I would be there for more than three months. Thereafter, Professor Leidy tried to persuade me to take up medicine. He said that "the law school's mission was to train judges and legislators." Leidy saw no role as judge or legislator for a black woman. Leidy believed that if I went into medicine I would always have colored people to work for.

I recall that in 1938 there were five women in the entering law class at the University of Michigan. After the first year only Pat Potter survived. All of the women students sat on the first row seats in all the classes. Pat Potter also took abuse. Potter's father was a lawyer in Detroit. One professor said more than once

---

An original submission to this volume.

during class that at least Potter would have a chance to work in her father's law office as his secretary. I was not really welcomed at the law school.

Two black male law students in the third year class really helped me get through the first year, Cecil F. Poole[1] and William Martin. I studied with them.

I left the law school in 1938 without graduating because my father had a stroke. I transferred to the Robert H. Terrell Law School, a black law school in Washington, D.C., so that I could work to make more money to help support my family. I do not regret that I left the University of Michigan's law school because had I remained, I would have missed so much of the civil rights action going on in Washington, D.C. It was during my student days at Terrell Law School that I got to meet Thurgood Marshall, Charles Hamilton Houston, William Henry Hastie, and Belford V. Lawson. I saw them involved in the protest to eliminate Jim Crow, and because I was from Texas I understood all too well the importance of the civil rights work that these men were doing. Coming to Washington broadened my vision of the importance of the law and civil rights, a vision that I had not been exposed to at Michigan.

---

1. In 1976, Cecil F. Poole became a U.S. District Judge in California.

Breaking New Ground with Grace:
The University of Michigan's First Black
Woman Law Graduate

JANE CLEO MARSHALL LUCAS

(1994)

EARLY YEARS. I was born in Benton Harbor, Michigan, in 1920 and attended public schools there, except for my junior year in high school when I attended the Laboratory School at Atlanta University. My father, Edson S. Marshall, a native of Little Rock, Arkansas, was the window trimmer and ad writer at the local department store. He was a human sponge that absorbed information from all about him. My mother, Tina T. Marshall, was born in Benton Harbor, Michigan. She attended Fisk University for one year before she married. She worked as a nurse's aid, as a teacher's aid, and in a factory during World War II. She finally received her undergraduate degree from Western Michigan University at the age of eighty-five. She delivered the principal address at the graduation exercises with nary a note. I am their only child.

Benton Harbor was a small, predominately white, blue-collar town. There were two blacks in my graduating class at Benton Harbor High School. My parents wanted me to continue my education at the University of Michigan. I wanted to attend Howard University. One might say I wanted to "reach out and touch" more blacks. It was finally agreed that if I obtained a scholarship to Howard, I could do my undergraduate work there. However, I would have to enroll at the University of Michigan for further studies. I received a scholarship and entered Howard University in 1937.

Years before Law School. When I was a child of ten or eleven years of age, my parents told me that they wanted me to be a lawyer. Thus, I grew up knowing that I was expected to become a lawyer. The possibility of another career choice never occurred to me. I had no idea what subjects one should study as a pre-law student. For some reason, unknown to me today, I chose political science as a major. In retrospect I can think of more pertinent and practical areas of study.

An original submission to this volume.

My time at Howard was happy and carefree. Learning was a pleasure; many of the most brilliant black minds comprised the faculty. One of my favorite professors was Dr. Rayford Logan. In my senior year I applied for two scholarships—one to Cornell University Graduate School, the other to study in Puerto Rico the summer following graduation. I received the latter. When I told Dr. Logan of my disappointment in not receiving both, he said, "Jane, if you receive half of the things in life you want, you will be fortunate." As it turned out, I did go to graduate school. Puerto Rico was a great place for a twenty-year-old to spend the summer.

After graduating from Howard University in 1941, I entered the Horace H. Rackham School of Graduate Studies at the University of Michigan, where I received a master of arts degree in political science in 1942. That fall I entered the University of Michigan Law School, the only law school to which I applied.

Days at University of Michigan Law School.   I encountered no overt racial prejudice from students or the faculty. The only suggestion of prejudice I remember occurred when I registered. A middle-aged white lady who was probably the head clerk said to me, "You are not the first colored girl to enter the law school. None of them finished. We'll see what you do." I felt no gender prejudice.

There were several black male students; I was the only black female student. There were about eight or nine white female students. I was the only black female student. There were no blacks or women on the faculty.

Actually, some of the white students were quite friendly, although we did not socialize off campus. I recall one woman student telling me how much she hated Jews. This did cause me to wonder what she said about blacks when I was not around.

At the time no women were allowed to live in the Law Quadrangle, living quarters adjacent to classrooms and library. I cannot remember whether any black male students lived there. My guess is that they did not. For a while I lived in a private home. Later I moved into a large rambling structure, called the "B" home, where a number of black women lived. It was run by the university as a dormitory of sorts. At about this time a few black undergraduate students were being accepted in the regular dormitories.

Shortly before graduating from law school, I went to Washington, D.C., for a visit. While there, I talked with Dr. Logan about job possibilities. He suggested that I go to Philadelphia and seek the advice of Sadie T. Alexander and her husband Raymond Pace Alexander, both of them were lawyers. She was the first black woman lawyer that I had ever met. She said that the best thing she could advise me to do was to "marry a black lawyer." I thought that was hilarious! At any rate I never met a black lawyer who showed any interest in marrying me.

In order to graduate as many men as possible before they were drafted to serve in World War II, the law school went on the trimester system. As a result,

I was able to finish in two calendar years. Because of the small number of graduates in the classes of 1943, 1944, and 1945, our class reunions are held together. I graduated from the University of Michigan Law School in 1944 and passed the Michigan bar examination shortly thereafter.

I did not return to the campus until 1989, to attend our forty-fifth class reunion. I was the only female and only black lawyer there. I had forgotten most of the men and knew none of their wives. Yet this was one of the most enjoyable experiences in my relatively long life. I did not get the impression that anyone was exceptionally nice to me out of a sense of duty. I was simply accepted as an integral part of the group.

After Law School.   My first job was in the law office of the only black lawyer in Alabama, Arthur Davis Shores. My father's sister, who lived in Birmingham, had written me that Mr. Shores needed an assistant. I wrote him about the position and began working in his office in the fall of 1944.

I applied to take the Alabama bar examination, but as fast as I met one qualifying hurdle, another presented itself. In the meantime I helped Mr. Shores draft pleadings on a variety of subjects. Sometimes I would accompany him to court. Mr. Shores was a gentle and kind man, who was well liked by whites as well as blacks. He was in great demand as a speaker; I assisted in writing his speeches on social and legal issues. I worked for Mr. Shores for about a year, after which I married and moved to Fairmont Heights, Maryland. Ironically, just before I left Alabama, I received notice I was eligible to take the bar examination.

In 1946 four or five black men and I took the Maryland bar examination. To my knowledge one man, a graduate of Northwestern University Law School, and I were the only blacks to pass. I have often wondered if the criterion for admitting blacks to the bar was the school attended. It is my understanding that no black female had previously passed the Maryland bar.

In the fall of 1946, I received a call from Dean George M. Johnson inviting me to join the law faculty of Howard University. H. Elsie Austin was originally scheduled to teach, but for some reason she decided not to in late summer. At that time the law school was committed to adding a woman to the faculty. However, I am sure anyone would have been welcome under the circumstances. Fortunately for me, an unemployed black female lawyer living in the outskirts of Washington, D.C., was brought to their attention.

Thus I became the first woman to teach full-time on the law faculty. Other members of the faculty were distinguished and brilliant men: James A. Washington Jr., James M. Nabrit Jr., Spottswood W. Robinson III, Herbert O. Reid Sr., Howard Jenkins, and Charles Quick. Our relationship within the law school was pleasant. Some of the men often had lunch together. Occasionally I was invited. Outside of the law school we attended many of the same social functions. Often we were guests in each other's homes.

During my first two years of teaching, the law school offered day and night classes. This was done in an effort to help World War II veterans to catch up on their education. My husband and I did not own a car. Each morning at eight o'clock I would walk along a dusty, unpaved road with no sidewalks to catch a street car. After about an hour's ride I would arrive at the campus where I stayed until ten o'clock at night. Then I reversed the procedure and came home. It was indeed kind of Dean Johnson not to give me an early morning class.

As I recall, I taught personal property, wills, torts, and domestic relations. Most of the male students were older than I; most of the female students were younger. All were serious students. My own experience in the law was limited. My method of teaching was to concentrate on the basic principles of common law. I did not feel I was shortchanging the students because other members of the faculty had many theories about many subjects, which they freely expressed in the classroom. At various times, my former students have told me that they always passed those sections of bar examinations based on courses taught by me.

After World War II, there was a common saying that "Daddy goes to school; mother works." A large number of the students were married; some had children. My husband, a veteran, was a medical student. As a result of this similarity in our lives, students related to me as a person, not just a teacher. I was their Ann Landers.

In 1950, I resigned from the law faculty. My husband and I moved to Staten Island, New York, where he did his internship.

Other Work Experiences.   We settled permanently in the Washington, D.C., area. Marriage to a man who no longer wanted me to work and my own indifference to law combined to make further work sporadic and mundane.

I worked in the Women's Division of the Labor Department. During that time I helped to write a handbook on women's rights.

Later I worked at the Civil Rights Commission. What I remember most is counting the heads of little black children entering desegregated schools. At any given time we knew with almost exact precision how many black children were enrolled in every public school in the South. This information was used by law enforcement agencies of the government. Actually, it was fascinating to watch the total picture develop.

My last job was with the newly created Equal Employment Opportunity Commission in the late sixties. I reviewed discrimination complaints to see if further action was warranted.

Conclusion.   If I broke new ground, it was not because I strove to do so. It simply happened. One of my high school English teachers defined a grace as "an unmerited blessing." Whatever my accomplishments may have been, they are just that—graces.

Neither a Whisper Nor a Shout

Joyce Anne Hughes

(1995)

IN 1971 WHEN I BECAME the first Black[1] woman tenure-track law professor at a white school,[2] I did not know the history that would locate me along a continuum of previous Black women who taught law. An African-American, Lutie A. Lytle was "America's first woman law professor in 1897."[3] However, Sybil Jones Dedmond has been identified as the first African-American woman tenure-track law professor.[4] She taught from 1951 to 1964 at an ABA approved

---

The title was inspired by a passage from ELLIS COSE, THE RAGE OF A PRIVILEGED CLASS 9 (New York, HarperCollins 1993): "Racial discussions tend to be conducted at one of two levels—either in shouts or in whispers. The shouters are generally so twisted by pain or ignorance that spectators tune them out. The whisperers are so afraid of the sting of truth that they avoid saying much of anything at all." While this exposition is not a "racial discussion," race has had a major role in much of my history.

    1. I use the term Black with a capital "B" to indicate African-American, as contrasted with the term black with a lower case "b" which I used for a color.

    2. It may be a misnomer to use this term for any school whose enrollment includes Black students. However, I use it to exclude the predominantly Black law schools of Howard, North Carolina Central, Southern, and Thurgood Marshall School of Law at Texas Southern.

    3. J. CLAY SMITH JR., EMANCIPATION: THE MAKING OF THE BLACK LAWYER, 1844–1944 18 (Philadelphia, University of Pennsylvania Press 1993). Lytle taught at a Black law school, Central Tennessee College, located in Nashville, Tennessee. Id. at 57, 58, 344, 353. Central Tennessee's law school continued until 1921. Id. at 58. Lytle is the first woman of any race to teach at a chartered law school in the nation's history. In 1886, a year before she became a law professor, Ellen Spencer Mussey, white, and Emma Gillett, also white but a graduate of Howard, a Black law school, instructed students in their law office. Id. at 88–89 n.263. See also Herma Hill Kay, The Future of Women Law Professors, 77 IOWA L. REV. 5, 5 (1991) [hereinafter Kay]. The first woman tenure-track law professor at an American Bar Association (ABA) approved and American Association of Law Schools (AALS) school was Barbara Nachtrieb Armstrong who was appointed an instructor in law and social economics at the University of California, Berkeley in 1922. Id. at 5–6.

    4. Id. at 9 (Kay).

Black law school, North Carolina Central.[5] Unlike Dedmond, whose students "accepted her, in part because many of these black men had been taught by black women in undergraduate school and the segregated primary and elementary schools of the American South,"[6] in my early years of teaching, my students were primarily white males. So the challenges I faced were unlike my Black female predecessors who taught at Black law schools. Indeed, I was the first Black woman graduate of the University of Minnesota Law School, where I started law teaching. Not only was I the first Black professor, I was the first woman professor of any race. So I suffered the "double jeopardy"[7] of both sex and race. That "double jeopardy" still exists. In 1994 women were 26% of full-time law professors[8] but only 177 were Black women.[9] Thus we are only 3.5% of all law professors.

When I joined the faculty at the University of Minnesota Law School, the appointment received some attention.[10] Overlooking its significance in Black history, a Minneapolis paper called it "a gain for women's lib . . . "[11] But some University of Minnesota Black law students were reported to have "preferred a black man on the faculty."[12] In the academic year I started law teaching, women were 9% of total law school enrollment; about half were first year students.[13] Black enrollment was one-half that: in all ABA-approved schools in 1971–72

---

5. *Id.* at 9 n.21.

6. Emma Coleman Jordan, *Images of Black Women in the Legal Academy: An Introduction*, 6 BERKELEY WOMEN'S L.J. 1, 13 (1990–91).

7. Frances Beale, *Double Jeopardy: To Be Black and Female, in* TONI CADE, ED., THE BLACK WOMAN 90–100 (New York, The American Library, Inc. 1970).

8. AMERICAN BAR ASSOCIATION, A REVIEW OF LEGAL EDUCATION IN THE UNITED STATES 67 (1994) (Published by the ABA Section of Legal Education & Admissions to the Bar) [hereinafter ABA].

9. J. OF BLACKS IN HIGHER ED., Winter 1994/95, at 29. For a collection of essays by Black women law professors, *see Symposium, Images of Black Women in the Legal Academy,* 6 BERKELEY WOMEN'S L.J. 1–201 (1990–91).

10. Brian Anderson, *Three Women Named by 'U' Regents,* MPLS. TRIB., Apr. 17, 1971, at 1A; Floyd Egner, *Regents Appoint 3 Women during 'Nonroutine' Session,* MINN. DAILY, Apr. 19, 1971; *First Black Woman Graduate of 'U' Law School Named,* MPLS. SPOKESMAN, Apr. 22, 1971, at 1; *Joyce Hughes to Join Law School Faculty,* TWIN CITIES COURIER, Apr. 24, 1971, at 1; *Black Woman to Join Law School Faculty,* U. OF MINN. ALUMNI NEWS, May, 1971, at 50. *See also, At the University of Minnesota Law School: A 'Together' Prof.,* EBONY, May, 1972, at 39.

11. *Editorial,* MPLS. STAR, Apr. 19, 1971 (on file with author).

12. BLACK TIMES (Albany, Calif.), Aug., 1971 at 18. My response was quoted as "[I]t is important that the brothers know that I do not want to gain one inch at their expense. We cannot allow a wedge to be driven between us for mutual respect and shared responsibility is (sic) essential in the struggle for liberation." *Id.* Cf. Barbara J. Williams, *Black Women in Law,* 1 BLK L.J. 171 (1971) in which the author emphatically states, "THERE IS NO PROBLEM BETWEEN BLACK MEN AND BLACK WOMEN. THE PROBLEM IS BETWEEN BLACK PEOPLE AND WHITE SOCIETY."

13. ABA, *supra* note 8, at 67. Total J.D. enrollment was 91,225 of which women were 8,567. Of that number, 4,326 were first-year students.

Blacks were 4.1% of all students and almost half were first year.[14] It is not known how many of the country's Black students were female or how many women students were Black. The number was probably small, if judged by the number of African-American women lawyers and judges in 1970—only 500.[15] Challenges faced by Black women law professors are cumulative of those encountered by Black male professors and women professors.[16] In summarizing the June 1973 "hearing"—my second year of teaching—a section of the American Association of Law Schools reported the expectations of me:

> [T]o be a counselor to individual black and other minority students, as well as a tutor, a friend, a companion and a champion; to be a recruiter for black and other minority group students and for women students; to be available for unscheduled consultation on the "black question", or the "woman question"; to participate in formal and informal seminars on race relations and sex stereotyping; to endure with grace and tolerance both inadvertent and overt racial slurs; to serve on all special committees relating to minority groups and women; and, of course, to teach her regular classes, serve on the regular faculty committees, publish scholarly articles and be "one of the boys."[17]

That "hearing" was characterized by the dean as a special meeting of the University of Minnesota Law faculty. It was nine and one half hours long. There were fourteen (14) observers who attended all or part of the meeting, including representatives from the Association of American Law Schools, the Association

---

14. Edward L. Littlejohn and Leonard S. Rubinowitz, *Black Enrollment in Law Schools: Forward to the Past*, 12 THURGOOD MARSHALL L. REV. 415, 435. Total enrollment was 91,225 with Black enrollment being 3,744 or 4.1%. However, these were all ABA-approved law schools, which would include some predominantly Black law schools.

15. Stacey M. Brooks & Maurice Foster, *Another Dimension*, NBA MAGAZINE, Sept., 1992 at 20.

16. Speaking of being both Black and female in our early years in the profession, Prof. Patricia King of Georgetown said, "The combination is deadly, or can be deadly. I catch it from both sides. . . . I have found that being a woman as well as Black is a double barrier." *Proceedings of Minority Group Law Teachers Planning Conference* Sept. 19–20, 1974, Harvard Law School, 4 BLACK L.J. 575, 584 (1975) [hereinafter cited as Minority Group Law Teachers]. *See generally, Symposium, Black Women Law Professors: Building a Community at the Intersection of Race and Gender,* 6 BERKELEY WOMEN'S L.J. 1–201 (1991). For all "people of color" law professors, Professor Reginald L. Robinson said, "we get questioned more, doubted often and dismissed quickly." A.A.L.S. SEC. ON MINORITY GROUPS NEWSLETTER, Oct., 1995 at 2.

17. *AALS, Proceedings* 1973 at 145 (Report of Section on Minority Groups). More than 10 years after this event, the added duties of minority faculty still existed. *See* Derrick Bell, *Introduction* to Richard Delgado, *Minority Law Professors' Lives: The Bell-Delgado Survey*, 24 HARV. C.R.-C.L. L. REV. 349, 352 (1989) [hereinafter cited as Delgado]. *See also* Cheryl I. Harris, *Law Professors of Color and the Academy: Of Poets and Kings*, 68 CHI-KENT L. REV. 331, 342 n.31 (1992) [hereinafter Harris].

of American University Professors, the Minneapolis Urban League and students.[18] I was seated at a table in front with the then dean—the person who had replaced the dean in office when I was hired, a person who had been my professor when I was a student and who, a year after the special faculty meeting, made statements about affirmative action which "greatly angered many law students."[19]

The genesis of the June 1973 meeting was a University of Minnesota Law School Grievance Committee handling of a student petition six months earlier in December 1972. Actually, the saga starts in September 1972. I was teaching one of two sections of Legal Professions, a course dealing with lawyers' ethical responsibilities and then the only *required* third year course. At the beginning of the academic year 1972–1973 students sought faculty approval to change the evaluation from the normal grading to a Pass/Fail system. A faculty committee recommended approval and both the professor teaching the other section and I remained neutral[20] when the issue was brought to the full faculty. However,

---

18. Not all observers remained throughout the lengthy meeting. Outside observers were:

A.A.L.S.—Dean Walter J. Leonard, Chair, Sec. Minority Groups
*A.A.L.S.—Prof. Paul Oberst, representing Ass'n president
A.A.U.P.—Prof. George A. Donohue
U. of M. Federation of Teachers—Prof. Hyman Berman
*U. of M. Equal Opp. & Affirm. Action—Ms. Lillian Williams
*U. of M. Ofc. V.P. for Academic Admin.—Ms. Nancy L. Groves
Mpls. Urban League—Mr. William E. English

Student observers were:

*Michael Hoover, Law School Council
Joseph Hudson, Black American Law Students' Association
Theodore Massey, Black American Law Students' Association
Trina Chope, Black American Law Students' Association
*Dennis Peck, Grievance Committee
*William Pickell, Grievance Committee
*Stephen Chapple, Grievance Committee

Those with an asterisk were there at the invitation of the Dean. The others came upon my request.

19. *"Request to the Dean,"* MINN. DAILY, Nov. 18, 1974 at 8 (Letter to editor, signed by 92 law students). *See also* Carl A. Auerbach, *Dean Clarifies Stand,* MINN. DAILY, Nov. 18, 1974, at 9 (Letter to editor); *"Auerbach Reiterates Questioned Lecture,"* MINN. DAILY, Nov. 19, 1974 at 1; *"Auerbach's Sincerity Questioned about AA,"* TWIN CITY OBSERVER, Nov. 20, 1974 at 1. Cf. Carl A. Auerbach, *The Silent Opposition of Professors and Graduate Students to Preferential Affirmative Action Programs: 1969 and 1975,* 72 MINN. L. REV. 1233 (1988) [hereinafter Auerbach]. An irony is that since his retirement from the University of Minnesota, Carl Auerbach comes each fall to Northwestern Law School as a Visiting Scholar and occupies an office a few doors from my office!

20. U. of Minn. Law School Faculty Minutes, Sept. 29, 1972 (on file with author) provide in part:

Professor Bryden next stated . . . that a large number of students had apparently indicated a desire that the Legal Professions course be offered on a P-N basis. He added that Professors

it rejected the student request.[21] Then on a Friday in December, three months later and seven days before the scheduled exam, students requested that the faculty grant Pass/Fail grading *in my section alone* because of (a) my alleged excessive cancellation of classes or ill-timed make up classes and/or (b) that I was unprepared to teach a course in Legal Professions. A "supplemental allegation" was added complaining that students who had registered for the other section were assigned to mine.[22] Although the matter of Pass/Fail grading for both sections had been decided at the beginning of the academic year, the faculty decided this was now a matter directed to me individually and referred it to the Grievance Committee.[23] The Monday after the student petition was presented to the Friday Faculty meeting, the Grievance Committee met with some students[24] and because it found the petition "too vaguely drafted to serve as a fair basis for a hearing,"[25] took oral statements from the students and rewrote the petition. I received a copy two hours before the hearing. The "supplemental allegation" mentioned above was added one hour before the hearing. At that hearing

> The grievants were called upon to present a case-in-chief. Professor Hughes and Mr. Joseph Hudson [Black male president of Black American Law Students Association] cross-examined them. Professor Hughes presented a defense.
>
> The Committee did not follow general rules of evidence. It did not follow standard procedures for taking objections to testimony. This was both because the shortness of time seemed to call for less formal procedures to

---

Hughes and Schoettle were neutral on the issue and that the Scholastic Requirements committee had voted 3 to 2 to recommend approval. A motion was made to permit the students in Legal Professions to opt for a pass-fail grading system. The motion was seconded and following discussion failed of passage, thus leaving the course on the normal grading system. . . .

21. *Id.*

22. Of course, the other section was taught by a white male. There were 134 students in my section. 90 persons signed the petition, but in response to a question at the "hearing," the dean acknowledged that no one had checked the signatures on the petition to determine if they were in fact students in my class. Draft Minutes of U. of Minn. Law School Faculty Meeting June 11, 1973 (on file with author) [hereinafter cited as Draft]. No final minutes of that meeting were ever made or adopted. At my request, the entire proceeding was tape-recorded.

23. William B. Lockhart, who was dean when I was hired, had returned to teaching and at the time of this episode was Chairman of the Grievance Committee. He disqualified himself and in fact testified in my favor before the Committee. A student who had signed the petition was also a member of the Grievance Committee so he was disqualified.

24. I inadvertently stumbled upon the meeting which was in a professor's office next to mine. The Committee never met with me prior to the hearing.

25. Statement of Facts prepared by Prof. Fred Morrison, June, 1973—Part I. Grievance Committee Proceedings, 4 (on file with author).

insure fairness and because the Committee viewed its function as partially conciliatory, as well as adjudicative.[26]

The Committee submitted its report to the faculty two days later. Its recommendation that the student petition for Pass/Fail grading be denied was adopted by the Faculty, but the full report was not submitted for faculty action.[27] That report said that the Committee's "proceedings may have augmented the hostility already present in this matter."[28] It also attempted to explain "why Professor Hughes was chosen for particular attention by the students" by noting that I was a second year teacher; that the course Legal Professions was subjective; and that the Code of Professional Responsibility had recently been revised.[29] Of the two sections of the course, only the first "explanation" applied to me alone. The other two were equally applicable to the white male teaching the other section, but of course he was not chosen for "particular attention."[30] Importantly, there were two other second year teachers, persons younger than I but who had started teaching at the same time I did. Both were white males. Neither was subject to the outrageous treatment I endured.[31]

I was incensed that the student petition was referred to the Grievance

---

26. *Id.* at 4. I know of no precedent that says "standard procedures" can be relaxed because of "the shortness of time." Moreover, the committee's desire to "insure fairness" seemed to be directed only toward the students and not me. In addition, no conciliation was ever attempted with me.

27. The report concluded "that the students failed to show that Professor Hughes' absenteeism was excessive, or that make ups were ill timed . . . " Actually, the students were unable to indicate how many classes had been canceled and the Committee had to rely upon my records. About a month before the hearing, on October 30, 1972, the dean had distributed a memorandum indicating there was no specific law school policy on class cancellations and quoting the general University policy that provided in part "Each individual faculty member must have reasonable latitude to cancel a scheduled class. . . . " Two years after my Grievance Committee hearing a student wrote to the student newspaper that "The faculty's habit of canceling classes and rescheduling them at their convenience has again reached the frustrating point." *Of the Essence,* QUARE, Dec., 1975 at 8. To my knowledge, no other law faculty member before or since me has had the matter of class cancellations determined by a Grievance committee.

On the other issues, the report concluded "that the students failed to show that Professor Hughes was unprepared to teach a course in legal professions." As to the assignment of students to my section, the Committee decided that it was not "a justiciable controversy." Memo to Faculty from Grievance Committee re Report of Committee, Dec. 6, 1972 (on file with author).

28. Report of Grievance Committee to Faculty, Dec. 6, 1972, 4 (on file with author) [hereinafter Report].

29. *Id.* at 5. One member of the Grievance Committee abstained from this section of the report.

30. I disagree that the course was subjective. This was a pejorative way of saying that something taught by a Black woman imparts a perspective which is different from that of a white male. Even the white male teaching the other section testified on my behalf before the Grievance Committee about the nature of the course.

31. One is now deceased. The other is a professor at the University of Connecticut School of

Committee. The initial attempt to receive Pass/Fail grading undoubtedly occurred because I had started teaching a section of the Legal Professions course.
No such attempt was made in prior years when both sections were taught by
white males. The Faculty made its own decision to require the usual grading
with no prodding from either me or the other professor.[32] If the faculty had chosen the Pass/Fail route for *both* sections, it would have treated equally me and
the white male teaching the other section. The attempt to obtain Pass/Fail grading in my section alone indicates student unwillingness to have a Black woman
judge performance in a required course. What was most distressing, however, is
that the faculty failed to treat a "colleague" with courtesy and lent support to
student prejudices by referral to the Grievance Committee.[33]

Following the faculty's adoption of the recommendation of the Committee, I distributed a memo "to correct . . . an inadequate record of the events, and
to express my severe dissatisfaction with the faculty's method of handling the
matter."[34] It made particular reference to the fact that it was not indicated any-
where "that the character or quality of teaching will be determined in an adversary setting, precipitated by a student petition."[35] BALSA, Black American Law
Students Association, also distributed a memorandum to the Faculty and said,
inter alia, the action was without precedent and pointed out that the hearing
"denied Professor Hughes the type of courtesy usually given to a faculty member."[36] There was no response by the Faculty to me or to BALSA. In conversations with the dean, he asserted I had no complaint since I "prevailed" and no
malice was intended. He advised me to forget about the matter.

The special Faculty meeting of June 11, 1973, was because I would not for-

---

Law. In 1974 when he heard I would be visiting elsewhere he wrote to say "I'm sorry you're leaving—
not simply on a personal basis, since I hardly know you . . . but because I fear that it will mean that
. . . someone else will have to come and put up with all the flak that you've been taking over the past
three years." Letter from Loftus E. Becker Jr. to Joyce A. Hughes (Apr. 13, 1974) (on file with author).

32. My first year teaching the course, the other professor had proposed that we both go to a
Pass/Fail system but I did not agree. I do not know what involvement, if any, he had in the initial
student petition to the faculty which was directed at both our sections. At the faculty meeting that
acted on the petition, he was "neutral."

33. In addition, the report of the committee addressed some specious issues. Although the faculty as a whole did not adopt that report, still its existence was known and it is part of the record.

34. Memorandum from Joyce A. Hughes to Faculty, Dec. 14, 1972 (on file with author). One
concern was that the initial petition to the full faculty was considered without my prior knowledge
that it would be presented and at a time when I was absent from part of the meeting because I was
teaching a make-up class. Moreover, the dean allowed a scheduled agenda item to be deferred so the
student petition was considered during my absence from the meeting.

35. *Id.*

36. Memorandum from Black American Law Students Association, U. of Minn. Law School
to The Faculty, U. of Minn. Law School, Jan.19, 1973 (on file with author) [hereinafter BALSA
Memo].

get. The only motion adopted at that meeting did extend me an apology but only for lack of adequate notice.[37] Much of the meeting avoided discussion of the question of race and disparate treatment. Toward its conclusion the President of the Minneapolis Urban League stated that the black community believed there had been unequal treatment. He labeled the hearing "a travesty of justice." But "justice" was probably not a reasonable expectation from the same Faculty which permitted the Committee to act in a "75% adversary [*sic*] manner"[38] on a student petition requesting Pass/Fail grading.

That petition was not about lack of qualifications.[39] When I started teaching my credentials were as good as the white males on the faculty—and better than some.[40] But those paper credentials did nothing to protect me from hostile students nor did they persuade the faculty and dean to treat me as a colleague.[41] Rather, they chose to align with white students rather than a Black pro-

---

37. It provided:

> It is most regrettable that, due to the faculty's imposition of time limits, the Grievance Committee did not provide timely notice to the parties to the Grievance of December 1–6 of the precise allegations of the petitioners and of the time for hearing. Since the committee found no substance to the allegations made, it is difficult to describe the failure to provide adequate notice as a denial of due process to Professor Hughes. However, a colleague has been subjected to a process which was defective and emotionally distressing. The Faculty apologizes to Professor Hughes for the inconvenience and disruption to her caused by these defects.

Draft, *supra* note 22.

38. Prof. Fred Morrison, member of the Grievance Committee stated that the committee acted in a "75% adversary [*sic*] manner." *Id.*

39. Edward W. Lempinen stated that a single standard "has defined excellence among law faculties for several generations. [That standard is:] Graduate with superior grades from a superior law school. Serve on law review. Clerk in a prestigious court. . . . Have a successful run in big-firm private practice." Edward W. Lempinen, *A Student Challenge to the Old Guard*, STUDENT LAWYER, Sept., 1990, at 16. *See also* Deborah J. Merritt & Barbara F. Reskin, *The Double Minority: Empirical Evidence of a Double Standard in Law School Hiring of Minority Women*, 65 S. CAL. L. REV. 2299, 2306–10 (1992); Bruce Comly French, *A Road Map to Achieve Enhanced Cultural Diversity in Legal Education Employment Decisions*, 19 N.C. CENT. L.J., 219, 258 (1991); Robert J. Borthwick & Jordan R. Schau, *Gatekeepers of the Profession: An Empirical Profile of the Nation's Law Professors*, 25 U. MICH. J.L. REFORM, 191, 197 (1991).

40. Professor Michael Olivas concluded that "for most schools, white candidates with good (but not sterling) credentials are routinely considered and hired, while the high demand/low supply mythology about minorities persists." Michael Olivas, *Hispanic Lawyers' Group to Designate Its Second List of 'Dirty Dozen' Law Schools*, A.A.L.S. SEC. ON MINORITY GROUPS NEWSLETTER, May, 1990, at 10.

41. Commenting on the failure to hire, promote, and grant tenure to minority candidates, Professor Roy Brooks says:

> There are simply too many minority candidates with qualifications too similar to many white male candidates who do not do as well as the latter for one to seriously suggest that the dearth

fessor. Nor was it about investing a course with racial perspectives.[42] Rather, I believe the students were simply rejecting the idea of having a Black woman pass judgment upon their performance,[43] particularly in a course that was essential to graduation given that Legal Profession was then a third year required course. As others have noted, there is no presumption of competence for Black professors as there is for whites. In fact, there is a presumption of incompetence. Simply being good at what one does generally will not be acknowledged for Black law professors.

Some people had difficulty understanding my protest over the Grievance Committee matter, particularly since the committee denied the student petition for Pass/Fail grading.[44] To have remained silent would have been taken as acquiescence in the propriety of the Grievance Committee even addressing the issue.[45] It is clear that they were dealing with the competency question since the

---

of minority law professors, especially tenured minority law professors, is entirely due to a lack of qualifications.

Roy Brooks, *Anti-Minority Mindset in the Law School Personnel Process: Toward an Understanding of Racial Mindsets*, 5 LAW & INEQ. J. 1, 30 (1982).

42. I did not then explicitly point out racial features of an issue. Now, when talking about the fact courts usually say that flight is relevant on the question of consciousness of guilt, in the Evidence course I call to students' attention the introduction to John Williams's book THE MAN WHO CRIED I AM (Boston, Little Brown [1967]), which gives a description of a Black man who happens upon someone lying wounded in the gutter but who suppresses a natural inclination to help and runs away for fear that his presence will lead to the conclusion that he was responsible for the harm. Also, I give students reading on eyewitness testimony that includes a summary of Gordon W. Allport's classic study in which persons on a subway report that a razor is in the hands of a Black man, rather than a nearby white man who actually carries it. *See* Robert Buckhout, *Eyewitness Testimony*, SCI. AM., Dec., 1974, 23–31.

43. "Minority teachers can expect difficulties from many white students who have never had a non-white peer, much less a non-white in a position of authority over them." *Minority Group Law Teachers, supra,* note 16, at 577. It may be that in the 20 years since this statement was made, students and faculty have now come to accept certain non-white persons. But I agree with Derrick Bell that "the ends of diversity are not served by persons who look black and think white." Statement of Derrick Bell, Harvard Law School, Apr. 24, 1990, reprinted in A.A.L.S. SEC. ON MINORITY GROUPS NEWSLETTER, May, 1990, at 4. As he has noted, some "interests and perspectives are already well represented on law faculties. . . . The new diversity of thought that many minority scholars bring to legal academia is not served by minority professors who represent white agendas." DERRICK BELL, CONFRONTING AUTHORITY—REFLECTIONS OF AN ARDENT PROTESTER 112 (Boston, Beacon Press 1994) [hereinafter CONFRONTING].

44. While the Grievance Committee denied the requested Pass/Fail grading, it nonetheless entertained the issue of competency and made gratuitous remarks that BLSA said "leaves a very negative impression of Professor Hughes' performance and ability as a teacher." BLSA Memo, *supra* note 36, at 1 "We further object strenuously to the negative innuendoes and free extemporizing in the final section of the report. It is transparent that this is a subtle attempt to find fault where none had been shown." *Id.* at 2.

45. In his article on affirmative action, the person who was then dean at the University of Min-

faculty had previously rejected Pass/Fail grading for the course. Nonetheless, it was considered, assuming the complainant's allegations could be shown.[46] The Grievance Committee episode also underscored the importance of the person heading a law school. William B. Lockhart, who was dean when I was hired, had stepped down from the deanship he held from 1956 to 1972. Had he still been at the helm, I question whether the student petition would have been handled as it was. It was his replacement who allowed faculty consideration of the student petition against me and who advised me to forget the matter.[47]

The next academic year after the grievance matter, tenure was considered. Rather than grant tenure, the decision was to renew my probationary appointment. The dean said he and the Faculty had obtained the impression that I did "not care to participate in [the] life" of the law school apart from my "classroom and special tutorial duties."[48] He claimed that he and the faculty "are also most anxious to cultivate with you the same informal, warm spirit of free communication and true collegiality that the rest of the Faculty enjoys."[49] Such a desire would have been welcome if it meant that one could retain viewpoints influenced by the Black experience and retain one's personhood as an African-American woman. But to the extent that such "free communication and true collegiality" requires masking of one's ideas and demands that one become an "honorary" white male,[50] then the offer must be rejected. To be the only Black

---

nesota said that "Silence is interpreted as agreement." Auerbach, *supra* note 19, at 1278. Certainly I did not want him or the faculty to assume acquiescence based upon silence by me. Moreover, "silent suffering does not beget reform. . . ." Delgado, *supra* note 17, at 350.

46. The Grievance Committee did question whether the requested action was an appropriate remedy, assuming incompetency could be shown. Despite doubts about the requested remedy, the committee then proceeded to determine matters of competency.

47. The Grievance Committee matter was not my only issue of concern. *See, e.g.,* Letter from Joyce A. Hughes to Carl A. Auerbach, Jul. 12, 1974 (on file with author):

> . . . My patience, however, is running thin. After watching the faculty devote two meetings trying to devise a method to exonerate Professor Cound from successive violations of its late grading rule, I find it inexcusable that a member of the staff would broadcast the malicious statement that I am consistently late. As you know, once the faculty adopted its own rule, I have complied fully and completely. My only argument in the past was with the attempt to single me out and to force me to comply with student rules which the faculty as a whole had rejected as not being binding on it.
>
> . . . [P]lease instruct the clerical staff that until they begin the practice of calling all other professors by their first names, they can refrain from calling me Joyce and address me as Professor Hughes.

48. Letter from Carl A. Auerbach to Joyce A. Hughes, Mar. 4, 1974 (on file with author).

49. *Id.*

50. Before Nelson Mandela became President of South Africa in 1993, if an African-American were to be sent to South Africa on business for his/her U.S. employer, he/she would be given the status of "honorary white." Cf. Beverly I. Moran, **Quantum Leap:** *A Black Woman Uses Legal Education to Obtain Her Honorary White Pass*, 6 BERKELEY WOMEN'S L.J. 118 (1990–91).

and the only woman and the only Black woman law teacher in an environment generates even additional pressure to approximate a white male norm. A critical mass of Black persons facilitates individual Blacks in that mass to retain our uniqueness. Although the numbers were small, there was a "mass" at Northwestern University School of Law when I arrived in 1974 as a visiting professor,[51] compared with the University of Minnesota law school.[52] That was one factor in my acceptance of its offer to join the regular faculty.[53]

The mere presence of a Black woman law professor can be instructive.[54] Her presence is instructive to the extent that she brings that which majority students often obtain from majority professors—that African-Americans and other minority students are capable and competent. In addition, simply seeing a Black woman law professor means other Blacks may be assisted to consider it a career option.[55] *All* students—and the legal academy itself—deserve exposure to professors who are committed to truly educate—a word whose root means to "lead forth." My experience suggests that the leadership of one person can draw out others from entrenched misconceptions.[56]

Black women law professors can be in the vanguard of those who lead the

---

51. Associate Dean Thom Edmonds was African-American. So too were Professors Ronald Kennedy and Samuel Thompson. The latter is currently Dean at the University of Miami School of Law. Unfortunately, cancer claimed the life of the former in his prime. Dean Edmonds left academia. James A. Rahl was dean of Northwestern law school when I joined the faculty and served from 1972 to 1977. At a memorial service for him Jan. 3, 1995 his commitment to affirmative action was noted.

52. Northwestern's law library had Black staff; many secretaries were Black; and at the time, all the maintenance people at the law school were Black. In contrast, there were no African-Americans working in *any* capacity at the University of Minnesota Law School other than me.

53. The Minnesota dean expressed a hope "that the year at Northwestern will help you to gain perspective on your problems." Letter from Carl A. Auerbach to Joyce A. Hughes, Oct. 1, 1974 (on file with author). My response was that "It was . . . disappointing for you to suggest that this year will only be of benefit to me in *my* problems. . . . [T]hose problems are shared by the University of Minnesota, if not caused by it. . . ." Letter from Joyce A. Hughes to Carl A. Auerbach, Oct. 16, 1974 (on file with author).

54. Bell, Confronting, *supra* note 43 at 212. There, Professor Bell states: "The new diversity of thought that many minority scholars bring to legal academia is not served by minority professors who represent white agendas."

55. Currently there are at least six Black persons (5 women and 1 man) who are now law professors who were students at Northwestern Law School during the time I have taught there. I did nothing to assist any of them to obtain law teaching positions and make no claim that I caused them to choose law teaching. Yet I do believe my presence helped them to see law teaching as a viable career option, if only subconsciously.

56. My career has benefitted from persons who took actions not then usual. There was Jane Andrews, Placement Director at Carleton College, Northfield, Minnesota; Judge Earl R. Larson, U.S. District Court Judge, District of Minnesota; Herbert Lefler of the firm of Lefler, Lefevere, et al.; Dean William B. Lockhart, U. of Minn. Law School 1956–1972; Dean James A. Rahl, Northwestern U. School of Law 1972–1977; and former Supreme Court Justice (1962–65) Arthur Goldberg, head of the U.S. Delegation to 1977 Belgrade, Yugoslavia conference on the Helsinki Accord.

legal academy forth from the erroneous belief that rationality implies "point-of-viewlessness."[57] Black women professors can begin to develop a pedagogy that addresses the "intense alienation"[58] of minority students whose "values, beliefs and experiences clash not only with those of their classmates but also with those of their professors."[59] Such a pedagogy may in fact be beneficial to all students.[60]

While each Black woman law professor must develop her own method to cope with the demands of the academy, we can and should be uniquely who we are—Black women[61]—and bring that to bear on what we do—teach law. Often it is believed that people are what they do. To the extent that teaching law is equated with being a white male (or even a white female), then Black women law professors must insist on the dichotomy between who we are and what we do—a distinction I tried to maintain even in the beginning. "Because the past is with us in the present,"[62] we need to keep past experiences in our minds as we speak in neither a whisper nor a shout.

---

57. CATHERINE A. MACKINNON, TOWARD A FEMINIST THEORY OF THE STATE 162 (Cambridge, Harvard University Press 1987), as quoted in Harris, *supra* note 17, at 343 n.35.

58. Kimberlé Williams Crenshaw, *Foreword: Toward a Race-Conscious Pedagogy in Legal Education*, 11 BLACK L.J. 1 (1989), *reprinted in* 4 S. CAL. REV. L. & WOMEN'S STUD. 33, 35 (1994).

59. *Id.* at 34.

60. A white male student related that he and others feel more comfortable in my classes than others taught by white male professors and thus participate more. Of course, this is a double-edged sword as some majority students may feel they have license to "question more, doubt often and dismiss quickly" in a class taught by a Black woman. Thus I find it necessary at the start of a course to lay down firm ground rules. I have had to insist that students can not speak unless I first recognize them, as often students think they can speak out whenever they please in my classes. However, the fact remains that I do not need to bludgeon a student with my superiority. By definition I am superior since he/she must learn that which I already know.

61. A survival strategy employed by some is "racelessness." "A raceless persona develops when People of Colour minimize their connections with their racial/ethnic background and assimilate into the dominant group. They take on the attitudes, behaviors, and characteristics that are attributed to the dominant culture." Shelina Neallani, *Commentaries—Women of Colour in the Legal Profession: Facing the Familiar Barriers of Race and Sex*, 5 CANADIAN J. WOMEN & LAW 148, 258 (1992).

62. Harris, *supra* note 17, at 333.

Antioch's Fight against Neutrality in Legal Education

JEAN CAMPER CAHN

(1974)

*A*T ANTIOCH LAW SCHOOL, WE now have a year of experience in our effort to produce a new breed of lawyers. In the process of freeing ourselves from historically rooted restrictions, we are now encouraging new ways of perceiving learning and the law.

You may feel that you have stumbled through the Looking Glass as I describe a law school organized around a teaching law firm. Students are called interns. We talk about billable hours for professions. Our clinical classes are called grand rounds, petit rounds, or post mortems. Our librarian worries about random-access indexing systems and non-hierarchical indexing for case files. We have an Associate Dean for Professional Affairs. The interns have offices and typewriters and secretarial support. Ethics is a hot subject for debate in the halls. And we are insured for malpractice by Lloyds of London.

No, you have not fallen through the Looking Glass. Antioch is alive and well in Washington, D.C. Antioch is the direct result of the affiliation of the Urban Law Institute of Washington, D.C. with Antioch College, Yellow Springs, Ohio.

The Urban Law Institute has pioneered in the practice of poverty law by acting as corporate counsel for the poor in a variety of settings. The school is organized around the Institute for a twelve month year, and its objectives are: to produce a new breed of lawyers and legal technicians committed to the use of law as an instrument of justice; to generate a new body of empirically based scholarship (first book to be published this fall); to deal with problems of social injustice, and to act as a catalyst nationally to change the nature of legal education [;] to avoid the post mortem approach to legal studies, which is so far removed from the traumata of human events . . . Antioch will continue the tradition of developing legal analytical skills. However, from the beginning of the

---

1 LEARNING AND THE LAW 40 (1974).

third month of the students' first year, our students are required to apply these skills to real life situations.

Students start with one case in November; two cases in January; three cases by March. Academic and professional tasks expected of each student are extremely demanding—but so is what is expected of each attorney/professor. Sixty-two hours a week is the average expected load of each student. In a two month period, students are expected to amass a minimum of 104 hours in the clinic. This time is spent as interns on call, special process service and the rendering of service to individual clients.

The most difficult problem the school has faced is not the availability of suitable students (1,400 applicants for 140 spaces). The real problem is building an appropriate faculty. The role of attorney/professor at Antioch is a much more difficult role than at other law schools. Faculty members are expected to perform the usual faculty functions of writing for scholarly journals, recruiting of students and teaching. In addition this year, the 19 full-time faculty, with the help of a small corps of associate faculty (mostly government lawyers and Federal Bar Association members), are expected to guide 260 students and be responsible ultimately for service to clients in approximately 8 to 12,000 cases. Faculty must handle grand rounds, analyze discussions of live cases, produce and direct video performances of interviews, negotiations and law office counseling, and systematically teach students the skills involved in the lawyering process . . .

[T]he Antioch faculty will increasingly abandon appellate case books as the faculty produces more and more material especially designed for a clinical law school.

Several points need to be stressed in any discussion of a law school which has as its central pedagogical device a teaching law firm—very much like the great teaching hospitals.

1. Most law schools only have one clinical year (the third), so that the clinical method never gets a chance to be used beyond Band-Aid cases. 2. The attempt to use the clinical method throughout law school and to produce graduates with a full range of basic competencies requires that some things must give way (since money, manpower and time are necessarily limited). 3. The things that can give way are the so-called advanced courses which are intellectually pleasurable but, in fact, are sterile when it comes to knowing how to practice law. Understanding the real institutional dynamics that the practitioner lives with, or dealing with the basic problems in a given specialty regarding the viability of legal institutions and the rule of law, are central to the clinical concept. 4. All this poses a direct threat to the lifestyle of professors. It makes the teacher accountable for wrestling with legal problems at the rate and pace generated by the changing world and makes him accountable for the competencies which he creates or fails to create in students. 5. Those who enter the teaching of law see it as a profession different from lawyering. Indeed, practicing lawyers who be-

come faculty members may change their entire images of themselves. They have become professors, and they tend to see that role in conventional terms. Too often, they do not hold themselves accountable for developing in their students professional competence. Instead, they may tend to go back to more comfortable ways of teaching which, of course, do not include the competence factors we, at Antioch, find so important.

How do we deal with this problem? How do we make certain that our law professors see their roles in much the same way as doctors do in clinical settings?

First, our faculty recognized the legitimacy of affective as well as cognitive modes of knowledge. However, if one is interested in the use of law for social change, then one must recognize emotive expressions of problems before they become intellectual, respectable and neatly analyzable. The job of the lawyer is to convert those incoherent or inarticulate realities into statements of equities and causes of action that enable decision-makers to respond with remedies.

If one is interested in the individual client, then one must learn to listen to the emotion as well as the surface thrust of his statements—to the latent as well as the explicit. Otherwise the lawyer deals with what the client thinks the lawyer wants to hear, rather than with what is really troubling the client. The proposition is professionally threatening to men of "reason."

Second, both our pedagogical needs and service needs at Antioch have forced us to examine all the incentives and rewards built into the school's structure. Are they antithetical? Do they militate against providing a substantial volume of quality service to clients while teaching the students basic professional competency?

We found that because of the traditional view of appropriate faculty lifestyle and behavior, a limited number of cases were often massaged to death.

In private practice, the professor's motive creates the primary pressure for moving cases. But a school dealing with poor clients has no such pressure. In fact, faculty members who move cases risk being tagged as "bad" teachers since students want the security of knowing all there is to know about a given case. However, since the client's interests aren't served as well by making the cases more complex, a teacher is in fact "bad" who allows the students to prolong a case . . .

The teaching law firm has been divided into three divisions: criminal, civil-private and civil-public (statutory entitlement). We have started a clinical library to serve as an institutional memory capable of retrieving memoranda, written prototype case files, video materials dealing with professional behavior and its analysis. Thus, we will, in time, have a library reflecting our teaching methodology rather than the appellate case method. We have centralized quality control functions in one person, our Associate Dean Nathan Paulson. In a sense, he guards the courthouse doors for us—assuring the quality for each faculty member's and each student's performance. We have decided that those clinical classes we call grand rounds will be used to teach interviewing, negotiation, handling ethical problems, research, drafting pleadings, discovering, preparation for trial, etc. We have brought about an integration of clinic and classroom through centralized admission.

For all these changes, we're merely on the edge of a new frontier . . .

It is most difficult for most law schools to truly face the fact that when a student graduates, he is not a professional in the true sense of the word. He does not understand the whole doctrine of accountability to clients. He is not prepared to deal with the unstructured reality of this society and to make those crucial moral judgments that each of us, in our role as practitioner, must make.

Unfortunately, the typical faculty recruitment system only rewards those who achieve by the standards of intellectual dexterity: who have made law review, served out a clerkship, practiced for a year or two (during which little or no contact with live clients was permitted by the firm) and who have finally, sought the fullest serenity and sanctuary of like-minded souls. Whatever motivations call people to teaching law, they rarely attract those who would emulate Stephen Douglass going to "encounter for the millionth time the reality of experience and to forge in the smithy of my soul, the uncreated conscious of my race."

The Antioch Law School has not produced the millennium, nor is likely to . . . Our only boast is that we have made a beginning at creating a deeper kind of legal education.

There Is a Future for Black Lawyers

Arthenia Lee Joyner

(1985)

*T*HE NATIONAL BAR ASSOCIATION (NBA) welcomes the opportunity to offer testimony at this hearing sponsored by the American Bar Association (ABA) Board of Governors Task Force on Minorities in the Legal Profession. Since 1925, the year the NBA was founded, it has sought to persuade ABA and every state bar association in America about the worth of the Black Lawyer. Our efforts have resulted in increasing the number of minority judges at the state and federal levels. These efforts, however, have not been without difficulty. Bar associations have resisted the upward mobility of Black lawyers, law firms have shunned them, government has been slow to appoint Black lawyers to work in specialized areas of the law.

The testimony that we give today is far from sufficient to cover each of the four categories the ABA called upon the NBA and others to address. It is difficult to trace each of the four categories back to 1844, the year Macon B. Allen became the first Black lawyer in American history admitted to practice law. Our hope is that the ABA Task Force studying the problems faced by minority lawyers is a sincere effort to do something which might open windows of opportunity to minority lawyers in America.

At this time in American history, we see the winds moving the clouds backwards rather than forward in time. We hear the leaders of our country, and the Department of Justice, urging the courts to forget about the racism of the yesteryear as it relates to present effects on American Blacks. We are witnessing a focus on materialism and a rejection of the concerns for the human element in our society.

In spite of these ominous signs, we are participating in these hearings in

THE SPECTRUM, AMERICAN BAR ASSOCIATION, YOUNG LAWYERS DIVISION NEWSLETTER, Fall, 1985 (pages unnumbered).

hope that change will come as a result of this fact finding exercise. We are encouraged by your efforts to raise the moral question associated with too few Black lawyers in the legal profession.

Access to legal education by Black men and women is not increasing at a rate in proportion to the percentage of Blacks in the nation. There has been progress, but the fact of entry is limited by a host of factors which should concern the American bar as a whole. The educational system of this nation has not created materials or books in which a positive image of the Black lawyer is projected.

Black lawyers are rare or nonexistent in several communities in the nation. Moreover, many communities with sizable Black populations have no Black judges, and law firms within such communities make no effort—indeed are not even conscious of the need to recruit Black lawyers to apply for law firm positions. Hence, many Black youth infer that the law is a profession of and for "white men."

This is a regrettable inference. This inference is also drawn from the lack of Black professional role models in common textbooks and in other teaching aids, the failure of teachers to expose Black students to the history of the Black lawyer, and a general lack of understanding that there is an affirmative need to suggest law to Black students as a career.

The recruitment, hiring and retention of Black lawyers in the private sectors is a moral imperative.

The problem is one of moral commitment of American law firms to change their image by casting off the yoke of bias against Black law graduates and Black lawyers. So serious is the dearth of Black lawyers in certain regions of the country with large Black populations that there is talk about boycotting the companies represented by such firms until they clean up their act.

It is a shame that talk of boycotts has surfaced as a remedy to get qualified Black lawyers into majority law firms. However, each year the record shows hardly any change by the law firm industry to alter existing discriminatory patterns. Consequently, Black law graduates are discouraged from applying to large and medium size firms as options for employment. This effectively limits Black lawyers from specializing in several areas from litigating in federal courts, from influencing the law in the same areas, and from qualifying for the federal judiciary under ABA standards.

American law firms must recognize that they are part of the problem limiting Black lawyers in the legal profession. This is not a perception. It is a fact.

Career patterns in the public sector are slightly better. The public sector has benefitted from the discriminatory hiring patterns of the law firm industry. In recent years the number of Black lawyers has increased at the state level. The pattern developing in state governments suggests that after the race barrier was lifted allowing Black lawyers an opportunity to work, they found a high performance and production level among Black lawyers. Private law firms would do well to use some state governments as models for their own hiring practices.

Career development is vital to Black lawyers hired by large firms and government agencies. Most lawyers, and particularly minorities know when they are present for show or accommodation as opposed to "on the ladder" for partnership or promotion.

It's time to start packin' when no partner suggests that you attend continuing education seminars, takes you to Judicial Conference meetings, or includes you in discussions with clients. Career underdevelopment may be designed to eliminate a Black lawyer from partnership consideration, and built-in failure.

On the other hand, law firms recognizing the delicate need for Black lawyers in the profession should affirmatively expose Black lawyers in the firm in continuing legal education activities and client exposure as soon as possible. Every effort should be made to assure early and fair evaluations of their work and offer encouragement, and if need be, an opportunity to attend graduate law training.

The Black law firm is being neglected by corporate America.

On June 25, 1984 author Charles W. Stevens of the *Wall Street Journal* published a front page story entitled, "Black Lawyers Begin To Enter Mainstream of Legal Profession."[1] The article painted a rosy picture of what is really a grim situation. The heart of Stevens's article is buried in two sentences. One sentence states that "Precisely how many black firms are developing corporate practices isn't known." A second sentence states that "[B]lack firms have existed since post-reconstruction, and they have faced a dogged battle for survival since that time because corporate America has been slow to recognize and to utilize the services of Black lawyers." Today, there is a dearth of Black lawyers in corporate legal offices, and few Black general counsels. Therein lies the problem.

Corporate board members and corporate counsels select law firms among these groups. If they are among these groups, Black lawyers are still not considered as candidates for corporate legal services. Unless corporate executives, board members and general counsels become more sensitive to the exclusion of Black lawyers from among their ranks the growth and development of predominantly Black law firms appears grim. A small law firm (and majority of Black firms are small) cannot easily develop a corporate practice unless corporations have confidence in the firm. Confidence may be generated by the amount of dollars the firm earns, where it is located, list of corporate clients, law school affiliations, political affiliations, and a host of other personal factors.

As mentioned in the Stevens article, a few Black law firms may boast of annual billings of $500,000. However, this is a far cry from billings of white law firms that gross $10 to $20 million dollars per year. The bottom line is that Black

---

1. WALL ST. J., June 25, 1984, at 1.

law firms cannot develop corporate practices because corporations are simply not sending any significant business to them.

The lack of corporate clients impedes Black law firms from obtaining acceptable ratings from lawyer directories, and unofficial behind-the-scene inquiries. Naturally, corporate clients want and deserve the best and most efficient lawyers to represent them. Since Black law firms are not utilized by corporate America, it is difficult to meet the competition of their white counterparts, no matter how good, brilliant or efficient the firm is.

Secondly, as the Stevens article points out, Black law firms are recent recipients of retainers from municipal governments where Blacks control city hall. While Black control should and ought to bring change in the society, white law firms have not lost any financial position representing these same cities. On the other hand, in cities that are controlled by non-Blacks, Black law firms receive little or no consideration by city administrators for retainers. Why?

The answer to this question is far from certain. The reason for non use of Black firms by cities may be the same reason why corporations do not retain Black law firms. These firms are often invisible to the commercial and political world. However, all this may be changing given the awareness of minority communities to spend their money with companies who do not put blinders on to Black capitalism; and to vote for political candidates who respond to the support of Black people. But, by-and-large, Black law firms are not being retained by corporate America, state and local governments and this is reflected by the disappointing growth of Black law firms in the past 100 years.

If Black lawyers are to increase their numbers in America, Black youth must see that they can succeed as corporate lawyers. If the legal community is the guardian of the rule of law, it must take the lead in opening corporate doors for the employment of Black lawyers and retention of Black law firms. If the corporate ethic is to be accepted by minorities in this country, it must put its money where its mouth is to enlarge the free enterprise system wherein Black law firms struggle to survive.

Corporations that have made an effort to use the services of Black law firms are to be commended. However, much more awareness of the use of these firms is required by corporate America.

ABA's discriminatory acts alone limited the upward mobility of Blacks in the legal profession as a whole. Black lawyers were affirmatively shunned by ABA and nearly every bar association of this country. Black lawyers survived because they refused to allow racism to impede their personal quests for intellectual advancement and collegiality. So it is today. However, the ABA through its affiliates continue to maintain considerable weight in all aspects of law in this country. We therefore look to you to correct the obvious . . .

The Black lawyer is going to have something to say about American jurisprudence. The sooner America realizes that Black lawyers hold a key to peace in this land, the sooner the definitions of freedom and liberty will be understood by all. As a former president of NBA stated in 1937, "Disfranchisement, segregation and discrimination are issues which must be fought in American courts. The hope of colored Americans for a square deal depends almost entirely upon the proper interpretation of the law."

Today, the "square deal" is not solely that of the courts. It is now shared by all institutions of the society who recognize a moral commitment to correct the evils cast upon Blacks by a racist past. . . .

Members of the Epsilon Sigma Iota Legal Sorority, founded on November 19, 1920, at Howard University School of Law. *Left to right, sitting:* Alice B. Brantley, Julia P. Cooper (Mack), Lillian Skinker Malone, Hazel Tucker (Smith) *(sitting behind Malone)*, Lucille Williams, Romae Turner, Wilada Bradley; *sitting, second tier, at far right:* Etta B. Lisemby, Shirley E. Jones (Mann), Isadora A. Letcher; *left to right, standing:* Mertice L. Jones (Duggans), Dorothy Wheeler, Ena St. Louis, Peggy S. Strauss (Griffith), unknown, Ollie May Cooper, and Annie Brown (Kennedy). Photograph circa 1955. *Courtesy Judge Julia P. Cooper Mack.*

Above left, Marilyn V. Yarbrough, Dean of the University of Tennessee School of Law (1987–91). *Courtesy University of Tennessee School of Law. Above right,* Goler Teal Butcher, Professor of Law, Howard University School of Law (1990). *Courtesy of photographer, Harlee Little. Right,* Jean Camper Cahn, Co-Dean of The Antioch Law School. *Reproduced courtesy of photographer, Roland Freeman.*

Left, Lutie A. Lytle, Professor of Law, Central Tennessee Law School (1897). *Courtesy of Ollie May Cooper and Mr. and Mrs. Paul F. Cooper. Below,* Ollie May Cooper. *Courtesy of Ollie May Cooper and Mr. and Mrs. Paul F. Cooper.*

Above left, Veva Izelle Young, practicing Lawyer in Chicago for forty years. *Photograph by the author. Above right,* Sadie Tanner Mossell Alexander, 1946. *Photograph by B. Marshall Wilson, reproduced courtesy of The University of Pennsylvania Archives. Right,* Patricia Roberts Harris, Secretary of the Department of Housing and Urban Development. *Courtesy of the National Archives.*

Left, Issie Lee Jenkins in 1978, Equal Employment Opportunity official, first woman to act as the Commission's Executive Director. *Courtesy of Issie Lee Jenkins. Below,* Pauli Murray, 1944. *Courtesy of Ollie May Cooper and Mr. and Mrs. Paul F. Cooper.*

This page:
Right, Jane Marshall Lucas, first African American woman to graduate from the University of Michigan School of Law (1944). *Photograph by the author. Below, right to left,* Arthenia Lee Joyner and Arnette Rinehart Hubbard. *Photograph by the author.*

Facing page:
Mary Frances Berry, Member of the U.S. Commission on Civil Rights. *Photograph by the author.*

Facing page:

Top left, Karen Hastie Williams, a former law clerk for Justice Thurgood Marshall. *Courtesy of Karen Hastie Williams.* Top right, Lani Guinier, Professor of Law, University of Pennsylvania School of Law. *Photograph by the author.* Bottom, Jewell Rogers Lafontant (Mankarious), on a panel during the National Bar Association meeting in 1960. Ms. Rogers was the National Secretary of the National Bar Association. *Left to right, standing,* Thomas Miller Jenkins, Florida A&M Law School Dean, Vernon Z. Crawford, of Mobile, Alabama. *Seated,* Leroy G. Charles, of Chicago, Jewell S. Rogers (Lafontant-Mankarious), Elmer Jackson Jr., president, NBA. All are lawyers. *Courtesy of Ollie May Cooper and Mr. and Mrs. Paul F. Cooper.*

This page:

Left, Eleanor Holmes Norton, delegate to Congress from the District of Columbia and former chair of the U.S. Equal Employment Opportunity Commission. *Courtesy of Eleanor Holmes Norton.* Below, Helen Elsie Austin, circa 1930s. *Courtesy of Ollie May Cooper and Mr. and Mrs. Paul F. Cooper.*

Facing page:
Jane Edna Harris Hunter.
*Reproduced courtesy of the
Western Reserve Historical
Society, Cleveland, Ohio.*

This page:
Left, Marian Wright Edelman,
President, Children's Legal Defense
Fund. *Courtesy of photographer,
Harlee Little. Below,* Judge
Constance Baker Motley, U.S.
District Court, Southern District
of New York. *Courtesy of
photographer, Harlee Little.*

Above, Barbara Charline Jordan, U.S. Congresswoman, Texas. *Courtesy of Congresswoman Barbara Jordan.*

Facing page:
Top, Carol Moseley-Braun, U.S. Senator, Illinois. *Courtesy of Senator Moseley-Braun. Bottom,* Margaret Bush Wilson, Chair of the National Board of Directors of the NAACP. *Courtesy of photographer, Harlee Little.*

This page:
Right, Judge Consuelo
Bland Marshall. *Courtesy
of Consuelo Bland Marshall.*
Below, Althea T. L. Simmons.
*Courtesy of Howard
University, Moorland
Spingarn Research Center.*

Facing page:
Edith Spurlock Sampson,
U.S. Delegate to the United
Nations (*right*), with Eleanor
Roosevelt, 1950. *Courtesy of
the National Archives.*

Barbara Mae Watson, Assistant Secretary of State, U.S. Department of State, being sworn in by her brother, Judge James Watson, 1966. Secretary of State Dean Rusk is in the middle.

Problems within the Legal Profession

Cora T. Walker

(1985)

I HAVE BEEN A MEMBER OF THE New York Bar almost 38 years. At that time, the American Bar Association denied membership to Blacks. Consequently, my introduction to the benefits of the nationally organized bar group was through the National Bar Association.

I believe my NBA experiences have served me in good stead. It enables me as a senior Bar member, to address the resulting shortfalls and limitations created within our profession. Even after many years of ABA membership, for the minority lawyer there is a short-fall of meaningful fellowship. I have a basis for comparison, particularly as this relates to career development. As a Black female, I have also shared the sexism experience.

We applaud this excellent opportunity to articulate our concerns in the area which is the parent of all the other problems. It is probably the area over which ABA can offer the greatest assistance, by creating a movement to eradicate the racism, that Black lawyers particularly in private practice have the least control. For, while an initial observation is that these hearings are a naive approach to serious problems, we think it is better than no approach at all.

We remain pessimistic about opportunities for advancement of Blacks to partnership status in majority law firms, until these problems are addressed.

We ask that the ABA Task Force focus upon the paucity in the number of large and small corporations that employ minority lawyers and law firms as outside counsel. Needless to say, vocal public encouragement from ABA would bring about substantial changes in the existing practices.

Many lawyers in the ABA leadership, because of the institutional racism that exists in the nation are undoubtedly not aware on a personal basis of the

THE SPECTRUM, AMERICAN BAR ASSOCIATION, YOUNG LAWYERS DIVISION NEWSLETTER, Fall, 1985 (pages unnumbered).

seriousness of this problem. We urge you to voice to the corporations, which you advise as to their legal affairs, that the employment of Black law firms is a viable means of broadening the base to obtain quality legal services at fair and moderate costs. In that direction, an important activity that ABA could do is to assist minority firms to develop aggressive approaches to promote the corporate use of Black lawyers.

This group would then be able to assist in providing job opportunities, for clerks, legal support staff personnel and employment in associate positions for the new entrants to the legal profession. There is no doubt that this kind of assistance and the training will aid in the development of new admittees.

The problem of bridging the gap between law school and the practice for minorities would be assisted. Everyone knows of the scarcity of employment opportunities for Black law school graduates. Some are even forced to leave the legal field after law school graduation or admission.

In addition, the various public entities must also be informed of the injustices in this area. We must see that more Black lawyers are hired and promoted fairly in the use of legal services in the private sector and for government financed work. Municipalities (and their affiliated agencies) and private corporate entities, whose constituencies are primarily Black people, should be encouraged by the ABA and NBA to retain law firms that have adopted hiring and promotion policies which ameliorate racist and discriminatory policies that are characteristic of many major law firms in this country.

We know these problems within the legal profession are only microcosmic of our American system that has been in existence for centuries. Remember it was necessary for the ABA to change its discriminatory membership policy. Now the time has come to update the legal services it renders to its growing Black and minority membership. This affects ABA in its ability to service a large segment of the Bar. . . .

PART 4

On Presidents and Judges

Black women and black women lawyers are no strangers to American presidential politics. They have always understood that the president and Congress have not been representative of all Americans, particularly the political concerns of black American women. Hence, black women have judged the Congress and U.S. presidents by their actions to enlarge black rights, and to enforce the law against racial discrimination and other lawless conduct against black people. Black women were at the center of debates on the right to vote prior to the ratification of the Fifteenth and Nineteenth Amendments to the Constitution. During the nineteenth century, they organized themselves into federations, not only to advance the interests of black women, but also to protect their families and themselves against the infamous Ku Klux Klan and the callous disregard of national leaders to the civil rights of black people in the South and North.

Until recently, there has been a dearth of public statements and writings by black women lawyers on the potential effects on black people resulting from judicial appointments by the president. With few exceptions, public scrutiny of nominees to federal judicial posts appears to have been left to black male lawyers. That has all changed since the tumultuous judicial nomination hearings of Robert Bork and Clarence Thomas to the U.S. Supreme Court.

Herein, six women of different political persuasions discuss prominent black and white public figures, such as Presidents Ronald Reagan and William Jefferson Clinton and Judges Robert Bork and Clarence Thomas, from their vantage point as women who happen to be black lawyers. Common among almost all of the articles is a concern about the general lack of empathy for black people by each of these public figures. An article presenting an inspiring memorial to Thurgood Marshall is the only exception.

The Most Dangerous Election in History

Juanita Jackson Mitchell

(1984)

*T*HIS IS A MOST DANGEROUS and most critical election . . .
The Ku Klux Klan has openly endorsed Ronald Reagan for President. We are in danger of losing all our gains in civil rights and everything else.

President Reagan has already set in motion the plan of the Republican right to put us back on the plantation. Haven't you heard their battle cry?: "We want to take America back!" For anyone who has read, or lived long enough to know our history, the cryptic message behind this slogan from the Rev. Jerry Falwells, the Jim Bakkers and the Republican administration is that blacks have made too much progress too fast. "They are taking this country away from us. Let's take it back," is the undercurrent flashing around this nation. The enemies of our progress mean business. To them, Jesse Jackson and what he represents is a threat. The same is true of women.

There is a backlash from the men of this nation to the nomination by the Democrats of Geraldine Ferraro (to be vice president of the United States). "Women are trying to run this country," many men are either whispering or loudly proclaiming.

Labor is in the same frying pan with the blacks and women. All of the hard-won advances we have collectively made which have improved the quality of life for all, are threatened. Let no one forget it. Labor has been our ally in getting the civil rights bills through a reluctant Congress. The enemies of labor are our enemies.

Walter Mondale as U.S. Senator and as Vice President in the Carter administration, was indispensable in helping us get the Civil Rights bills through Congress, knocking out bad legislation, and getting passed the strengthening amendments to the Civil Rights laws. It is sad that our memories are so short or

---

WASHINGTON AFRO-AMERICAN, October 20, 1984, at 5.

that we do not know what a great civil rights record Mondale has. Yet, the publishing of his civil rights record sets up a terrible backlash. So we are between a rock and a hard place.

It can happen again. By 1900, the 17 black U.S. Congressmen and the 2 black U.S. Senators that were in the Reconstruction Congress, had disappeared. It took 54 years of the worst cruelty, racial segregation, and lynching in the history of man before we began to advance again . . . [1]

---

1. Mitchell refers to Brown v. Board of Education, 347 U.S. 483 (1954) as the "Second Emancipation Proclamation."

Surviving the Reagan Years

MARY FRANCES BERRY

(1989)

COMMITTEE REPORT INTERVIEWED Mary Frances Berry at length to discover what she views as the successes and failures of the civil rights community in the 1980s and the direction we need to assume in the 1990s.[1]

Q: You told a *Ms. Magazine* interviewer, for an article in which you were featured as "Woman of the Year," that the "happiest day of my life was when [President Ronald] Reagan fired me. I was fired because I did what I was supposed to do, his firing me was like giving me an A and saying 'go to the head of the class.'" Can you elaborate?

A: When I first came onto the Civil Rights Commission in 1980 it never occurred to me that the Commission was going to become the focus of the President and the Attorney General's energies and efforts. I would have thought that they might be upset with some of the things that the Commission had done, because I knew the Commission's history and I knew presidents had been upset before, but it never occurred to me that they would spend their time undermining and attacking the Commission. They began to do that in 1981 and 1982 because they didn't like the Commission reports. For instance, they did not like a report we did on police practices and how the use of deadly force and other practices might interfere with people's civil liberties by killing innocent bystanders.

Edwin Meese (former U.S. Attorney General) did not like that report—he thought we were nosing around into law enforcement. And then when we came

Civil Rights Agenda, 3 COMMITTEE REPORT: LAWYER'S COMMITTEE FOR CIVIL RIGHTS 10 (Fall, 1989). The interview was conducted by Emily Epstein.

1. *See* William Raspberry, *Free the Civil Rights Commission,* WASH. POST, May 30, 1983, at A17; Bob Jones University v. United States, 461 U.S. 574, 596–602 (1983). (In an 8–1 decision, the United States Supreme Court held that it was wrong to allow tax breaks for the racially discriminatory Bob Jones University.)

out with an affirmative action report that had been in the works for a number of years, they did not like that because they were busy opposing affirmative action and the report talked about how affirmative action is the law and needs to be enforced.

They also didn't like the Commission pointing out on the Bob Jones issue that they were completely wrong when they told [Senator Robert] Dole and the Congress that we needed new legislation to make it illegal to give tax credits to racially discriminatory schools. It turned out that the Commission was right, of course, and they were wrong. So when they kept on pursuing these policies, the Commission criticized them, which is what the Commission is supposed to do. I was very vocal in my criticisms, and it didn't matter to me what we kept hearing directly or indirectly from people in the White House.

Mr. Reagan told a reporter that "we served at his pleasure and we weren't giving him very much pleasure." That didn't bother me too much because I knew we were supposed to be the watchdog for civil rights so we kept doing this and finally he fired us for criticizing him. I just simply thought it showed how well we were doing our job. So I didn't mind at all, I was very proud of it.

Q: You won the battle against Reagan's firing of you in federal court and were reinstated.[2]

A: Yes, and the reason we sued Reagan was not, as some people thought, because we needed the jobs. We had jobs. I have always been a professor—I was during that time and I still am. But it was a matter of principle. Someone should not be fired for carrying out their responsibilities. That just doesn't make any sense.

Q: What were your greatest personal victories as Commissioner during the 1980s and, conversely, your greatest personal defeats or setbacks?

A: I think the greatest success was being able to survive the Reagan years. I remember at various times during the Reagan years people who were involved in civil rights and social justice simply despaired. When Reagan was first elected none of us thought we would get through that first term, but we did and we made it through the second.

To have gotten through all of those battles and maintained some of the progress that was there and not have it completely eroded was, I thought, very important for all of us.

I think also one of my greatest successes was my involvement in the Free South Africa Movement.[3] When we went to the embassy on the eve of Thanksgiving and started that whole thing, it was right after Reagan had been reelected.

2. *Id.* (Raspberry). Berry v. Ronald Reagan, 32 EPD (CCH) ¶33,896 (D.C. D.C.), vacated 732 F. 2d 949 (D.C. Cir. 1983). (The judgment of the District Court was vacated because the authorizing statute of the U.S. Civil Rights Commission had expired.)

3. *See, e.g., Antiapartheid Sit-In,* WASH. POST, Jan. 15, 1986, at 7; *Seeing S. Africa for What It Is,* WASH. POST, June 7, 1987, at C3.

To be able to get sanctions, to change public opinion and to set in motion a course of events which have led now to real changes and at least the possibility of eventually overcoming apartheid, I think is absolutely phenomenal.

In terms of defeats, the most bitter defeat was to lose the battle over the Civil Rights Commission and to watch people violate, in my opinion, the public trust by catering and kowtowing to the Administration.

My next biggest disappointment was not being able to do anything about the judicial appointments. While it wasn't my role as a commissioner to do anything about the appointments, it was very difficult to watch the civil rights community not be able to do much either.

Q: What is your view of what the primary civil rights issues are going to be in the 1990s? Last Term's Supreme Court decisions have placed us in a historical watershed in that victories that we thought were secure are being undermined and we are now on shaky ground. I'm wondering what sorts of battles you think we will be facing and what your advice is to the civil rights community?

A: Let me begin with the old issues that we have been working on for a long time that have not been resolved.

First of all, there will be an immediate battle in the beginning of 1990 over legislation to remedy the Supreme Court decisions of last Term. There will be a battle over the legislation being proposed on Title VII, as well as a battle over the minority set-aside decision in Richmond, Virginia[4] and, of course, a continuation of the battle over abortion rights.

Next year, on the federal plateau, there will be a lot of issues about enforcement of the new Fair Housing Act. The Department of Housing and Urban Development has not engaged in effective enforcement of the Fair Housing Act and there are millions of housing discrimination complaints that need attention.

Then there is the Americans with Disabilities Act which, as soon as it is passed, will be another area that will need monitoring in terms of its enforcement. Those are the straightforward civil rights issues involving enforcing equal opportunity and access for people.

Then there are the old issues like school desegregation, which hasn't happened yet. Most of the schools to which Black and Hispanic kids go are racially segregated or only minimally desegregated. We still have to deal with that.

It is a tough issue because there is so much resistance to the idea. Even a lot of African-Americans have given up on the notion that the schools can be desegregated and have turned their attention away, both because of the resistance and because of all the bad things that happened in terms of busing Black kids out of their own neighborhoods. In order to turn this issue around we need a

---

4. City of Richmond v. J.A. Croson Co., 488 U.S. 469 (1989) (striking down an ordinance allowing minority set-asides).

change in attitude and a recommitment to the issue. This is not a strictly legal approach. Law can influence this issue and we can respond to the issue legally. But changes in climate and changes in leadership on this issue are going to be the necessary challenges.

Then there is the issue that I think is the most important one: quality and equality of schools for all children. We need a legal strategy to try to compel school systems to pay as much attention to this issue as they do to other important issues. Most schools have instituted some kind of school reform, but in almost every state we still have deficiencies in the schools. Now we have the school choice movement that President Bush keeps talking about but we haven't seen enough results yet.

So, the old issues are the laws which are already on the books but are not being adequately enforced and the new issues are things like affordable housing. We need to start to consider what kind of strategy and what kind of analysis is necessary to increase the housing supply for people so that the reality of equal opportunity in housing will come to pass.

We ought to focus on 1) civil rights enforcement for everybody, 2) education, training, and doing something about the drug problem, 3) responses to the needs of single parents to support their children and get the job training they need, and 4) a more responsible fiscal and budget policy for the country. If we do those things, I think we might move the social justice agenda . . .

Q: Define for me briefly what you see is the state of affirmative action right now in this country. Is it going to remain intact at the state and local levels?

A: Yes. I think affirmative action in employment is here to stay. Private business and corporations are accustomed to operating in terms of affirmative action and they don't see it as being controversial. They are also very much aware of the need to include women and minorities in the work force.

There will continue to be confrontations over issues like promotions. State and local governments will continue to be under political pressure from people who have jobs and who already have upper level positions and who feel that women and minorities will interfere with their opportunities. We will still have fights about that. If the legislation is passed to eliminate the Supreme Court decisions, I would suspect that we would continue to make slow progress as we have in the past. If the legislation isn't passed, then it's going to be extremely difficult to win these cases. We will be in trouble.

Q: Are you familiar with Julius Wilson's book, *The Truly Disadvantaged?*[5]
A: Yes, I am.

Q: What do you think about his criticism of the reliance by the civil rights community on affirmative action in employment to solve the problems which

---

5. WILLIAM JULIUS WILSON, THE TRULY DISADVANTAGED: THE INNER CITY, THE UNDERCLASS AND PUBLIC POLICY (Chicago, U. Chicago Press 1987).

minorities face in this country? Wilson argues that affirmative action really isn't meaningful to a large segment of the minority population, especially to those who are unemployed. Do we need to be shifting our focus for the 1990s?

A: I think Julius Wilson's book is interesting, but I think that he is wrong. I think that we need both things. This argument about either having a focus on opportunities for educated and trained people or having a focus on the underclass is simply misguided. We have to do both. For people who are educated and trained, we have to worry about them being discriminated against in terms of being alienated and not given opportunities either to get jobs or to move up when they have jobs.

For people who are not educated and trained, of course, we have to worry about educating them and training them. That's the first thing before we worry about full employment.

I think full employment has been a goal of the movement for social justice for years; for example, the Humphrey-Hawkins Full Employment Bill passed in 1978. No one disagrees with the need and the desire to restructure the economy to try to get full employment. The goal of working on full employment is going to be made even more difficult because of the kind of budget and fiscal policy decisions that were made by President Reagan, and now President Bush, along with the international problems of Japanese competitiveness—both Japanese and West German—as well as the changes in Eastern Europe.

The pressures on the American economy are going to make it even more difficult to try to increase employment and to compete in the world for everybody as well as for people who have been locked out. I don't see any signs in the administration or in the Congress of anybody wanting to restructure the economy. Let me tell you, I also think that for most people, politically, to argue that you ought to restructure the economy because it will benefit the underclass is a losing argument. If people are comfortable already and feel that they are doing fine in the economy as it is, to argue with them that they need to restructure it, to help somebody else, when you don't know the consequences for them, I don't think it's a good argument . . .

Q: What are your goals? What are the goals of the Commission for the next ten years? Can you speak to me about how you see your role and the role of the Commission in the 1990s?

A: Whether the Commission on Civil Rights will again become a force for change in the direction of solving some of our problems depends on the appointments that will be made, and we will know that over the next two or three months. If Mr. Bush appoints people who want to take hold and be part of the progress, I, of course, will join with them. I've already suggested to the Commission that we focus the agenda on the issue of Hispanic and African-American education. While we think that the education summit that Mr. Bush had was okay, we haven't seen anybody doing anything since then . . .

Q: During this last decade we saw a real focus on safeguarding private interests to the exclusion, many would argue, of the public good. If you buy Arthur Schlesinger, Jr.'s theory that politics work in a cyclical fashion, do you anticipate for the 1990s a revitalization of interests in public good, a swinging back of the proverbial pendulum?

A: Well, I've been waiting for Schlesinger's cycles to come again, and I believe in cycles but I'm not entirely sure that the wheel is turning.

I see the most recent elections as a sign that progressive politics is very healthy in this country. I also see the successes over the last eight years in the civil rights community of defeating everything—almost everything—that Reagan proposed. So, I'm not sure the wheel had turned entirely in the other direction because there is a difference in this country between who people elect as president, and who we elect to Congress.

Our main problem right now is that the Congress agreed to Mr. Reagan's tax policies in 1981, which means that even the people who want to promote social programs can't because there isn't any money to do anything, and Mr. Bush has his "no new tax" plan. All the polls show that large numbers of Americans want to do something about social justice issues, like education for everybody. People want to do things about health care, about housing, and the homeless, but there isn't any money . . . The major problem now is that Reagan wrecked the enforcement agencies and made the civil rights groups spend all their time trying to defeat things or trying to get policies despite him, instead of moving on to new issues.

President Clinton's Doubt;
Lani Guinier's Certainty

LANI GUINIER

(1993)

" *F*ROM NATIONAL PUBLIC RADIO in Washington, this is a special report. A news conference from the Justice Department by Lani Guinier, who, until last night, was President Clinton's nominee to head the Civil Rights Division of the Justice Department. Ms. Guinier just began addressing a gathering of reporters. She introduced her family. Now we're going to hear what she has to say:"

Guinier: . . . Had I been allowed to testify in a public forum before the United States Senate, I believe that the Senate would also have agreed that I am the right person for this job, a job some people have said I have trained for all my life.

I would also like to thank all the Americans, those who have known me all my life and those who have only just heard of me, for their support and encouragement. I am blessed with many loyal friends, fine colleagues, dedicated allies, and, as I've said earlier, a wonderful husband and son. Their support has helped me to endure this process with some measure of dignity, and I am grateful.

I deeply regret that I shall not have the opportunity for public service in the Civil Rights Division. I am greatly disappointed that I have been denied the opportunity to go forward to be confirmed and to work closely to move this country away from the polarization of the last twelve years, to lower the decibel level of the rhetoric that surrounds race, and to build bridges among people of goodwill to enforce the civil rights laws on behalf of all Americans. In particular, I had been excited about the possibility of working closely with Attorney General Janet Reno, a woman of outstanding integrity, a woman of principle, a woman whose vision of a more just society has been an inspiration to us all. In many ways it is her example of strength and courage that has inspired me and has allowed me to remain true to my principles in the difficult days following the announcement of my nomination on April 29 [1993].

I have always wanted to be a civil rights lawyer. My father's experience at Harvard College in 1929, as he recounted it to me, was an early lesson in the indignity and inhumanity of racism. My father was denied any financial aid on the grounds that one black student had already been awarded a full scholarship. He was not allowed to live in the dormitories on the grounds that no black, except the relative of a United States senator, had ever resided. He was the victim of a racial quota, a quota of one. I have never been in favor of quotas. I could not be, knowing my father's experience. My commitment to civil rights, to democratic fair play, to cross-racial coalition building, were all forged in the crucible of those memories.

I have been fortunate to have had the opportunity to pursue my ideals as a civil rights lawyer, first as a Civil Rights Division attorney and special assistant to Drew Days when he was head of the division in the Carter administration, and later as counsel for the NAACP Legal Defense Fund, where I litigated many cases and lost only two. In all my work I have been inspired by the civil rights movement of the 1960s, by the Voting Rights Act of 1965, and by the amendments to that act which I worked with Congress to produce in 1982, with the vision of those amendments of an integrated legislature in which all of its members work together for the common good.

I have been fortunate to have many heroes and mentors, heroes like Dr. Martin Luther King Jr., Justice Thurgood Marshall, and Judge Constance Baker Motley; mentors like Judge Damon Keith, Solicitor General Drew Days, former Ford administration transportation secretary William T. Coleman, and Elaine Ruth Jones, director counsel of the NAACP Legal Defense and Educational Fund. These are people who committed their hearts, their considerable intellectual energy, and their professional lives to a vision of a just society, a society in which America makes good on her promise to be a true, generous, and inclusive democracy.

I have always believed in democracy, and nothing I have ever written is inconsistent with that. I have always believed in one person, one vote, and nothing I have ever written is inconsistent with that. I have always believed in fundamental fairness, and nothing I have ever written is inconsistent with that. I am a democratic idealist who believes that politics need not be forever seen as "I win, you lose," a dynamic in which some people are permanent monopoly winners and others are permanent excluded losers. Everything I have written is consistent with that.

I hope that what has happened to my nomination does not mean that future nominees will not be allowed to explain their views as soon as any controversy arises. I hope that we are not witnessing the dawning of a new intellectual orthodoxy in which thoughtful people can no longer debate provocative ideas without denying the country their talents as public servants. I also hope that we can learn some positive lessons from this experience, lessons about the importance of public dialogue on race, in which all perspectives are represented and in which no one viewpoint monopolizes, distorts, caricatures, or shapes the outcome.

Although the president and I disagree about his decision to withdraw my nomination, I continue to respect the president. We disagree about this, but we agree about many things. He believes in racial healing and so do I. Last year in an interview with Bill Moyers, then candidate Bill Clinton was asked, "Is there one thing on which you would not compromise?" He answered, without flinching, "Yes—racial equality." I believe that he and Attorney General Janet Reno will use the opportunity of this presidency to act on that commitment, to act affirmatively to move this country forward, to work with and for all Americans to go beyond the polarization and divisiveness of the past few years and the poison of racism that has so infected our society.

There are real problems affecting real people in this country, people who are still the victims of unlawful discrimination on the basis of their race, their ethnicity, their gender, their sexual orientation, or their disability. I hope that despite the unfairness of the way that I have been treated by the political process that people will, nevertheless, work within that system to resolve the more important unfairness that others continue to suffer in their daily lives. We have made real progress toward Dr. Martin Luther King's vision of a society in which we are judged by the content of our character, not by the color of our skin, but we are not there yet, and we need real presidential leadership, action, not just words, to heal the racial hemorrhaging and to realize Dr. King's dream, which is my dream, too.

Thank you.

Moderator: Lani Guinier, now taking questions from the press.

Q: The other side in this, your opponents, were able to define you because you didn't really get support from the administration in helping to explain the real Lani Guinier. Do you think that the administration did a good job? How would you rate their job of helping you as a nominee?

Guinier: I think that the administration has been supportive of my nomination, at least until yesterday, and that maybe they will have learned some lessons for future nominees who will benefit from some of the mistakes that were made with regard to my nomination.

Q: What do you think the mistakes were?

Guinier: I think that you're right that my opponents were successful in defining me in a way that even my own mother does not recognize.

Q: Ms. Guinier, what does the president backing down on your nomination say to you about his political courage, his loyalty, his toughness?

Guinier: I respect the president. I disagree with his decision to withdraw my nomination. I think he has the opportunity to be a great president, and I hope he takes advantage of that opportunity.

Q: Some of your supporters yesterday, one of them, Mary Frances Berry, a civil rights leader, said if the president backed down on your nomination, this will send a message that will undermine his ability to lead, as not willing to stick it out . . .

Guinier: I think the president will have many opportunities to lead, and again I hope he takes advantage of them. I hope he shows the important leadership that I believe he's capable of and that he is committed to exercising on behalf of civil rights enforcement in this country. I certainly think that working together with Attorney General Janet Reno that this administration can make a huge difference in the lives of many people.

Q: There has been much discussion about how the president is now moving "back to the center." What do you think the wisdom of that is, and how do you feel it affected your nomination?

Guinier: I really do not have any way of answering that question.

Q: If there is a movement on his part to move away from the political spectrum that you are said to represent, more toward the more conservative center of the political spectrum, what would you think of the wisdom of that?

Guinier: I think that I represent an important and mainstream tradition that this administration is also committed to, and that is vigorous enforcement of the civil rights laws as passed by Congress.

Q: Help us, if you can, to understand the relationship you had with the president. You have known him for twenty years, and yet yesterday he said that he had not read your writing on this subject of civil rights, enough, at least, to make judgment on your nomination. Do you think that it is possible for him not to understand or really know what you stood for during the course of this personal relationship that you had with him?

Guinier: I think the president knows what I stand for, and I think the president agrees with what I stand for, and he has said that.

Q: Yet yesterday he did say that if he had read what you have written, he would have not nominated you.

Guinier: That's something that you're going to have to ask the president.

Q: Professor Guinier, you just enumerated today what your writings don't say. Did the president misread your writings?

Guinier: I think that the president and many others have misinterpreted my writings which were written in an academic context, which are very nuanced, which are very ponderous. I'm certainly flattered that the president sat down and read a law review article that I have written. Most law professors don't have that privilege. I can assure you that it's even difficult to get my own mother to read my law review articles, and to say that the president of the United States has read one of them is a real honor.

Q: Has there been any discussion of another possible position for you in this administration?

Guinier: We have not had any discussion about that, but I am committed to working with the president and with the attorney general in any way that I can.

Q: Did you ask for this forum? Did the Justice Department offer it to you? Since you're a private citizen, why are you here?

Guinier: I did not arrange this press conference, so you will have to ask the people who did arrange the press conference that question.

Q: The president said yesterday that had the nomination proceeded, it would be on grounds upon which—and he pounded his fist on the podium— he could not defend. You've said that he stands for racial equality and you've also said that in your conversation with him, he understood where you were coming from and he agreed with you. Upon what did he come to the conclusion that a battle over you would be something he could not defend, and what do you think about that statement?

Guinier: I think that what he has said about the divisiveness of proceeding with my confirmation hearings is something that I disagree with, but I understand. He has suggested that to pursue my confirmation might have inappropriately reopened and polarized the condition of racial relations, or reopened old wounds and polarized the condition of racial relations in this country. I certainly agree that we need to have a debate and a conversation and a dialogue about race, and I agree that we need to do that in a forum in which we can hear each other without shouting at each other.

Q: When you said, "I need a hearing to defend myself," what did he say back, particularly with regard to the question of fundamental fairness?

Guinier: He said he understood my position.

Q: Are you going back to the University [of Pennsylvania] full time or what?

Guinier: I am a tenured full professor at the University of Pennsylvania Law School, and I look forward to going back to Philadelphia with my husband and my son. . . .

Robert Bork Should Sit on High Court

Jewell Rogers Stradford Lafontant (Mankarious)

(1985)

*J*UDGE BORK HAS ASKED ME to appear on his behalf. I have reviewed most of the relevant court cases; I have read his writings; and I have watched and listened to his testimony as well as that of many witnesses who have appeared before you. There has been a thorough discussion of the cases in which he has been involved and an unending criticism of much of his writings. I must say that I don't recognize the Judge Bork I know from so much of what has been said by his opponents here.

You see, I knew him well. Let me tell you about the heart of the man. In 1973 after I left the United Nations, I came to the Office of the Solicitor General. I was a rarity, if not an oddity: there never had been a woman, black or white, Deputy Solicitor General of these United States. And my presence here is due to the high regard I have for Judge Bork, based upon my personal experiences with him.

Judge Bork placed me in charge of the entire Civil Division where I reviewed hundreds and hundreds of cases that had been determined first in the United States District Courts and then in the United States Courts of Appeal. I say I was an oddity—and it's not just my assessment; it appeared that there was also the perception of the staff in the offices of the Solicitor General. You see, attempts were made to isolate me. On one occasion, a secretary who had warmed up to me after a few months after my arrival, she said: "I am going to tell you something, Mrs. Lafontant, that you are not going to like—the other deputies meet regularly, and you are not included." How do you like this, I asked. She continued: "I was told to call the deputies in to a meeting and the names were called, and I said: and Mrs. Lafontant? The response was: 'Oh, no, just the men.'" The response could have been: Oh, no, just the whites.

Statement, Hearings before the Comm. on the Judiciary, U.S. Senate, 100th Cong., 1st Sess., 2884 (1987).

I immediately reported this to Solicitor General Bork, and it is an understatement to say that he was appalled. And though he is usually a calm and even-tempered person, he exhibited strongly his dismay and sputtered his unhappiness about this attempt to exclude me and to discriminate against me. The very next day was the beginning of my attending so many briefings–I was bombarded with meetings—that I wondered to myself whether I had been wise in complaining in the first place.

But those meetings were very important, not only because the current cases were discussed, the relevant law reviewed, but the cases for argument before the Supreme Court were assigned at those meetings, and those in charge of assigning have the pick of the cases to present to the various lawyers.

By being kept out of these discussions, my education of course was being limited, to say the least, and I was not given the choice cases to argue.

But Judge Bork handled this in his usual low-key, quiet but determined and fair manner—no confrontation, no embarrassing accusations—things just changed. He had seen to it that I was treated the same as the others.

And during my entire tenure there, Judge Bork exhibited complete fairness and openness. He was always open for debate—actually enjoyed the give and take of debate. He believes, and has said: "Intellect and discussion matter, and can change the world." He doesn't have a closed mind.

Bob Bork's devotion to women's rights was further exhibited in his support of the Federal Women's Program of the entire Department of Justice. In fact, the Federal Women's Program was founded in my quarters of the Solicitor General's office, and I became its first Chair, which could not have happened without the blessing and encouragement of Judge Bork . . . I do believe that Bob Bork, by putting the weight of his office behind this program, caused the Department heads to sit up and take notice.

All of my life I have been involved in civil rights organizations, having served for many years as secretary of the Chicago branch of the NAACP, on the Board of Directors of the American Civil Liberties Union and its Legal Redress Committee, and as Chairman of the Illinois Advisory Committee of the United States Civil Rights Commission, as well as being a Commissioner of the Martin Luther King Holiday Commission. I have no hesitancy in supporting Judge Bork's nomination to the Supreme Court.

Not only is he a supporter of equal treatment for women, I sincerely believe that he is devoid of racial prejudice, or else I would not be here.

But what I like about him further is that he can be persuaded. In his 1963 *New Republic* article, he opposed the Public Accommodations Provision of the proposed 1964 Civil Rights Act, but then years afterwards, in '73, while I was in the Solicitor General's office, he changed his mind. He admitted he was wrong, and he has been severely criticized for his change of heart. To me that is a sign of true intellect, that you can admit you made a mistake. Bork said: "I was on the wrong track, the civil rights statute has worked very well. Were it to be proposed today . . ."—and he was talking in 1973—"I would support it . . ."

[N]o matter how well you know a person, in evaluating the judicial competency and suitability of one who is being considered for appointment to the Supreme Court, there is no looking glass into which we can gaze and with accuracy and credibility determine or predict with certainty how an associate justice will perform, reason, decide, and vote in the abstract. The justices, as I understand the situation, decide cases on the basis of the facts before them, the nuances of the circumstances, and the controlling precedent . . . As a woman and a black woman, I have no fear of entrusting my rights and my privileges to Robert Bork as an associate judge of the Supreme Court. I believe in him. . . .

Clarence Thomas Should Not Sit on High Court

PATRICIA A. KING

(1991)

*A*S A BLACK WOMAN, IT IS DIFFICULT for me to oppose the nomination of a black individual who has known great personal struggle. Nevertheless, Judge Thomas's extensive record and personal posture is so antithetical to the interests of women and blacks—especially black women—that I feel an obligation to testify against his nomination.

Much has been said of Judge Thomas's rise from Pin Point, Georgia to the federal bench. Without question, the Supreme Court should include people who have endured such struggles. But we must recognize that that alone is not enough.

I don't often talk publicly about my own background, but I think it is necessary here to put Judge Thomas's life story—dramatic and compelling as it is—into the context of life in black America. Judge Thomas's background is not unique among African Americans of our generation. And virtually all of us over the age of forty have had at least one exceptional grandparent who has been injured and severely humiliated by racism in America.

I grew up during segregation with my sister in a female-headed household in a public housing project in Norfolk, Virginia. I attended segregated schools through high school and never knew any white contemporaries. I was able to apply to only one college because we did not have the money for multiple applications. I was able to attend Wheaton College in Norton, Massachusetts, because my uncle put a second mortgage on a house he owned—the only piece of real property owned by anyone in my family—in order to pay college bills.

I am reluctant to parade that family history in public, but not because I am ashamed of my background. I am very proud of my mother's strength and

Statement, HEARINGS BEFORE THE COMM. ON THE JUDICIARY, U.S. SENATE, 102d Cong., 2d Sess., 266 (1991).

tenacity and the love and determination she employed in raising my sister and me. I am grateful to my uncle for what he did and to the other members of my family for the encouragement they gave me. I am profoundly grateful to the high school teacher who taught, inspired, and pushed me to achieve. And I am proud of them all as strong black people who battled through racism and material poverty to hold themselves in dignity and to forge spiritually rich lives. I don't talk about it simply because it has no impact on my capacity to function effectively as an adult or professionally as a lawyer and a legal educator. Moreover, my story is not unique in the black community and, frankly, I don't want either people's sympathy or their condescension.

My background was not a predictor of my performance as a government worker in the State, Justice and Health, Education and Welfare Departments or during the time I worked at the Equal Employment Opportunity Commission. Some of that government service, by the way, was rendered during the Nixon and Reagan administrations. Nor could that background have served as a predictor of success in my eighteen-year career as a law professor at Georgetown University or in my service on a broad array of government commissions and panels dealing with the most complicated and delicate problems of medical and legal ethics that our country has faced in the last decade and a half.

And, frankly, I don't think Judge Thomas's background is any more a predictor of his future service on any bench than mine has been for my career.

Though there are similarities between Judge Thomas's background and my own, it seems to me that there is an attitudinal difference that separates us. I readily acknowledge that some of my successes resulted from affirmative action—my admission to Harvard Law School, for example—and from the help and support I received from others. In remembering where I came from, I also remember very bright young black people who were not as fortunate as I. They did not have my mother or my aunts and uncles, but if they had had a chance, they could have made some real contributions to this society. But affirmative action came too late for them; they had slipped away before it was firmly established in the late 1960s when I went to law school. Somehow Judge Thomas seems not to remember those he must have encountered along the way who were lost to the darkness simply because there was no help for them. I surely worry about that lack of memory and empathy in someone of my race who is proposed as a Justice for the Supreme Court. Even his behavior towards his own family raises serious concerns. While Judge Thomas gives his grandfather great credit for his success, he has not been so generous to his sister, Emma Mae Martin. In describing his rise from humble beginnings, he has frequently criticized her need to turn to welfare for a period in her life, saying, for example: "She gets mad when the mailman is late with her welfare check. That's how dependent she is." He has criticized her children as well: "What's worse is that now her kids feel entitled to the check, too. They have no motivation for doing better or getting out of that situation."[1]

Judge Thomas's willingness to castigate his sister publicly for personal gain is deeply troubling not only for its opportunism, but also for what it reveals about his lack of compassion and understanding about his own sister's struggle to overcome great obstacles. Similarly, Judge Thomas's ability to extend compassion to others whose cases may come before the Court is also in question since the situation faced by Emma Mae Martin is one shared by many other black women.

Judge Thomas's father abandoned his family when he and his siblings were very young. As is the case in many female-headed households, the family was poor. Judge Thomas's mother supported her family by picking crabs at five cents a pound. When a fire destroyed their home and their belongings, Mrs. Thomas could no longer support her family on her salary (she moved from picking crabs to cleaning houses), and sent the children to live with relatives. While the boys lived with their grandfather, an independent middle-class businessman, Judge Thomas's sister was sent to live with her aunt. She graduated from high school, married, and had children. When her husband left, she supported her children by holding down two minimum wage jobs. Only when that aunt suffered a stroke and needed care was Ms. Martin forced to turn to welfare; like many women, Ms. Martin had no choice but to quit her job in order to provide such care. She was on welfare for four or five years before returning to the workforce; she is now employed as a cook.[2]

The story of the women in Judge Thomas's family demonstrates an ethos of family support, resourcefulness and interdependence—not dependence. When husbands left the family or relatives fell ill, it was the women who carried the burden for the family—at great cost to any personal ambition. At the same time, though, their story makes plain the limited range of opportunities and choices available to black women, especially those who are single heads of households. Judge Thomas, however painful his personal experiences were, and are, because of racism, did not face the multiple barriers of race and poverty when compounded by sex discrimination and family responsibility. Moreover, in his oft-repeated recitation of his personal history, little space or respect is given to the intense struggle of these women. Yet stories like these are at the heart of the heroic rise of our people and Judge Thomas's insensitivity to that aspect of his personal and our communal life is deeply troubling.

Judge Thomas's record shows no understanding of the imperative to provide opportunities and choices to black women. The notion of "choice," usually

---

1. Neil A. Lewis, *Thomas's Journey on Path of Self-Help*, N.Y. Times, July 7, 1991, at 12.

2. Karen Tumulty, *Sister of High Court Nominee Traveled Different Road*, LA Times, July 5, 1991, at 4.

perceived as limited to issues of reproductive freedom, is really a much broader concern for black women:

> Choice is the essence of freedom. It's what we African Americans have struggled for all these years . . . the right to select our own paths, to dream and reach for our dreams. The right to choose how we would or would not live our lives.[3]

Black women understand that no matter how hard they work, and no matter how well prepared they might be, workplace choices and opportunities for them may be limited. The work experiences of Judge Thomas's mother and sister are not unique. African-American women historically have been represented in substantial proportions in the labor force; however, we have yet to reap the full economic rewards of that participation. While it is true that many of us have improved our status as workers, many more remain in low wage jobs.[4] Even when women hold equal amounts of education, job training, and work experience, they are three times more likely to earn low wages as white men.[5] African-American women are four times as likely to be low wage workers.[6] The average family income for black women is less than that of white women.[7] The unemployment rate is higher for black women than for white women.[8] Black women—like Judge Thomas's sister—are more likely to hold several low-wage part-time jobs with no health insurance or other benefits.

As demonstrated by Judge Thomas's own experience, the status of black women in the workplace contributes to their poverty and to the poverty of their families. The number of black women who head households is growing; to the extent that single parents fare badly in the labor market, or are unemployed, their children suffer. That Judge Thomas's mother and sister have worked as crab pickers, cooks, and maids, as have thousands of other black women, is not

---

3. "We Remember," Statement of African-American Women for Reproductive Freedom (1989).

4. For example, in 1989, 27.3 percent of employed black women were in low-paying service occupations, as compared to 16.1 percent of white women. M. Power, *"Occupational Mobility of Black and White Women Service Workers"* (presented at the Institute for Women's Policy Research Second Annual Women's Policy Conference, June, 1990) (unpublished manuscript).

5. *"Low-Wage Jobs and Workers: Trends and Options for Change,"* National Displaced Homemakers Network and the Institute for Women's Policy Research, Washington, D.C. 1989.

6. *Id.*

7. On average, the 1989 median annual earnings of black women working year-round and full-time was $17,389—61% of white men's annual earnings of $28,541. The figure for white women for the same period was $18,922, or 66% of the annual earnings of white men. National Committee on Pay Equity, NEWSNOTES (March, 1991) at 6.

8. Overall, 11 percent of black women who desire to work are unemployed, compared with 4 percent of white women. *The Economic Status of Black Women: An Exploratory Investigation,* STAFF REPORT, UNITED STATES CIVIL RIGHTS COMMISSION, October, 1990.

an accurate indication of their abilities, but rather a reflection of the dearth of choices available to them as black women—in particular black women heading households in rural Georgia.

Judge Thomas's positions on affirmative action, wage discrimination, class action litigation, and other proven remedies for discrimination may possibly become law and public policy that would further limit the choices for black women in the workplace. For example, Judge Thomas has repeatedly attacked well-established Supreme Court case law on affirmative action—even when developed to remedy proven egregious discrimination and despite its demonstrated effectiveness in expanding equal employment opportunity. As head of the EEOC he deliberately chose not to seek goals and timetables in settlement agreements and consent decrees, changing course only in reluctant response to vigorous objections from members of Congress. He drastically cut back enforcement of the Equal Pay Act, the law that prohibits gender-based differentials in jobs that are equal or substantially equal; and, notwithstanding the EEOC's obligation to enforce the laws prohibiting gender- and race-based wage discrimination, he adopted a cramped analysis of Title VII's application to such discrimination that left the claims of many women unremedied. And, in spite of the proven effectiveness of class action litigation, Judge Thomas criticized the EEOC's reliance on that strategy and reduced the resources devoted to it—causing a substantial reduction in the number of class action cases filed by the agency. Of equal concern to me is Judge Thomas's record on reproductive freedom. That issue is all too often viewed through the narrow prism of abortion and thought to be of interest only to white women. That is not the case. The fundamental right to privacy, including the right to abortion, is at the core of equality for women, including black women and other women of color.[9] If women cannot control their own bodies, it is difficult—if not impossible—for them to fight for or enjoy the other rights to which they are entitled.

Black women interpret this right as the right to choose to have a baby, as well as the right to choose not to. For black women, the right to reproductive freedom also means access to information about family planning options and to safe and affordable health care, including pre-natal and post-natal care.[10] No one needs a broad array of reproductive choices more desperately than black women, poor women, and women with children.[11] When women's reproduc-

---

9. *"Women of Color Reproductive Health Poll,"* National Council of Negro Women and Communications Consortium Media Center, August 30, 1991. The survey respondents included African-American women, Latinas, Asian women, and Native American women. About three-fourths of those responding to the survey agreed that the decision to have an abortion is one that every woman should make for herself.

10. *Id.*

11. Statement of African-American Women for Reproductive Freedom, *supra* note 3; Women of Color Reproductive Health Poll, *supra* note 9.

tive freedom is curtailed, black women and other women of color and their families suffer first and most deeply.

Before he was nominated to the Court, Judge Thomas made speeches, wrote articles, and signed on to reports that criticized or attacked constitutional protections of reproductive freedom that have enhanced the power of black women over their own lives. His post-nomination retreat from his record, his refusal to discuss Roe v. Wade[12] to any meaningful degree, and his claims that he has never thought seriously about these issues provide us with scant comfort. A decision to overturn Roe will have drastic implications for our lives and our health. Women who are captives of poverty or geography, including many women of color, would be robbed of their choices and again forced to risk their lives in back alleys.

In conclusion, I want to repeat that this has been a most difficult decision for me to make. Our role models are all too few, and Judge Thomas's personal achievements are indeed impressive. However, we cannot afford to let those achievements blind us to the reality of his record on issues of critical importance to black women—including, but not limited to, his apparent lack of compassion and understanding of the struggle of the black women in his life. Our role models and our Supreme Court justices should include not only those men and women who have demonstrated personal achievements, but also those men and women who have demonstrated an understanding of what it takes to rise up and out of oppressive circumstances. All of us who have "made it" have an obligation to help others, and to recognize that others need our help. Judge Thomas has been able to dream and to reach for his dreams; yet he has ignored the need for or worked to deny that choice to others. He should not be confirmed.

---

12. 410 U.S. 113 (1973).

In Clarence Thomas You Hope
for a Miracle

Adjoa Artis Asantewaah Aiyetoro

(1991)

CHAIRMAN BIDEN AND MEMBERS of the Judiciary Committee, thank you for allowing the National Conference of Black Lawyers, through me as the director, to present this testimony before the Committee. The National Conference of Black Lawyers is an organization of lawyers, judges, legal workers, and law students that was formed in 1968 specifically for the purpose of advocating for the rights of black people specifically and people of color, the poor, and the disadvantaged generally. The organization has participated on all levels of advocacy, including litigation and public education . . .

I would like to briefly address two main issues . . . in opposition to Judge Thomas's nomination. First, it is important that the significance of the nominee's race to this process be explicitly stated in the record. We are disturbed that the assessment of this candidate may be less strenuous by those who view themselves as anti-racist because he is a black person who, like many other black people in his age group or who come before him, have risen to occupational levels that far exceed those of their parents and even their siblings. We are disturbed that those who have adopted in deed, if not in word, the philosophy of white supremacy are embracing him because his blackness serves to mislead many in assessing his record, a record which demonstrates in large part a disdain for the very remedies he utilized to advance when applied to persons of color other than himself. Those who are confused, well-meaning of all races, hold onto the hope not supported in his record that somehow, if confirmed to the Supreme Court, he will support the law as it is now for people of color, women, and those in the fringes of society. They hope for a miracle. We urge you to determine whether and how you are using this candidate's race, and to decide to refuse to confirm

Statement, HEARINGS BEFORE THE COMM. ON THE JUDICIARY, U.S. SENATE, 102d Cong., 2d Sess., 945 (1991).

based on a record that demonstrates support for lawlessness and behavior that is below the standard to be demanded of a Supreme Court justice. It is true that the National Conference of Black Lawyers finds a number of Judge Thomas's views to be in direct contradiction with the positions of this organization. We know you know this . . . But his views also reflect a character that is below the standards this body should demand. He is a man who, despite the law of the land, refused to act to protect the rights of groups for whom he had responsi- bility, a man who ignored codified ethical requirements and withheld informa- tion about the relationship between himself and the family of the principal shareholders in a lawsuit potentially costing them more than $10 million, a man who sat on the advisory board of the *Lincoln Review* and attended a reception of the South African ambassador, yet indicates to this Committee that he did not know of any position in support of apartheid by the leadership of the *Lincoln Review,* and he himself did not support apartheid. He is a man who re- tracted position after position that he took prior to this nomination and urged you to look at only his and other nominees' comments as a judge since they would be less offensive, a man who humiliated his sister and family, but now flaunts the sister, indicating her character is stronger than his.

This nomination is an insult to not only black people, not only the tradi- tion of high integrity and character set by Thurgood Marshall, but to the ideals of the Constitution and the constitutional convention, that those who sit on the highest court will be those with whom we can look with pride and respect, al- though we may not always agree with them. We cannot look with pride and re- spect at Clarence Thomas, but only with fear and trepidation for how he will continue to trample the rights of people [of] color, the disadvantaged and women; not in conformity to the law, but in disdain for it and their collective rights.

Thurgood Marshall Spoke
for Humble People

KAREN HASTIE WILLIAMS

(1993)

*T*HE PROPHET MICAH INSTRUCTS us to do what is just, to show constant love, and to live in humble fellowship with our God. Thurgood Marshall embodied this direction as his guiding principle, and inspires us to follow his extraordinary example.

T.M., as he was known popularly in chambers, was larger than life. A legendary champion of civil rights, his towering achievements as an advocate for equal opportunity for African-Americans was surpassed only by the enormous inner strength and endurance that kept him focused on his mission.

From poor sharecroppers in Mississippi, who sought the right to vote, to frightened parents in Little Rock, who asked only for the right for a decent education for their children, the clarion call of hope sounded when Americans oppressed by racial discrimination heard the inspiring words, "the lawyer is coming." They didn't have to say his name. They all know who he was.

Justice Marshall's arrival at the Supreme Court in 1967 changed more than the complexion of the men sitting around the Friday conference table. He changed the nature and focus of the debate. Both because he was at the table, and because he spoke from the heart for the humble people who could not be there to speak for themselves.

Thurgood Marshall also made it clear to his brethren that outstanding, well-credentialed law clerks could be as diverse as America—female or male, black, brown, yellow, or white, Christian, Jewish, or Hindu.

As the 1970s and 1980s witnessed a political environment with increasing hostility to the cause of individual rights and liberties, he never lost faith in the fundamental decency of women and men of good will, or in the integrity of the

---

Thurgood Marshall and His Legacy: A Tribute, 2 TEMPLE POL. & CIVIL RIGHTS LAW REV. 159 (Spring 1993).

Constitution, the Bill of Rights, and the institutions of our American democracy. Even in dissent, the vigor of his arguments, and the unyielding language of his opinions left no doubt as to his commitment. Whether the issue was equal opportunity in education, housing, or employment, the death penalty, women's rights, or religious freedom, his words confirmed that he was indeed the conscience of the Court and of the broader American population.

Close contact with a living legend is not easy . . . With humor, wit, and sarcasm he taught us the serious task of analyzing the law from a very human perspective. If we suggested a more traditional approach, he often reminded us who signed the opinion. He demanded much of us, but no more than he demanded of himself . . . God bless you and be with you, Thurgood Marshall.

Part 5

Race, Equality, Justice, and Freedom

This part is dedicated to four core areas that overlap in importance to black women lawyers. Each topic is represented by a cluster of black women lawyers, who discuss views on race, equality, justice, and freedom. Under the subject of race, the authors address the deadly force of racism, democracy and race, symbols of racism, its direct impact on employment opportunities and political rights for minorities, and its osmotic, anti-Semitic impact as well.

Under the subject of equality, the authors address the dual discrimination borne by being women and black; a new male aggressiveness against black women; and the historical impact of Jim Crow education of black children. One author declares that, given the continued presence of racism, "radical solutions are a natural response to a hostile environment."

The section on justice presents diverse statements on the role that politics and economics play in the fundamental value system of the American society, the loss of justice and civil liberties when government officials have contempt for law and order, the meaning of "political correctness," and the justification of reparations for black people as a remedy because of their enslavement and mistreatment.

The subject of freedom is introduced by a rare document. In 1883, Mary Ann Shadd Carey graduated from Howard University School of Law and was admitted to the bar of the District of Columbia. Shadd was one of the first black women to join with white suffragettes for the right to vote. "Give Colored Women the Right to Vote" (circa 1870) is her testimony, perhaps the first direct testimony that a black woman presented before Congress. Shadd was not yet a lawyer when this testimony was presented before the Senate Judiciary Committee, but it reveals the depth of her commitment as an advocate on matters involving the liberation of women and the restraint on freedom. Another statement dating back to 1932 affirms that the quest for the right of blacks to vote has long been a crusade by black women lawyers.

The remaining articles about freedom discuss the important role that federal courts have played in black freedom, critical expressions about how the system stifled freedom before the passage of the Civil Rights Act of 1964, the need for greater vigilance by black leaders to protest against the failure of federal enforcement of civil rights laws, and the right of gay citizens to be free from discrimination.

Race

Racism Is a Deadly Force in America

HELEN ELSIE AUSTIN

(1944)

OUT OF THE NIGHT THAT THREATENS US, one of the things for which we can be truly grateful and in which we may find courage is the brave and wise stand which has been taken by the race's militant leaders and organizations in this period. They are looking back on the gestures and rejecting the emotional propaganda. They rise to insist and to bring home to the American people that democracy must demonstrate its value as a way of opportunity for all if it is to be saved. Future historians will, I am sure, pay great tribute to this militant and honest spirit as it is now being expressed by the NAACP, the National Urban League, the National Negro Congress, and our labor organizations. Individually and as organizations, we must not let them down. They should be given the support and cooperation so vitally necessary to their success.

However, along with these efforts on our economic front, there should be developed a large "follow through" program to entrench these new victories and to root out the most dangerous and deadly force in America. That poisonous force which is as much as anything a factor in the collapse of the present civilization. Many years ago, 'Abdu'l-Baha the great Persian scholar visited America.[1] He traveled and spoke extensively in the promotion of a new world faith and world unity. In addressing a group of white and colored leaders he said these words:

From handwritten notes of speech delivered in Washington, D.C., in 1944.

1. 'Abdu'l-Baha, referred to by many as an Ambassador to many, visited the United States in 1912. *'Abdu'l-Baha to Give Last Lecture*, THE WASHINGTON EVENING STAR, Apr. 24, 1912, at 4. On April 23, 1987, The Baha'l Club of Howard University commemorated the Seventy-Fifth Anniversary of his visit address at Howard University. See Memorial Program, "The Baha'l Club of Howard University Commemorates the Seventy-Fifth Anniversary of the Visit of 'Abdu'l-Baha to Howard University and His Address in Andrew Rankin Memorial Chapel, April 23, 1987." Courtesy of H. Elsie Austin, Nov. 16, 1995.

In America, I told the white and colored people that it was incumbent upon them to be united or else there would be shedding of blood. I did not say more than this so that they might not be saddened. But indeed, there is a greater danger than the shedding of blood. It is the destruction of America. Because aside from racial prejudice, there is another agitating factor. It is that of America's enemies, these enemies are agitating on both sides, they are stirring up the white against the colored and the colored against the white. But of this the Americans are submerged in a sea of ignorance. They will regret it. But of what use will their regret be after the destruction of America. Now is the time for Americans to take up this matter and unite both white and colored races. Otherwise destruction and devastation.

This force of disunity especially as it is generated from racial prejudice is the most dangerous issue in America today. The race issue has become the most subtle and powerful contact of the American people used by the forces most opposed to democracy in any form. Through it we can see the thing 'Abdu'l-Baha spoke of actually coming to pass. Black and white, we are being played against each other and against ourselves. For every group which rises to liberalize and unite the people there are others surely at work under cover dividing and agitating. The newest example and most amazing by far is the new pure African society which in a recently issued periodical makes a scurrilous attack upon the mulatto. It announces a campaign to purify the black race and to oppose the leadership of mulatto Negroes and to get them removed from places of prominence with respect to the race. So the already deplorable division within the Negro's ranks is to be increased. This is the only symptom of what is at hand. For pressure on America will eventually force the race issue into prominence and create an alignment of opinion. It is for this period that we must prepare.

Now is the time for every bit of organization, strength and for all types of leadership to unite in an educational campaign to mould new ideas of Americanism and race and to develop a sense of unity in the American people. Prejudice will not be checked until the ideas of difference and prestige which cause it are replaced with new ideas of unity, cooperation and justice. Brotherhood is no longer an ideal in this age, it is a social necessity without which all men will be in danger of extermination. We must make the demonstration of democracy a popular thing and call attention to the importance of actions rather than words. This means a new and persistent vigilance and pressure on the control centers of the American mind. The schools, the churches, the press, the radio, the community, and the administration of government, they must make democracy work. In such a campaign, everyone has a part to play. And, the playing of this must be for us the most important cause of life in this period.

When the time for showdown comes as it must we shall not be able to hold these victories in the face of heightened tension, bitterness and strain unless we have developed a powerful force of public opinion between white and black America and a strong sense of unity.

How shall we proceed in this campaign against prejudice? There are three things we should do immediately. We must first of all increase the opportunities for intelligent contact between the races. Only through association and development of mutual interest and cooperation will some of these distorting ideas on race which exist on both sides disappear. It should be stressed that white and black America have a common patriotism, citizenship, language and religion and that it is sheer folly for them to be divided upon the accident of color. Insidious propaganda which embitters and distorts must be exposed and attacked wherever it is found. And while blacks are being denied the right to vote, those men in public office who use their positions to entrench prejudice and further it should be opposed by both white and black. Wherever association is possible, we must use it to develop a new standard that recognizes the blend of the best which is found in a background made up of all the races and nationalities which exist.

Democracy and Race

MABEL DOLE HADEN

(1947)

*T*HE CHILD LIVES AND GROWS, and grows as long as he lives. He will grow anyway whether his concepts are shaped to fit the pattern of living in a Democracy or in a Communistic state. In one way or another he will carry on. The problem which faces parents and teachers at the very outset is, "How shall he grow?"

The home is the greatest single factor in the life of the child. Of necessity, it is here that his awakening intelligence receives its first stimuli, and his earliest lessons in social adjustment begin. It is here that the Negro parent begins to ask herself: "When shall I let him know that he is considered different from the little boy whose father owns the corner grocery store?" And, "If I must tell him that, how can I make him understand? How can I put this over without giving my boy a complex? I cannot tell him that he is considered a better person than the boy on the corner, that would be a lie, nor can I tell him that he is not as important to the bulk of society, for this he could never understand. Then, shall I tell him at all, or allow him to become aware of the emphasis placed on this difference by some unforgettable experience without me to soften the blow?"

It is at home too where the white parent is helping her child mold emotional and behavior patterns. It is here that he learns confidence in himself and in many instances he is taught lack of confidence in his little playmate whose skin is of a different hue . . . for example, we are all familiar with the incident of Mrs. Mary M. Bethune's childhood. The white playmate was generous with all her toys, but could not stand to see little Mary pick up a book, and literally snatched it away, exclaiming: "You can never read that!"

Teaching the white child that there is a recognized and alleged difference

Mabel Haden Covington, *What Shall We Teach Our Children*, THE AFRAAMERICAN WOMEN'S JOURNAL 20 (Summer/Fall 1947).

based on the question of color, is not nearly so painful to or carefully planned by his mother, as is this teaching which is done by the Negro mother. Each mother anticipates where the blow will fall when trouble comes because of lack of understanding between racial groups. The Negro Mother can see her son being lynched in some sort of way because of lack of justice in our American courts and hearts. The white mother feels secure as she erroneously precludes disturbing results keeping her child from the goals she has set. She seldom feels the importance of placing emphasis upon likenesses rather than differences when she talks about the colored child around the corner.

When the Negro mother teaches her child that all humans are basically alike, and that we are guaranteed the right to life, liberty, and the pursuit of happiness, what does she say when her son insists on seeing a movie, which his pal on the corner has told him was simply great, or when he is exhausted from hunger and wants to eat in a downtown restaurant in a city where races are like Washington, D.C. separated?

The school is next important to the home in determining the degree of adjustment to life which the child will attain. Working hand in hand with the home, it can accomplish much to ensure emotional health and character balance. Both should be characterized by a live-and-let-live policy. The school is a larger world than the home. The child's personality is already established when he reaches school, but it is here that his personality is challenged with new and different personalities and experiences. The teacher, in many instances must work hard to add to what the parent has done for her child, and in many instances should work hard to unravel what the parent has done to her child. When we tally what we hope the results of our teachings will be, we ask ourselves then, "What shall we teach him at school?" What are the ingredients that make up an intelligent democratic citizen? What can we do with this interesting, complex personality to make it get along well with others, speak clearly and correctly, start a job and finish it, to read and write well, to understand science, to grow well and strong, and to be a decent human being? What scheme can we formulate to extract the poison of racial superiority and hatred which has taken root in the minds of many? Poison like that which must have been planted in the minds of the seven children of defendant Fleming in the South Carolina Lynch Trial and other children of the defendants who attended the trial. There they were drenched with the Southlands conception of democracy, that white is right, and that it is easy to get away with murder if the victim has black skin. Aren't they being taught to be proud of the democratic South?

The objectives of schools are a form of social policy based on some accepted scale of values. The school aims to produce efficient, expedient, and fair-minded citizens. Democracy is consistent with justice. Such teaching involves planting cooperative desires, a desire to help whenever and wherever help is needed; respecting the rights of others as he faces his responsibilities; to settle issues through reason, rather than force. It is all important that the teacher of all groups of children bear in mind these general objectives as she guides from day to day toward a perfect democratic America, whose theories are consistent with a functioning democracy, and not just talk, talk, talk.

I feel certain that a white lady with whom I was dealing recently, would have been more embarrassed if some one from Russia had been present when her little grandson exclaimed, when he heard that I was a teacher: Are you a teacher? I didn't know they had "N - - - er teachers!" He probably was surprised, for he repeated it over and over. He seemed to like me, but he knew nothing of respecting the dignity of a person who was not white. And indeed, why should he? He has been taught at home, at school and through the movies that any human being who is not 100 percent white has no dignity.

This theory of a non-functioning democracy leaves the Negro teacher in never, never land. Nothing could be easier than repeat our educational theory, to have the child pledge allegiance and loyalty to the flag and to his country. This sort of thing is bearded. The task before the teacher, any teacher, is to formulate a national theory that will work. The child must know democratic ideals, and understand why he believes in them. Teach the child, especially the Negro child to question the validity of facts, and not believe everything he reads and hears.

When pupils are acquiring the historical background of American Democracy, they should enjoy an abundance of new experiences in democratic living, but from the development of the English colony in the New World, down to recordings of present day accomplishments, the glory and heroism of the white man has always been portrayed as the epitome of a self sacrificing, daring, noble and perfected martyr of surviving hero. No other person, Negro, Hindu, Chinese, or otherwise could ever conquer the weaknesses of the flesh as could he. As a result of this teaching then, all the rights granted by the Constitution of the United States should rightly go to the Miss Ann's and Mister Charlie's of America. During Elementary School days, I read so much of the patriotism of the Southern generals in the Civil War, it was hard to believe that the Northerners were right. The Uncle Toms and Little Topsies were presented in such a way, that eventually I began accepting the implications as matter of fact that such people were born to be servants. The suggestions were vivid that I would grow up to be a sickening little "Butterfly," "yes maaming" and "no maaming" all the white folks, until I became alarmed . . .

Whether education will succeed in its aim to make a functioning democracy is a question still to be answered. One thing certain however, is that parents and teachers are on their own to fashion means of egress from the staleness which has overcome the primary good for which our theories stand.

The Confederate Flag as
Racist Symbolism

CAROL E. MOSELEY-BRAUN

(1993)

*M*s. *MOSELEY-BRAUN.* Mr. President, I would like to respond to this amendment and to suggest that it is absolutely ill-founded and to oppose the amendment . . .

The real bottom line with regard to this amendment and to the request for a design patent extension by the United Daughters of the Confederacy is that it is not needed . . .

I submit further that the design patent is not needed in terms of the work of the organization. The Senator from South Carolina has gone on at great length to talk about the charitable work of the United Daughters of the Confederacy. The fact of the matter is the refusal to extend this extraordinary honor by this body does not stop them from doing whatever it is they do, from continuing their work in the community . . .

When members of the United Daughters of the Confederacy came to my office to discuss this issue when we were involved with consideration of the issue before the Judiciary Committee, they could not even then answer the question why it was necessary to have a design patent. They can continue to fundraise. They can continue to exist. They can continue to use the insignia. Nothing changes in terms of what it is they do. The only issue is whether or not this body is prepared to put its imprimatur on the Confederate insignia used by the United Daughters of the Confederacy.

I submit to you, Mr. President, and the Members who are listening to this debate, as I did in the Judiciary Committee, that the United Daughters of the Confederacy have every right to honor their ancestors and to choose the Con-

---

Speech of Senator Moseley-Braun on the floor of the U.S. Senate on July 22, 1993, opposing a grant to extend a patent to the United Daughters of the Confederacy, referred to as Amendment No. 610, in 139 CONG. REC. S9253 (1993).

federate flag as their symbol if they like. However, those of us whose ancestors fought on a different side in the Civil War, or who were held, frankly, as human chattel under the Confederate flag, are duty bound to honor our ancestors as well by asking whether such recognition by the U.S. Senate is appropriate.

The United Daughters of the Confederacy did not require this action to either conduct the affairs of their organization or to protect their insignia against unauthorized use . . .

So this is not an issue about protecting the insignia of the United Daughters of the Confederacy, nor is it an issue about whether or not they do good works in the community, nor is it an issue of whether or not the organization has a right to use this insignia. I think the answer in all those cases is they have a right to use whatever insignia they want, they have a right to organize in any way they want, they have a right to conduct whatever business they want. But at the same time it is inappropriate for this Senate, this U.S. Congress, to grant a special, extraordinary imprimatur, if you will, to a symbol which is as inappropriate to all of us as Americans as this one is.

I have heard the argument on the floor today with regard to the imprimatur that is being sought for this organization and for this symbol, and I submit this really is revisionist history. The fact of the matter is the emblems of the Confederacy have meaning to Americans even 100 years after the end of the Civil War. Everybody knows what the Confederacy stands for. Everybody knows what the insignia means. That matter of common knowledge is not a surprise to any of us. When a former Governor stood and raised the Confederate battle flag over the Alabama State Capitol to protest the Federal Government support for civil rights and a visit by the Attorney General at the time in 1963, everybody knew what that meant. Now, in this time in 1993, when we see the Confederate symbols hauled out, everybody knows what that means.

So I submit, as Americans we have an obligation, No. 1, to recognize the meaning, not to fall prey to revisionist history on the one hand; and also really to make a statement that we believe the Civil War is over. We believe that as Americans we are all Americans and have a need to be respectful of one another with regard to our respective histories, just as I would.

Whether we are black or white, northerners or southerners, all Americans share a common history and we share a common flag. The flag which is behind you right now, Mr. President, is our flag . . .

So I come back to the point I raised to begin with. What is the point of doing this? Why would we give an extraordinary honor to a symbol which is counter to the symbol that we as Americans, I believe, all know and love, which would be a recognition of the losing side of the war, a war that I hope—while it is a painful part of our history—I hope as Americans we have all gotten past and we can say as Americans we come together under a single flag. And this organization, if it chooses to honor the losing side of the Civil War, that is their prerogative. But it is inappropriate for that organization to call on the rest of us, on everybody else, to give our imprimatur to the symbolism of the Confederate flag.

Symbols are important. They speak volumes. They speak volumes to the people in our country. They speak volumes to the people outside of our country who follow and who care about what happens in this, the greatest Nation in the world. It seems to me the time has long passed when we could put behind us the debates and arguments that have raged since the Civil War, that we get beyond the separateness and we get beyond the divisions and we get beyond fanning the flames of racial antagonism. I submit that to use the insignia of the United Daughters is their prerogative. However, it is not their prerogative to force me and the other Members of this body to assent to an extraordinary honor of their own revisionist history. That is the purpose of the design patent.

I submit to the body that the Judiciary Committee, in voting 13 to 2, recognized how singularly inappropriate it would be to renew the patent for the United Daughters of the Confederacy and it is singularly inappropriate for this amendment to be accepted.

Ms. Moseley-Braun. Mr. President, I, therefore, move that amendment 610—this amendment—be tabled . . .[1]

I am really stunned how often and how much the issue of race, the subject of racism, comes up in this U.S. Senate, comes up in this body and how I have to, on many occasions, as the only African-American here, constrain myself to be calm, to be laid back, to talk about these issues in very intellectual, nonemotional terms, and that is what I do on a regular basis, Madam President. That is part and parcel of my daily existence.

But at the same time, when the issue of the design patent extension for the United Daughters of the Confederacy first came up, I looked at it. I did not make a big deal of it. It came as part of the work of the Judiciary Committee. I looked at it, and I said, well, I am not going to vote for that.

When I announced I was not going to vote for it, the chairman, as is his due, began to poll the members. We talked about it, and I found myself getting drawn into a debate that I frankly never expected.

Who would have expected a design patent for the Confederate flag? And there are those in this body who say this really is not the Confederate flag. The other thing we did know was a Confederate flag.

I did my research, and I looked it up as I am wont to do, and guess what? That is the real Confederate flag. The thing we see all the time and are accustomed to is the battle flag. In fact, there is some history on this issue. I would like to read the following quote from the "Flag Book of the United States."

The real flower in the southern flag began in November 1860, when the election of Lincoln to President caused widespread fear the Federal Government

---

1. Senator Barbara Boxer, of California, acted as the Presiding Officer shortly after this point

will try to make changes in the institution of slavery. The winter of 1860 to 1861, rallies and speeches were held throughout the South and, frankly, the United States flag was replaced by a local banner.

This flag is the real flag of the Confederacy. If there is anybody in this Chamber anybody, indeed anybody in this world, that has a doubt that the Confederate effort was around preserving the institution of slavery, I am prepared and I believe history is prepared to dispute them to the nth. There is no question but that battle was fought to try to preserve our Nation, to keep the States from separating themselves over the issue of whether or not my ancestors could be held as property, as chattel, as objects of commerce and trade in this country.

And people died. More Americans died in the Civil War than any war they have ever gone through since. People died over the proposition that indeed these United States stood for the proposition that every person was created equal without regard to race, that we are all American citizens.

I am sorry, Madam President, I will lower my voice. I am getting excited, because, quite frankly, that is the very issue. The issue is whether or not Americans, such as myself, who believe in the promise of this country, who feel strongly and who are patriots in this country, will have to suffer the indignity of being reminded time and time again, that at one point in this country's history we were human chattel. We were property. We could be traded, bought, and sold.

Now, to suggest as a matter of revisionist history that this flag is not about slavery flies in the face of history, Madam President.

I was not going to get inflammatory. In fact, my staff brought me this little thing earlier, and it has been sitting here. I do not know if you noticed it sitting here during the earlier debate in which I was dispassionate and tried my level best not to be emotional and lawyering about and not get into calling names and talking about race and racism. I did not use it to begin with. I do want to share it now. It is a speech by the Vice President of the Confederate States of America, March 21, 1861, in Savannah, [Georgia] "Slavery, the Cornerstone of the Confederacy," this man goes on to say:

> The new Confederate constitution has put to rest forever all agitating questions relating to our peculiar "institution," which is what they call it. African slavery as it exists among us, the proper status of a Negro in our form of civilization. This was the immediate cause of the date rupture and present revolution. The prevailing ideas entertained by Thomas Jefferson and most of the leading statesmen at the time of the formation of the old Constitution were that the enslavement of the African was in violation of the laws of nature, that it was wrong in principle, socially, morally, and politically.

And then he goes on to say:

Our new Government is founded upon exactly the opposite idea. Its foundations are laid, its cornerstone rests upon the great truth that the Negro is not equal to the white man, that slavery, subordination to the superior race is the natural and moral condition.

This was a statement by the Vice President of the Confederate States of America.

Madam President, across the room on the other side is the flag. I say to you it is outrageous. It is an absolute outrage that this body would adopt as an amendment to this legislation a symbol of this point of view and, Madam President, I say to you that it is an important issue. It is a symbolic issue up there. There is no way you can get around it.

The reason for my emotion—I have been here almost 7 months now, and my colleagues will tell you there is not a more congenial, laid back, even person in this entire body who makes it a point to try to get along with everybody. I make it a point to try to talk to my colleagues and get beyond controversy and conflict, to try to find consensus on issues.

But I say to you, Madam President, on this issue there can be no consensus. It is an outrage. It is an insult. It is absolutely unacceptable to me and to millions of Americans, black or white, that we would put the imprimatur of the United States Senate on a symbol of this kind of idea. And that is what is at stake with this amendment, Madam President.

I am going to continue—I am going to continue because I am going to call it like I see it, as I always do. I was appalled, appalled at a segment of my own Democratic Party that would go take a walk and vote for something like this.

I am going to talk . . . about the other side of the aisle and the responsibility of the Republican Party.

The reason the Republican Party got run out on a rail the last time is the American people sensed intolerance in that party. The American people, African-Americans sensed there was not room for them in that party. Folks took a look at the convention and said, my God, what are these people standing for: This is not America. And they turned around and voted for change. They elected Bill Clinton President and the rest of us to this Chamber. The changes they were speaking out for was a change that said we have to get past racism, we have to get past sexism, the many issues that divide us as Americans, and come together as Americans so we can make this country be what it can be in the twenty-first century.

That is the real reason, Madam President, that I am here today. My State has less than 12 percent African-Americans in it, but the people of Illinois had no problem voting for a candidate that was African-American because they thought they were doing the same thing.

Similarly, the State of California sent two women, two women to the U.S. Senate, breaking a gender barrier, as did the State of Washington. Why? Because they felt that it was time to get past the barriers that said that women had no place in the conduct of our business.

And so, just as our country is moving forward, Madam President, to have this kind of symbol shoved in your face, shoved in my face, shoved in the faces of all the Americans who want to see a change for us to get beyond racism, is singularly inappropriate.

I say to you, Madam President, that this is no small matter. This is not a matter of little old ladies walking around doing good deeds. There is no reason why these little old ladies cannot do good deeds anyway. If they choose to wave the Confederate flag, that certainly is their right. Because I care about the fact that this is a free country. Free speech is the cornerstone of democracy. People are supposed to be able to say what they want to say. They are supposed to be able to join associations and organizations that express their views.

But I daresay, Madam President, that following the Civil War, and following the victory of the United States and the coming together of our country, that that peculiar institution was put to rest for once and for all; that the division in our Nation, the North versus the South, was put to rest once and for all. And the people of this country do not want to see a day in which flags like that are underwritten, underscored, adopted, approved by this U.S. Senate.

That is what this vote is about . . .

If I have to stand here until this room freezes over, Madam President, I am going to do so. Because I will tell you, this is something that has no place in our modern times. It has no place in this body. It has no place in the Senate. It has no place in our society.

And the fact is, Madam President, that I would encourage my colleagues on both sides of the aisle—Republican and Democrat; those who thought, "Well, we are just going to do this, you know, because it is no big deal"—to understand what a very big deal indeed it is—that the imprimatur that is being sought here today sends a sign out to the rest of this country that that peculiar institution has not been put to bed for once and for all; that, indeed, like Dracula, it has come back to haunt us time and time and time again; and that, in spite of the fact that we have made strides forward, the fact of the matter is that there are those who would keep us slipping back into the darkness of division, into the snake pit of racial hatred, of racial antagonism and of support for symbols— symbols of the struggle to keep African-Americans, Americans of African descent, in bondage. . . .

The Issue of Race

ELEANOR HOLMES NORTON

(1986)

" WE ARE TALKING, OF COURSE, about the issue of what the black community can do in dealing with its own problems, and this is something very appropriate during the years of the [Ronald] Reagan administration, because the current philosophy in Washington seems to be that government should get out of people's lives. Let me ask you, very generally, as a philosophical question, how that strikes you. Do you buy the notion that government needs to get out of our lives?"

Eleanor Holmes Norton: It's a reactionary Darwinian notion that I don't think that most of the American people buy, but these are hard times. In many respects the American standard of living over the past ten years has actually decreased, so people are more open to such notions. The fact is that for fifty years, we, as a nation, have had precisely the opposite view, that government has a role in people's lives when they have been disadvantaged through no fault of their own. So I think in very specific ways the government still has a role. That role is often different from what it was twenty years ago, but I think the Reagan administration's view, that the government should have nothing to do with people, except, of course, when that administration seeks to interject its own policies into the lives of people, is wrongheaded, and I don't think, fortunately, that it represents the majority view of the American people.

The American people, for example, still endorse, profoundly, protection of the environment, civil rights, Social Security, the basic framework of the New Deal and the Great Society, so that while they apparently support this president,

From audio interview by Clarence Page from Wingspread, the Educational Conference Center of the Johnson Foundation in Racine, Wisconsin, in 1986.

I do not think they support him because of his views on social policy and the role of the government in ameliorating human misery.

Page: As former chairman of the Equal Employment Opportunity Commission in Washington during the [Jimmy] Carter years, you were a person very influential in trying to open up opportunities for people. I can't help but wonder what goes through your mind as you see others taking over your job and other areas of equal opportunity in government these days. What kind of thoughts run through your mind?

Norton: I left the government, of course, at the end of the Carter administration, and would have no problem whatsoever with people taking over my old position and the position of others who had civil rights positions in the government had those who now have replaced us had any semblance of commitment to enforcing the law. Their record on civil rights has been disgraceful, as a matter of fact. They have largely failed to enforce the law at all. Worse, they have often sought to overturn existing law. They have misapplied and misinterpreted the law. They have worked up racial polarization by making, or trying to make, the American people believe that numerical remedies, for example, are always unfair, when, in fact, these remedies have been approved by a conservative Supreme Court. They have distorted racial issues in a way that we have not seen at the federal level in this century.

Page: This Justice Department now is using the Memphis Fire Fighters case—and I should point out that the Memphis Fire Fighter[1] case was one in which a high court ruled that the local government should not lay off white firemen with more seniority first, ahead of those who had less seniority, I guess because those with less seniority happened to be minorities. Now [William] Bradford Reynolds, of the Reagan administration, the chief civil rights enforcer, has sent notice to governments all over the country saying, "Stop immediately all of your efforts toward affirmative action."

First of all, do you think it's fair for a white worker with more seniority to be laid off ahead of a minority worker with less seniority?

Norton: First let me make clear what had happened in the Memphis case. The blacks had been hired as a result of an affirmative action program following a consent decree signed by the city of Memphis, which, in effect, admitted that it had discriminated against black firemen in the past and kept those firemen from entering the department through normal routes. As a result, a quota for a specified period of time was put on the department. The blacks entered in that way. When a layoff occurred, it would have wiped out the very affirmative action program that the court had ordered.

Under those circumstances, many felt that though the court had long ruled that seniority matters could not be subject to race, that in a situation where the

---

1. *See* Firefighters Local 1784 v. Stotts, 467 U.S. 561 (1984).

court had, in fact, ordered the blacks on the job, they would not order them off or allow them to undo the court's own order. The court, of course, has interpreted a section of Title VII, the act that I administered, to mean that racial layoffs can never be done.

What do I think about racial layoffs? Very frankly, while I was human rights commissioner of New York City and when I became chair of the EEOC, I pursued an alternative remedy that I prefer. I understand that racial layoffs in a situation like the Memphis case can well be justified, given the prior discrimination that kept blacks from being on in the first place, but I prefer what has come to be known as short-term compensation, whereby instead of displacing any workers, black or white, a fire department would put those scheduled to be laid off, or a certain number of them, on a four-day work week, and on the fifth day they would be paid unemployment insurance at home. That way the minorities would be allowed to accumulate their seniority, nobody would be laid off, the savings that the employer needs to make would be made, and we would avoid the unique situation in affirmative action whereby somebody actually has to lose a job.

William Bradford Reynolds, to answer the second part of your question, has tried to apply this seniority decision to a totally different situation where there is no job loss as in hiring or promotion, but where pursuant to an affirmative action plan, a court orders blacks to be hired in some proportion to the whites who are hired, because the employer, in the past, discriminated against blacks or Hispanics or women or all three, on the basis of a decision that had nothing to do with hiring and promotion. Assistant Attorney General Bradford Reynolds has done exactly what you said: told states and cities that they should undo consent decrees that have been approved by federal courts, authorizing and, indeed, mandating racial hiring to correct discrimination, even though, of course, the courts have said no such thing with respect to hiring and promotion. It is a cardinal example of how this administration and its agents are seeking, through ways that are clearly, in my judgment, quite illegal—if not illegal, certainly unprofessional—to undermine twenty years of court decisions, as well as the 1964 Civil Rights Act itself.

Page: The major thrust of President Reagan's civil rights enforcers has been, they say in their own explanation, speaking here of William Bradford Reynolds, Clarence Pendleton, the rest of the establishment that we all know, that they are trying to guarantee equal rights for everybody, so they don't want blacks or other minorities to get more opportunity at the expense of whites, or women to get opportunity at the expense of males. That may sound to the average American as a very equitable way to approach the problem. What do you say to those people who agree with that philosophy?

Norton: What I say, I suppose, is what the Supreme Court has said, the [Warren E.] Burger court, the conservative Burger court has said, and that is that where you have discrimination, you've got to find a way, without defeating the rights of either group, to accommodate those who have been excluded. What the courts have said is in a situation where you had discrimination in the past, you cannot stop hiring whites in order to accommodate the blacks. What you can do is to hire some blacks and some whites for a certain period of time, usually that is a few years, until the blacks are brought up to some number, usually it will be a fraction of the work force, and then the work force will revert to its former self and you'll go forward.

If you don't do it that way, you never break the cycle of racial or sexual exclusion. You simply continue to have white males monopolize the jobs . . .

What this administration is doing is very scary. The administration is trying, in my judgment, to work up racial resentment on the parts of whites to remedies that have been ordered by courts. This is the kind of thing we expected from Southern racists all during the sixties, who stood in the schoolhouse door and otherwise defied the courts. We had come to believe that federal officials would not engage in such efforts.

Page: The same thing that [Governor] George Wallace, who stood in the schoolhouse door of the University of Alabama, after he became a person who was physically disabled, became a lot more sympathetic to the civil rights cause.

But there are those who feel that the bottom line of these court decisions is preferential treatment for minorities and women. What do you say to that? Even if only temporarily, is it not preferential treatment, to a degree?

Norton: It's not preferential treatment. Preferential treatment would mean that on the basis of race and nothing else, you're saying that we're going to prefer a certain number of blacks because we need a certain number of blacks as well as whites in order to have some kind of racial balance. This is remediation . . . I think the term "preferential treatment" is quite misleading, because what we are, in fact, doing is applying a court remedy to a proven legal wrong.

Page: This gets back to our question of self-help, what the black community can do to help itself. Coming from Chicago, I hear a lot of ethnic whites who are first- or second-generation immigrants who say, "My family came over here, we were discriminated against. We ran into all kinds of problems. We weren't here during the time of slavery. We had nothing to do with that. Yet now we are being penalized by the government because of our race," or because of sex. They say it's not fair, and this causes a tremendous collision between white ethnics and blacks in our major cities. What can you offer to kind of bridge the gap here?

Norton: The first thing I would offer is the certain knowledge that instances of remediation of the kind I've just described are quite rare relative to the total number of positions open, that you will not run into affirmative action programs ubiquitously. Secondly, what I have to offer is the notion that we are whites and blacks today in the transition generation that must dismantle racism or be content to live with it forever. We've got to find the fairest way to all concerned, to get from a society where race determined employment, to a society where race has nothing to do with employment. Thus, a period of remediation in which neither group experiences entirely its expectations will be necessary, or else we will be condemned to live in the same kind of racially exclusive society we have all pledged to move away from.

Page: We spoke earlier of the polarization that has been apparently encouraged by the Reagan administration now. We also see, in this light today, a lot of publicity about extremist groups on both sides of the racial line—the rise of the [Ku Klux] Klan and Klanlike groups. At the same time, [Minister] Louis Farrakhan and the more extreme type of Black Muslims are drawing bigger crowds than they have in many years. Do you think there is a connection here, that this is part of the atmosphere we're living in now?

Norton: I don't think that either whites or blacks embrace extremist groups of the kind you have mentioned. I do think there's a kind of curiosity about these groups which have been driven underground and have now emerged into the full light of day. I do also think they have some following, but I think that the following is tiny compared to the more balanced view of the majority of Americans, white and black.

Page: One thing that Louis Farrakhan has talked a lot about, he apparently agrees with President Reagan on the idea of self-help—"do for self," as he says, as Elijah Muhammad said before, that the black community should stop looking to the government for help and should try to build its own institutions, try to help itself. Do you think there's some merit in that?

Norton: I think that Louis Farrakhan is a little late. The notion of self-help, I find the expression quite demeaning. It implies that people have not been helping themselves. But the notion of community taking its own destiny into its own hands without government aid has been the rule, rather than the exception in American society. Out of 300 years, perhaps the last 30 have seen the government actively intervening, other than to impede black people. There may have been three or four years after the Civil War when that was also the case. Black survival has depended upon essentially the efforts of the black community.

Today I endorse—and I know of no black spokesperson or leader who does not endorse—the notion of blacks finding ways to deepen their own involvement in the elimination of their own problems, but I also believe that there are problems that no amount of so-called self-help could take care of . . .

We've got to apply self-help remedies where they are relevant and understand that government has to play a role in the lives of people who are often desperately poor. An example of what I might call a combination of self-help and government intervention is found in some recent experiences in the state of Massachusetts. Over and over again we were told we ought to get these people off welfare and make them work. The Reagan administration has a work fair program. It hasn't been terribly successful because the states have found it hard to implement, offers no permanent way off of welfare, so it hasn't been a particularly successful experiment . . .

Page: . . . When you look at the black community today, a number of us have been fortunate enough to be successful, an awful lot of others have not. What examples do you see of actions that we can take within the community to try to help ourselves over and above whatever we are able to get out of the government?

Norton: I think the community may be most excited about opportunities to deal with early pregnancy and teenage pregnancy. Probably the root cause of poverty in the black community is that 55 percent of black children are born to never-married black females, most of them poor. Many of them are very young.

There was a time when blacks were reluctant to speak about this problem, so it has grown and ballooned. There is no group in the black community that does not have a role in the elimination of early pregnancy to teenage girls and other young women . . .

Page: I can't help but think, also, obviously as far as family life goes, that's something we can really do to help ourselves. I wonder about economic opportunity. I see in our big cities a lot of small businesses and stores are struggling, and many outside people come in and serve as merchants in the black community and take those funds outside. I know you're familiar with this phenomenon. I wonder if there's anything that can be done within the black community to encourage more entrepreneurship.

Norton: That would appear to be one of the great priorities of the black community. Entrepreneurship, which was almost nonexistent except in Southern communities or all-black communities, and then in very limited fashion, began to really blossom and bloom with the set-asides, with minority business enterprise notions in the 1970s. I think that small business, though, business, for example, that serves on the corner of a ghetto street, is probably the most vulnerable kind of business there is. The notion that people come in, take the community's money, and go out, ought to be seen in some context. The business involves a lot of risk. Blacks are free to open those businesses if they want to, but they usually mean working twenty hours a day and sometimes not even making enough to live. Going into your own business is about working two or three times as hard as people who work for wages.

Without an entrepreneurial tradition—one of the legacies of slavery, by the way—you will get great problems when blacks who do not have the capital, do not have the credit, seek to enter business for themselves. I am, nevertheless, amazed by the extent of the entrepreneurial spirit in the black community, and I believe that black Americans are going to become capitalists in the American tradition like everybody else very shortly. . . .

Black Strategies: Responding to Thomas Sowell. I Know Where You're Coming from, But . . .

PAULI MURRAY

(1981)

*D*EAR TOM:
Although I have not seen you since we served together on Brandeis University faculty in 1969–70, I have followed your writings and public statements with an interest born of our mutual suffering during the crisis of black student militancy on predominantly white college campuses. I have now read and reflected upon your "Blacker Than Thou" pieces.[1]

I can understand your anger and pain over what you consider a "blacker than thou" syndrome on the part of many middle-class Negroes/blacks, reacting to a mass desire for a positive identity. As you know, I have resisted that syndrome, symbolized by stubbornly clinging to the term "Negro" as an acceptable (and dignified) identification. But I have come to understand that along with the elements of a passing fad, emphasis upon "blackness" has been a necessary corrective for a group in a nation that has traditionally identified "whiteness" with superiority.

When I was the age you are now, 50, I spent 18 months in Africa (Ghana), teaching but also coming to terms with my African ancestry and reflecting upon what it means to be an American. I listened to native Africans refer to the late Dr. Ralph Bunche as a "black white man," and heard myself described as *oburoni*, a term meaning stranger or foreigner. I discovered that aside from color and mutual victimization by colonialism/racism shared with black Africans, American Negroes were irrevocably products of the New World and that while there might be traces of African heritage in the black subculture of the United States persons of color had been shaped by the historical experience of chattel slavery, that "peculiar condition" that accounts for many of the complex racial problems

---

© WASHINGTON POST, February 26, 1981, at A19.
1. Thomas Sowell, *Leaders—or, 'Leaders'?* N.Y. TIMES, April 12, 1979, at A23.

we face today. This being the case, while it is useful and perhaps romantic to look at the African past, the answers to our racial problems lie in the American experience. Short of annihilation, our destiny is to become part of the mainstream of American life, working simultaneously for liberation and reconciliation, terms that have a theological as well as a political meaning.

If this is an agreed-upon goal, our differences lie in methods of reaching it. Your "blacker than thou" analysis reveals the diversity of backgrounds and approaches of people of color in the United States. For me, the goal can be reached by transcending "blackness" and "whiteness" and emphasizing "humanness." When one works for *human rights,* one necessarily tries to see the whole—the rights of Negroes/blacks, Hispanics, Native Americans, persons of Asian ancestry, women, the poor, the aged, the handicapped, homosexuals and all other oppressed or disadvantaged minorities. We discover that we do not have one identity but several overlapping identities. (At one and the same time I am a woman, a Negro, aged, left-handed, a human rights attorney and a priest!)

This leads me to point to the positive aspects of having a mixed ancestry. Those of us who, through accident of birth, are related by blood and culture to several races or ethnic groups are the natural "bridges" between the diverse peoples of the United States, however we may be classified in the census records. I am old enough to identify myself as "the granddaughter of a slave" and the "great-granddaughter of a slave owner."[2] This is an acceptance of my historical roots; it is also a reminder to white Americans that we are in fact related and cannot be excluded from the family table.

Because of the recirculation of genes over several centuries, most Americans of African ancestry also have European and Native American (Indian, or Amerindian) forebears. We are the modern "Ishmaelites." We can accept this fact of mixed ancestry, this "hybrid" background, as a group in historical transition, and use it creatively in our struggle for full human dignity, or we can reject it, continue a black–white polarization and permit white Americans to "get off the hook" by clinging to the illusion that persons of African ancestry are "different" and unassimilable.

I am convinced that how we view our identity will determine how we approach such thorny questions as affirmative action, busing, housing, education, politics and all the rest. We will seek not Black alternatives, but human alternatives to issues of health, welfare, minimum wage, etc. My chief quarrel with you, Tom, is that you are looking at the problems we face with a narrow lens. You have complained of the so-called "black elite" that "much of their demand for removing racial barriers was a demand that they be allowed to join the white elite and escape the black masses."

---

2. Pauli Murray, Proud Shoes: The Story of an American Family, x–xii (New York, Harper & Row 1978).

The so-called "white elite" who have long been my close personal friends and part of my extended family are individuals who believe that by virtue of their privileges and/or wealth they have a solemn obligation to reinvest in the human resources of the United States to enable others of all races (and sexes) to achieve as they have achieved. This is the finest of American traditions, and one to which I aspire. Moreover, historically, the close associations between individual blacks and whites have helped to alter relations between the races. In theology, we call this "bearing one another's burdens."

Finally, if I have anything to contribute to this discussion out of a life experience of 70 years in the United States, it is the firm conviction that the late Dr. Martin Luther King, Jr. was on the right track: He demonstrated the psychic, spiritual and political power of transforming negative, angry, hostile feelings into positive, creative energies in approaching the problems of human conflict. If we would only build upon King's earlier crude experiments in creative non-violence, refining the technique and, in his words, making it "a subject for study and for serious experimentation in every field of human conflict," it would be not only our distinctive contribution to the resolution of our racial problem but also a step forward in solving the issues of war and peace in the world.

White Racism; Black Dissent

FRANKIE MUSE FREEMAN

(1969)

A DISTURBING TREND HAS RECENTLY emerged in this country that places dissent on the same level as treason. It is a coldly calculated device to excommunicate dissenters from the company of decent men, a trick to divide Americans on the basis of their beliefs. We are being told that unless we accept every act of the government as correct, we are being un-American. We are being told not to criticize, that everything is being handled by our elected officials, and if we question them, then we indicate a shocking lack of confidence in our country. So far the device has been applied only against dissenters from the Viet Nam war, but if this "Operation Discredit" is successful, it will be turned against other dissenters, and particularly against those who dissent over the handling of racial problems.

The step from branding people who dissent on one issue as unpatriotic, to branding people who dissent on any issue as unpatriotic, is not a long one. Once the madness takes hold, and the fever begins, no one is safe except in total conformity. America has to be awakened to this danger, and we who are involved in civil rights activities have a particular responsibility in this matter, for as certain as it is that we sit here today, just as certain as it is that we will be the next on the list to be smeared as un-American.

This possibility does have an ironic overtone, for the majority of those who dissent over the handling of America's racial problems, do it out of a desire to reform the country, not destroy it. The great civilizations of mankind have all crumbled, not because of outside force, but because of their own internal weakness. America is no different, she too can destroy herself and it is

---

This article appeared in the Extension of Remarks, 116 CONG. REC. E2482 (1970). It is from an excerpt from a speech by Commissioner Freeman made at the 1969 NAACP Freedom Fund Dinner in Milwaukee, Wisconsin. She was a member of the U.S. Civil Rights Commission.

this that we try to avoid when we ask this nation to solve these problems while there is still time.

Whether the necessary actions will be taken, depends on whether White America can be convinced that she has permitted a racist society to develop and to continue to exist. She has supported institutions that have excluded Blacks, Mexican-Americans, Indians and other minority groups, and she has made a white skin the mark of excellence. The responsibility for changing this rests in her hands.

The responsibility, however, is only dimly perceived by the majority of Whites who find acceptance difficult because it calls into question their own conduct and challenges the sanctity of the institutions with which they feel most comfortable. If they admit to any degree of responsibility then they must have contributed to racism, and since this idea is abhorrent, they reject it. They cannot accept the possibility that their valued institutions, such as their schools, their churches, their all-White organizations, could have contributed to the present racial problems, and so they reject this idea as well . . .

Institutionalized racism often operates subtly, with few people realizing what is actually taking place. When schools almost automatically assign Black children to general courses while Whites are assigned to academic courses, this is racism. When police departments enforce the law one way in Black communities and another way in White, this is racism. When the only supply of housing available to Blacks is generally inferior and in the inner city, this is racism. When labor unions set artificially high standards and then confine their apprenticeships to relatives of members, this is racism.

These are examples of how racism operates, and as I have indicated, the responsibility for bringing about change rests with those who contribute most to the maintenance of such structures, the White community. . . .

African Americans Must Reject Anti-Semitism

Elaine Ruth Jones

(1994)

*H*ISTORY TEACHES THAT THE SEEDS of demagoguery take root in desperate times. For many African Americans, these are such times. Hyper-segregated black communities are plagued by high unemployment and economic devastation, by the double scourge of drugs and violence, by governmental and private-sector neglect and by the persistence of racism. Tempted by the demons of frustration and bitterness, some in the black community are giving voice to bigotry and anti-Semitic sentiments.

In late November, at a state college in New Jersey, such an individual delivered a speech, full of factual and historical misrepresentations, that vilified Jews, white people and black people who associated with them. The speaker, the Nation of Islam's Khalid Abdul Mohammad, denounced Nelson Mandela because of his vision of multiracial post-apartheid South Africa and called for the death of every white man, woman and child who had the temerity to remain in that country. The diatribe also contained remarks offensive to Jews, Catholics, Italians, Greeks and Arabs, as well as African Americans who do not think in the prescribed manner.

Ultimately, the significance of the speech at Kean College will not be found in its substance, but in our response to it. There are those in the African American community who may find the speech repugnant but are reluctant to publicly break rank with those who preach racial pride and self-reliance. Others may resent being held collectively and personally accountable for the statements of an individual with whom they have nothing in common other than ethnicity. Some believe that a speech insulting so many people in such an outrageously vile and ignorant manner should not be underscored by more attention than it deserves, while still others do not see why its anti-Semitism should be singled

Los Angeles Times, Jan. 28, 1994, at B7.

out for special response. Finally, some resent what they perceive to be patronizing pressure to repudiate views that they would reject anyway.

Whatever the merits of these positions, reasonable people cannot disagree on this fact: The message of racism, anti-Semitism and hatred delivered at Kean College must be condemned. We who work daily to eliminate the blight of bigotry know that in the struggle against racism, we cannot ourselves become racist. As African Americans, we oppose bigotry not simply because we historically have been its victims; we oppose it because it is morally wrong. If we are to condemn racism, we must condemn it no matter who the victims are or who the perpetrators may be. If we want others to denounce racism when African Americans are its target, we must be equally indignant and outspoken when others are its victims. Our struggle goes beyond self-interest; it is a struggle for what is right.

We must move beyond condemnation, however, to a meaningful dialogue about racism, anti-Semitism and other forms of bigotry. We must then move beyond dialogue to attack the conditions of poverty and isolation that produce the frustration and bitterness that provide such fertile soil for the seeds of divisiveness. As long as so many African Americans are profoundly alienated from mainstream America, the rhetoric of bigotry and hatred will resonate among some.

We must call upon the better angels of our nature to realize Dr. King's vision of a society in which "black men and white men, Jews and Gentiles, Protestants and Catholics" can join together in a celebration of freedom. Let us meet on the high road of racial and religious tolerance and mutual respect. Only there can we transform Dr. King's vision into reality.

Black Political Power

GLORIA E. A. TOOTE

(1982)

OUR RESPONSIBILITY AS MEMBERS of the National Black Republican Council is to make the Black vote less predictable. Blacks are not a monolithic group. All blacks do not share the same views on any issue, nor do all Whites. This is as it should be. We must recognize that the one-dimensional approach by Blacks to Party Politics was born of necessity, not choice. Unlike America's White ethnic groups whose votes were sought by both major parties, the Black vote in the past has consistently been sought by only one party at a time. The negative socioeconomic impact upon the Black community of maintaining a one-party identity is not insignificant, and it is important to America that it not go unchallenged. The Democrats in perpetuating the myth of the value of a one-party system to Black America are not only stifling the positive benefits of political competition, but are also impeding Black progress . . .

There is a Black political power! Public cynicism and Black political ineffectiveness could however eventually bring about its demise. The continued alienation between Blacks and the Republican Party is an ominous threat that we must recognize; and that can seed a negative national climate . . .

To the Republican Party I say Blacks are not arrogant . . . we are proud. Our loyalty can not be purchased . . . Our success is your success. Our failure is your failure . . .

The Black political perspective must become an agenda item for this nation. This will be achieved only when forced as such by Blacks. If Black communities are to economically and morally survive patience can exist no longer! We must drive our indifference. Those who would be free *themselves* must strike the blow! We must translate our thoughts into action and make the political

Excerpt from speech before the National Black Republican Council, Washington, D.C., September 16, 1982.

arena our key to power dynamics . . . If it were left to some there would be no freedom of political choice for Black America . . .

The Black vote can be a powerful, positive force in this country. Racism is not about to disappear, but it clearly can no longer serve as the principal support of a political structure. Achieving first class citizenship *for all* Americans is the responsibility of *all* Americans, not just Blacks. But we are naive if we have been misled into thinking that anyone else is going to care more about our problems that we do.

Both major political parties in the past have managed to adopt themselves to the demands made upon them by external necessities . . .

Let it be known throughout the land that the Republican Party is determined to take those steps necessary to assure Black America that its involvement and participation is wanted: and that ethnic political power is an indispensable instrument of government . . . The success of the Black Nixon appointees in encouraging "Black Capitalism"[1] and in funneling federal resources to the Black community proved that a conservative Republican administration can and will address Black needs . . .

The zeal demonstrated by Blacks in the sixties and seventies must be re-aroused in a quest to master and persevere in the role as overseer of the political conscious and economic agenda for America. We cannot allow the system nor those who recognize better than we the efficacy of this effort to thwart us. For ours though a self-serving crusade will ultimately benefit all, equally, affirmatively, and emotionally, to the betterment of America. . . .

---

1. *See* Theodore Cross, Black Capitalism: Strategy for Business in the Ghetto (New York, Atheneum 1969).

Equality

The Negro Woman in the Quest for Equality

PAULI MURRAY

(1964)

The Heritage

NEGRO WOMEN, HISTORICALLY, have carried the dual burden of Jim Crow and Jane Crow.[1] They have not always carried it graciously but they have carried it effectively. They have shared with their men a partnership in a pioneer life on spiritual and psychological frontiers not inhabited by any other group in the United States. For Negroes have had to hack their way through the wilderness of racism produced by the accumulated growth of nearly four centuries of chattel slavery and a century of illusive citizenship in a desperate effort to make a place of dignity for themselves and their children.

In this bitter struggle, into which has been poured most of the resources and much of the genius of successive generations of American Negroes, these women have often carried disproportionate burdens in the Negro family as they strove to keep its integrity intact against the constant onslaught of indignities to which it was subjected. Not only have they stood shoulder to shoulder with Negro men in every phase of the battle, but they have also continued to stand when their men were destroyed by it. Who among us is not familiar with that heroic, if formidable, figure exhorting her children to overcome every disappointment, humiliation and obstacle. This woman's lullaby was very often "Be something!" "Be somebody!" My friend and colleague, Mrs. Dovey J. Roundtree,[2] who tells

---

THE ACORN, June, 1964 (pages unnumbered).

1. *See* Pauli Murray & Mary O. Eastwood, *Jane Crow and the Law: Sex Discrimination and Title VII*, 34 GEO. WASH. L. REV. 232 (1965).

2. Dovey Roundtree is a 1950 law graduate of Howard University and practices law in the District of Columbia. *See A Long Life of Sweet Justice; Dovey Roundtree, Attorney and Role Model*, WASH. POST, Feb. 4, 1995, at D1.

this story of her own grandmother was never quite sure in childhood what it was she was supposed to be, but there was never any escape from the mandate.

Langston Hughes' poem, "Mother to Son" has great meaning for a generation which still recalls the washtub and the steaming wood stove as the source of hard earned dollars which sent it to school. It reveals the great gift of the Negro woman for mothering, consoling, encouraging:

Well son, I'll tell you:
Life for me ain't been no crystal stair.
It's had tacks in it,
And splinters,
And boards torn up,
And places with no carpet on the floor—
Bare . . . [3]

In the course of their climb, Negro women have had to fight against the stereotypes of "female dominance" on the one hand and loose morals on the other hand, both growing out of the roles forced upon them during the slavery experience and its aftermath. But out of their struggle for human dignity, they also developed a tradition of independence and self-reliance. This characteristic, said the late Dr. E. Franklin Frazier, sociologist, "has provided generally a pattern of equalitarian relationship between men and women in America." Like the western pioneer settlements, the embattled Negro society needed the strength of all of its members in order to survive. The economic necessity for the Negro woman to earn a living to help support her family—if indeed she was not the sole support—fostered her independence and equalitarian position.

In the human rights battle, America has seen the image of the Negro evolving through many women: Harriet Tubman and Sojourner Truth a century ago; Ida B. Wells in the latter part of the nineteenth century; Mary Church Terrell and Mary McLeod Bethune in an earlier generation; Mrs. Rosa Parks, Autherine Lucy, Mrs. Gloria Richardson, Mrs. Daisy Bates, Mrs. Diana Nash Bevel, Mrs. Constance Baker Motley, Mrs. Medgar Evers, Dorothy Height, Mrs. Anna Hedgeman, and many others in the contemporary struggle. Not only have women whose names are well known given this great human effort its peculiar vitality but women in many communities whose names will never be known have revealed the courage and strength of the Negro woman. These are the mothers who have stood in school yards with their children, many times alone. These are the images which have touched America's heart. Painful as these ex-

---

3. Langston Hughes, *"Mother to Son,"* in ARTHUR P. DAVIS ET AL., THE NEW CAVALCADE: AFRICAN AMERICAN WRITING FROM 1760 TO THE PRESENT 559 (Washington, D.C., Howard University Press 1991).

periences have been, one cannot help asking: would the Negro struggle have come this far without the indomitable determination of its women?

In the larger society, Negro and white women share a common burden because of traditional discriminations based upon sex. Dr. Gunnar Myrdal pointed out the similarities between the Negro problem and the women's problem in *An American Dilemma*. What he saw is common knowledge among Negro women, but it is interesting to see the United States through the eyes of a foreign observer. He said:

> As in the Negro problem, most men have accepted as self-evident, until recently, the doctrine that women had inferior endowments in most of those respects which carry prestige, power and advantages in society . . . The arguments when argument is used, have been about the same: smaller brains, scarcity of geniuses and so on . . . As in the case of the Negro, women themselves have often been brought to believe in their inferiority of endowment. As the Negro was awarded his "place" . . . [T]he myth of the "contented women" who did not want to have suffrage or other civil rights and equal opportunities, had the same social function as the myth of the "contented Negro" . . . [4]

Despite the common interests of Negro and white women, however, the dichotomy of the segregated society has prevented them from cementing a natural alliance. Communication and cooperation between them have been hesitant, limited and formal. Negro women have tended to identify all discrimination against them as racial in origin and to accord high priority to the civil rights struggle. They have had little time or energy for consideration of women's rights. But as the civil rights struggle gathers momentum, they begin to recognize the similarities between paternalism and racial arrogance. They also begin to sense that the struggle into which they have poured their energies may not afford them rights they have assumed would be theirs when the civil rights cause has triumphed . . .

Recent disquieting events have made imperative an assessment of the role of the Negro woman in the quest for equality. The civil rights revolt, like many social upheavals, has released powerful pent-up emotions, cross currents, rivalries and hostilities. In emerging from an essentially middle class movement and taking on a mass character, it has become a vehicle to power and prestige and contains many of the elements of in-fighting that have characterized labor's emergence or the pre-independence African societies. There is much jockeying for position as ambitious men push and elbow their way to leadership roles. Part

---

4. GUNNAR MYRDAL, AN AMERICAN DILEMMA: THE NEGRO PROBLEM AND MODERN DEMOCRACY 1077 (New York, Harper & Row 1962).

of this upsurge reflects the Negro male's normal desire to achieve a chance of personal worth and recognition of his manhood by a society which has so long denied it. One aspect is the wresting of the initiative of the civil rights movement from white liberals. Another is the backlash of a new male aggressiveness against Negro women.

What emerges most clearly from events of the past several months is the tendency to assign women to a secondary, ornamental or "honoree" role instead of the partnership role in the civil rights movement which they have earned by their courage, intelligence and dedication. It was bitterly humiliating for Negro women on August 28 to see themselves accorded little more than token recognition in the historic March on Washington. Not a single woman was invited to make one of the major speeches or to be part of the delegation of leaders who went to the White House. This omission was deliberate. Representations for recognition of women were made to the policy-making body sufficiently in advance of the August 28 arrangements to have permitted the necessary adjustments of the program. What the Negro women leaders were told is revealing: that no representation was given to them because they would not be able to agree on a delegate. How familiar was this excuse! It is a typical response from an entrenched power group.

Significantly, two days before the March, A. Philip Randolph, leader of the March, accepted an invitation to be guest speaker at a luncheon given by the National Press Club in Washington in the face of strong protest by organized newspaper women that the National Press Club excludes qualified newspaper women from membership and sends women reporters who cover its luncheons to the balcony. Mr. Randolph apparently saw no relationship between being sent to the balcony and being sent to the back of the bus. Perhaps if he had been able to understand what an affront it is to one's personal dignity to be sent to the balcony at a meeting concerned primarily with the issue of human dignity, he would set as a condition for his appearance a non-segregated gathering. He failed to see that he was supporting the violation of the very principle for which he was fighting: that human rights are indivisible.

In 1840, a somewhat similar issue arose in the anti-slavery movement. William Lloyd Garrison and Charles Remond, the latter a Negro, refused to be seated as delegates to the World Anti-Slavery Convention in London when they learned that the women members of the American delegation would be excluded and could sit only in the balcony. Mr. Garrison dramatized his protest by joining the women in the balcony. The seed of the Seneca Falls Convention of 1848, which marks the formal beginning of the woman's rights movement in the United States, was planted at that London convention. One wonders what similar decisions were made by the spiritual successors to Harriet Tubman and Sojourner Truth on August 28.

This was not an isolated incident. Women who have been active in local branches of NAACP have observed the efforts of men to push them out of positions of leadership. And from Atlanta came the recent announcement of Mrs. Ruby Hurley, veteran NAACP field worker, that she was organizing women's auxiliaries for NAACP because "Negro women and white women, too, have a responsibility to carry a greater share in the civil rights protest than they do." A woman's auxiliary implies an adjunct to a male organization. Can it be that the movement which Mary White Ovington, a woman, helped to organize has become so male-dominated that women no longer feel like first class members and can be roused to action only through an auxiliary organization in which they are at least treated as equals?

More recently, Mr. James Meredith, hero of the University of Mississippi crisis,[5] reportedly told the *Washington Post:* "My makeup won't allow me to go along with using women and children in certain exposed roles in our fight. I love them too much. I think it is the man's role to face danger and protect his women and children."

Two comments are relevant here. All Negroes are born involved in the civil rights fight and exposed to its dangers. Ironically enough, the very presence of women and children in the demonstrations has doubtless minimized the violence and aroused the sympathies of the American public. The grudging respect of some local police for an aroused public opinion has been a key factor throughout the mass demonstrations. No more dramatic illustration of the many roles which women have played in this struggle can be found than the news photos of Mr. Meredith himself in many tense situations with his legal counsel, Mrs. Constance Motley, at his side. The plain fact is that in today's wars and social revolutions there are no civilians. The tragic death of six children in Birmingham on September 15th made this painfully clear.

The second and more important fact is that in the civil rights revolution, it has been the individual commitment of men, women and children to the struggle for liberty and without regard to age or sex which has made the movement so spectacular and won the respect of the American people. It cannot be too strongly emphasized here that part of what has set the American Negro off from other Americans is their commonly held view that Negroes are not part of the significant American traditions and movements. It is pointed out that Negroes are the one group whose immigration to the New World was not voluntary. Negroes were not intended to be included in the Declaration of Independence, we are told. Although 200,000 Negroes fought in the Civil War and their emancipation was a result of the war, it was not their war it is said. All too often, upon reading American history one is left with the impression that Negroes are a group about which history has been made but who themselves have not

---

5. *See generally* JAMES MEREDITH, THREE YEARS IN MISSISSIPPI (Bloomington, Indiana University Press 1966).

taken the initiative in making significant history. Few people bother to read the historical materials which refute these general impressions . . .

To return to our central theme, it is also pointedly significant that in the great mass of magazine and newsprint expended upon the civil rights crisis, national editors have selected Negro men almost exclusively to articulate the aspirations of the Negro community. There has been little or no public discussion of the problems, aspirations and role of Negro women . . .

At the very moment in history when there is an international movement to raise the status of women and a recognition that women generally are underemployed, are Negro women to be passed over in the social arrangements which are to create new job opportunities for Negroes? Moreover, when American women are seeking partnership in our society, are Negro women to take a backward step and sacrifice their equalitarian tradition?

Negro women have tremendous power. How shall they use their power? How can they help Negro men and themselves to achieve mature relationships in the wider community without impairing this tradition? Or is it inherent in the struggle that Negro men can achieve maturity only at the price of destroying in Negro women the very characteristics which are stressed as part of American tradition and which have been indispensable to the Negro's steep climb out of slavery? And if these qualities are suppressed in the women, what will be the effect upon the personalities of future generations of Negro children? What are the alternatives to matriarchal dominance on the one hand and male supremacy on the other hand? . . .

Female Liberation and Human Survival

BARBARA MAE WATSON

(1975)

*F*OR TO BE BOTH A WOMAN and black in a world in which women are peculiarly disadvantaged is to impel a recital of wrongs where one of these two attributes compounds the complexities of the other . . .

I am . . . obliged to urge upon the conference special attention to the position of black women over and above those disabilities to which quite simply as women, we are already subjected.

When I consider the nuclear release of human energies that could follow in the train of more enlightened and thus, more equalitarian attitudes towards us by our male counterparts, I am astonished that this very obvious benefit has so far eluded the grasp of male intelligence. This intra-specific conflict within the human group is one of the prime causes of our present discontents. The great problems of war and peace, hunger and poverty, of crime and punishment, the redistribution of wealth, the constructive allocation of human resources, the building of a world society, these are tasks which can only be tackled with any prospect of significant success by an equal concert of effort on the part of men and women alike. The problem is, how to accomplish this crucial task before the sands in the hourglass run out, as indeed they are doing even as we debate these issues.

What steps are needed? How, in short, shall we achieve our liberation from this backward thralldom? If I may say so, as no coarse boast and in no spirit of overweening self-assertion, I am an inheritor of no mean renown. The numbers of black women who might have preceded me here—who indeed might have accompanied me to this rostrum—are legion. Some of the great historical fig-

---

This paper was delivered shortly after Barbara Mae Watson left the Department of State where she served as Administrator of the Bureau of Security and Consular Affairs from 1968 to 1974.

ures in the annals of my country—Sojourner Truth, Harriet Tubman, to name just these two, are surely not unknown to you. They, too, pleaded for the liberation of women even as they were working for the emancipation of their fellow slaves. In the contemporary era, the names of Mary McLeod Bethune, Mary Church Terrell and Rosa Parks have been equally outstanding and perhaps sounded in your ears. It is in their names that I speak. They are black as I am black. Yet the transcendent circumstance is not our blackness but our womanhood. And the crisis we confront today in the world at large is partly, insofar as we black women are concerned, a crisis of blackness. But far above and beyond this, it is a crisis of womanhood . . .

The exemplar of what is broadly described as the emancipated woman has varied from epoch to epoch, generation to generation. But the singular circumstance about these variations is that they have all been defined by males. We have played a pitifully small role so far in defining ourselves. Some of us, bolder than others, have struck out for ourselves in uncharted directions.

There have been a few great moments in the American woman's quest for equality, but progress generally has been slow and uneven. We have witnessed—and indeed are witnessing—an evolution of the spirit which, like the evolution of physical beings, is a slow and measured process. In fact, all movement is not necessarily in a forward direction—as I have previously pointed out. But against a long background of inactivity, the changes that have resulted in recent years have been dramatic . . .

These are beginnings—yes—but they are important beginnings because they indicate that American women finally have discovered the power of education and politics and how to use this power successfully. A committee of the United States Congress is currently trying to determine how best to improve the Government's role in advancing women's rights. Most of our laws—especially our federal laws—already demand equality. Compliance has brought with it opportunity and, in addition, the gradual shifting of attitudes that follows changes in law. One would expect this progress to be a rallying point, to bring women together—united. Yet, we cannot seem to agree among ourselves even on the basic fact that we do want true equality. We still are engaged in a heated debate over an equal rights amendment to the constitution of the United States. The amendment is very simple—only 26 words long. It says that equal rights should not be denied on account of sex. To date, the amendment has been ratified by 34 of the required 38 states. In many States, there has been bitter debate and, interestingly enough, some of the loudest protests have come from women. There appear to be two reasons for this state of affairs. The first is a great deal of misunderstanding about the true effects of the amendment. The second is an unwillingness by some women to trade the familiarity of the status quo for the uncertainties and responsibilities that greater freedom brings. Perhaps this feeling is uniquely a part of a nation where we are generally comfortable, a nation where we too often take our freedom for granted . . .

As much as anything, the key to real progress by large numbers of women lies in building our own self-esteem, our own belief that we are capable of success. A lack of self-esteem is our greatest handicap—greater than law or custom or attitude, although it is surely a result of all of these. The sad fact is that too many women do not accept themselves and their inherent human value. They do not know who they are and oftentimes, are afraid to find out. The progress women have made has helped to change this. True equality would help even more. Yet, I question whether true equality is possible for any of us until far more of us are ready to begin the search for our inner selves. If women do not truly believe in their own potential, that potential can never be realized. The next step in our search for equality is clear. We must spark a new reawakening that stretches beyond the recognition of inequities. We must focus instead upon our true human value as women and as full participants in life. And, as we reach out to one another, we must also take stock of ourselves. For true equality is something that cannot be given. It cannot even be earned by one woman for another. Only the opportunity can be given—each woman must be ready within herself to meet and grasp it. The world can ill afford the waste and loss of the brain power and superb energies which women have to offer. Indeed, the male of the species will benefit and prosper when full integration of the sexes will have been realized for they too, will be released from the imprisonment of stereotype . . .

Much of what I have been saying up to this point indicates the state of affairs which has led to revolutionary activities at the present time on the part of women in an attempt to achieve their liberation. I will not pretend that I endorse each and every activity of this nature in the identical terms in which it occurs. But I do endorse the intent and the goal. In my own case, my father made all the difference.[1] Would that all women had such a father who sought to encourage my full potentialities. That, however, might have been too arduous a task for him, energetic as he was. We need the present revolution. It would be still more desirable if it were carried out on a basis more instinct with the need for conciliation than confrontation. The latter expedient has been forced upon us by male intransigence . . .

We must free ourselves. The crucial task is one of inward liberation. The cruelest tyranny from which we must emancipate ourselves is the thralldom of a depreciated self-image. We are the mothers of the human race, its nurses, its guardians, and, it is no mere empty boast, its procreators. But this should not imbue us with arrogance. We may even hope as enlightenment slowly and

---

1. Barbara Mae Watson was the daughter of a distinguished lawyer and judge in Harlem, New York. His name was James Samuel Watson, a 1913 law graduate of New York Law School.

painfully dawns upon them, that it may endow our male counterparts with an unaccustomed sense of humility. Already there are changes in the wind some progress is being made slowly and painfully. We must continue unflagging efforts to achieve the ultimate goal. For if we let up, the game is lost and human survival will surely be at stake. . . .

When American Democracy
Becomes a Sham

JANE EDNA HARRIS HUNTER

(1940)

IN AMERICA, WE HAVE TWO different philosophies of social justice with but one standard of living. The white man's philosophy holds that the Negro needs only a third of the income required by the average white man. This takes no account of the fact that the black laborer has the same living necessities as does the white laborer. A white chauffeur will receive one hundred and twenty-five dollars, while the black chauffeur receives sixty-five dollars a month. Throughout industrial and other pursuits this disparity prevails. Despite this inequality of income, the Negro must pay the same for clothing, food, and often more for shelter and insurance. Such a condition indicates a blindness to the human rights of colored citizens.

Labor unions have measurably succeeded in establishing wage levels in the major industries; but these benefits have been available only in a limited sens. to the colored man. He has had to overcome barrier after barrier; some erected for selfish motives, and others born of the desire to prohibit him from entering a particular industry under any circumstances. White labor, in its mad rush to protect itself, seems to have forgotten that its black fellow laborer, if left out of consideration, proves a menace to any permanent adjustment of its struggles with capital.

In this situation is to be found a challenge to our leadership. Leaders must help the Negro laborer to hold such opportunities as he now has, and to discover new fields of service. The way to attract interest is to do something worth while, to create through joint efforts a demand for our commodities. The National Housewives' League is a notable example born of a grave necessity to save the Negro's pride, and to prevent many from dire want in the midst of the deepest depression.

JANE E. HUNTER, NICKEL AND A PRAYER 184 (Cleveland, Ellie Kani Publishing Co. 1940) (chapter 16).

The genius of Fannie B. Peck disclosed that the Negro housewife spends 80 percent of her earnings on the family, and that a large percentage of these earnings are spent with merchants who do not and will not employ Negroes. It did not seem wise to Mrs. Peck to spend her time in trying to abolish this unfair and unjust American policy, but she set herself to the task to make a way to help the Negro find employment.

Negro women were called together. They organized a National Housewives' League, with headquarters in Detroit, Michigan. Women there were convinced of the need for such an organization. It seemed an excellent plan to pool the interests and buying power of the race. The idea spread into the Eastern and Midwestern States where other groups were organized. The slogan, "Do not buy where you cannot work," was adopted.

The Rev. Peck organized the men into trade associations. Many of the organizations adopted the name "Booker T. Washington Trade Association," while others are known as the "Progressive Negro Business League."

From these efforts have come to the race additional shoe and grocery stores, laundries, furriers, and several credit loan associations. The refusal of store managers to employ Negroes as clerks, and the wholesale discharge of porters and maids, of necessity awakened the best in the leadership of the Reverend and Mrs. Peck. They realize that the ideal has not only provided jobs and re-awakened in the Negro a sense of self-respect; but the best thing that has come out of the movement has been the training of young men and women for usual citizenship . . .

The ideal of Negro leaders in this changing social order must be an unswerving desire to inculcate in their race self-esteem, created of the inner conviction which intelligence dictates.

The Negro in Northern States has remained indifferent too long to the call for intergroup action. He has contended for mixing of the racial groups. He has failed to visualize the opportunities within his race and reach. The Biblical injunction that "where there is no vision the people perish" applies to many of our leaders. As a race we can no longer depend upon the other race for our economic freedom. We may as well acknowledge that the white man is too busy with his own endeavors to be interested in the Negro. In most cases his interest does not extend much beyond that of a charitable impulse. Few are concerned with the economic improvement of the Negro. Thus the charity which he gives, at the same time in which he withholds economic opportunity, reduces the Negro's status almost to that of servitude.

Too often, alas, has the Negro been misled by leaders of his own race. There are those false prophets who would persuade us that some day the Negro will be absorbed by the white race. What the Negro really desires is a change of industrial and economic status so that he may enjoy the privileges and culture that other men possess. By thorough and complete miscegenation we should lose our richest heritage. The Negro must continue to make his distinct contribution to the world—as a Negro . . .

The foundation stone on which to build strong American citizens—whether the race be black or white—in my judgment, must be a thoroughgoing education, adapted to the peculiar needs of the individual. The masses of the Negro youth are today being trained without directed purpose. I observe them as they struggle through the elementary schools, junior and senior high schools, and finally, through the colleges of our country. Most of them return to their communities unfitted for the work the modern world needs to have done. I have considered over and over again plans for the proper education of the Negro youth in our American democracy. He has been more or less confused in two schools of thought. One idea is that a classical education is the means by which the full salvation of the race will be attained. The other emphasizes the need for vocational training, contending that practical education will enable the Negro to meet the challenge of our highly competitive society.

Across these two ideas of the proper training of Negro youth runs the peculiar American policy of racial segregation. I have found that in many northern communities in which exist the mixed school and non-mixed faculty little concern is shown for the future of the Negro child. The personal interest so vital to inspirational growth seems wholly lacking. Also in certain northern communities schools, presumably mixed but whose enrollment is predominately Negro, show a woeful lessening of the teacher's interest and discipline. Under these circumstances the Negro child completes his public school work without receiving the well-rounded education to which he is entitled. It is this situation that persuades me that Boards of Education in Northern States, in their attempt to segregate nationality and racial groups and to wage economy programs upon such groups, themselves would do well to restudy the purpose and meaning of public school education. Where segregation arises out of a natural and normal migration to a community, and when in such community there exists a need for a specialized school because of overaged and handicapped pupils, there should be provided by the Boards of Education the best experts in practical teacher training for that group. In the grouping of pupils on bases of nationality and race, there exists an opportunity for the development of group and race consciousness. This may prove an advantage, provided it is properly directed.

However, attempts to segregate nationalities and racial groups are generally used to afford opportunity to train cadet teachers and new principals, many of whom have little knowledge of the social and economic background of the students whom they attempt to serve. In the old American way of Negro segregation students are not only handicapped by denial of proper educational facilities but are victims of social and industrial prejudices. In recent years Negro teachers are gradually being inducted into public school systems in Northern States, due to migration of Negroes from Southern States. As the number of pupils increases Negro teachers are regimented into a district where buildings are aged and worn, equipment is meager, and liberal education is withheld. Despite the curtailed financial support in schools where pupils are predominately Negroid and where teachers are properly trained, regardless of race, students develop in a curriculum adapted to their ability and capacity. In my opinion, nationality plays an important part in group education when all things are equal. For instance, the Negro teacher reaches beyond the stereotyped, prescribed system and endeavors to inject into a Negro student that fuller meaning of education which lifts him above mere academic procedure to a richer realization of the needs of his soul. He inspires the child through the intimate and sympathetic relationship growing out of the suffering in which, as fellow Negroes, the teacher and pupil share.

In America the law of the land definitely prohibits discrimination because of race, creed, or religion; therefore, segregation that is based on race or religion should not exist. The Supreme Law of the Universe teaches that all men are created equal; and from this Law America wrote and established a Constitution giving birth to a democracy which has no color barrier when lived and practiced . . .

I am, therefore, fully convinced that we cannot make real advancement in our pursuit of education in cities where Negroes are segregated and their children are deprived of Negro leadership until Boards of Education provide equal educational facilities under the law. American democracy definitely promises equality of opportunity in public education. When she openly denies the Negro child this fundamental right, American democracy becomes a sham. . . .

The Underdeveloped Resource

Patricia Roberts Harris

(1966)

*N*EGROES . . . MUST NEVER MINIMIZE the fact that freedom of speech, petition and the press as guaranteed by the Federal Constitution, not guns and bombs, have been the weapons with which the Negro minority, with its friends in the majority, have assailed the walls of segregation. We must recall that it is the American commitment to the right of all to participate in community life through the use of the vote, not adherence to a class doctrine, which calls forth support of the cause of the disenfranchised Negro. We must remind us all, white and black, that it is a deep belief in the essential equality of all men which whips our consciences when we see men denied through no fault of their own, the right to sell their skills in the market place, and thereby to find security for themselves and their children.

For me, what is significant about American racial change is not the resistance to that change, a resistance which, in spite of my optimism, is still too great. What is significant is the fact that white Americans have no respect for their own arguments in support of the maintenance of racial discrimination, and are almost pitifully grateful for every evidence, no matter how small or how grudgingly achieved, of progress toward equality.

. . . Americans of Negro descent, and those devoted to the Negro cause . . . [know about this] because we have been forced, for many years, to be aliens in this land—aliens who were required to stand apart and look at that land with the critical eye of the rejected. What we saw, in addition to the weaknesses out of which came our problems, was the towering moral strength of a belief in

---

This address was made at Howard University on March 2, 1966, on occasion of its ninety-ninth anniversary. At the time of the address, Patricia Roberts Harris was the U.S. Ambassador to Luxembourg.

equality, even when these beliefs struggled with the wish for privilege, irrational prejudice, or a simple desire for the retention of the status quo.

Because we saw so well the real character of American society, we have the incredible phenomenon that most mature Negroes are politically and economically conservative, with all that term conveys. We wish to conserve the good in American society; we have no wish for radical solutions, as the failure of every far right and far left institution to recruit significant numbers of Negroes, attests.

Even today's flirtation by some Negro youths with radical theories represents far less than the fear mongering would have us believe. Considering the intransigence met by some civil rights workers in pockets of segregation, I find most of the so-called radical solutions a natural response to a hostile environment. Where guns are pointed at one's head, it is neither surprising nor a matter for condemnation, that a few of the people facing these guns think that change of the gun-wielding society is required. What is truly remarkable is that few of us who have faced these problems over the decades have lost belief in the system which gave rise to both the racial problem and its solution.

This continuing belief in the validity of the American democratic system, by those who are not yet fully in it, is a resource of incredible dimensions for the United States. It is a resource, which, for a variety of reasons, has not yet been adequately developed or utilized by this country. The resource consists of the fact that when we as Negroes speak of the vitality of American democracy, and describe its realities in terms of both general and specific change, we are believed . . .

We, the American descendants of a non-white race, can speak more persuasively of this reality to the non-white majorities of this world than can our white brethren, who, because of their past sins, are sometimes viewed with suspicion. While our psyches are American, our skins, those of most of us, are tinted, and when we can say that the "Man", the white man, has reformed, and when we say it from positions of substantial responsibility as American citizens, there is likely to be acceptance of the reality of change.

I cannot emphasize too strongly the importance of Negroes speaking as Americans on this subject. As Barbara Ward has said, the most truly prosperous part of the world, is this North Atlantic area in which we live, and which is inhabited primarily by whites. If the have-not despair of the poor of the rest of the world is not to emerge as a racial hatred because the haves are white, and the have-nots are non-white, it will be because we have been able to prove that race is truly irrelevant in the sharing of substantial power and prosperity. The emergence of the American Negro as an equal of his white peers and as a sharer of power [is the best evidence] in demonstrating the ultimate irrelevance of race.

My assumption is, of course, that once equality is achieved, we Negro Americans will find that we are culturally, politically and emotionally American, not Negro in any sense other than the genetic. That which we now see as

Negro culture is, in my judgment, but a strain of the American culture. There-fore, despite the recurring voices seeking a special identity and outlook for the American Negro, or those asking for orientation toward Africa or Asia, I believe that there is no difference between the long range interest of American Negroes and American whites.

Our fortunes as Negroes cannot be separated from the fortunes of the United States. Therefore, self-interest requires that we, as Americans, use all our resources to interpret the position of this nation.

If our experiences make more convincing this country's assertion of its de-votion to equality and the achievement of the good life for all, as citizens we will want to interpret this experience to the world. The choices that other men in other nations make about their future will depend upon their judgment about which of several competing systems and doctrines make more likely their achievement of the good life. That the American system can produce for its Ne-gro citizens the same level of prosperity provided for its white citizens, with, ad-ditionally, meaningful personal freedom, will not go unremarked . . .

But there are significant barriers to utilization of the Negro experience. First, there is a reluctance on the part of the beneficiaries of the old exclusive system to open the system to any newcomers. And this reluctance is intensified when the newcomer to the power arena is a Negro.

The second barrier to the effective utilization of the Negro is the failure of the American system to correct as quickly as it can the injustices which remain. It is difficult to persuade many young Americans to express their faith in the American system or to give service outside the civil rights movement until in-justice is eliminated in this country.

The third barrier is that the rest of the world wants, not propaganda, but proof. And part of that proof must be the fact that the Negro exemplars of the success of the system have skills which are useful, not only to the United States, but to the rest of the world . . .

Howard University was founded for and has served as a means of elimi-nating the disadvantage from which one-tenth of this nation has suffered. Now that the disadvantage approaches its elimination, we should use the experience of our past to serve the disadvantaged of other lands by bringing to them the understanding of the reality of American concern for their welfare.

With an increased awareness of the unique strength which this nation will possess when it completes the task of elimination of racial discrimination, and of the particular force with which we as Negroes can describe this strength, we must move quickly and wisely to make sure that we make the very best use of our racial experience in the interest of ultimate peace. . . .

Justice

Justice and Values in Government

Barbara Mae Watson

(1976)

WHAT, EXACTLY, DO WE MEAN when we speak of justice? It is easy enough to attach to this concept the traditional usages inherent in our customs, our contemplation and the canons of our jurisprudence. Any one of these preoccupations will raise at least as many difficulties as the semantic source from which they take their origin. No one as yet has formulated a universally satisfactory elucidation of the meaning of justice . . .

The crude pragmatism of the current situation is that your justice is my injustice; and the converse holds, of course, equally true. There are well known cynical translations into empirical terms among which the remark ascribed to Thucydides that "justice is the right of the stronger" is well known and, one regrets to observe, perhaps too widely accepted. But there are less disenchanted views of this fundamental concept of human relations between individuals, states or other collectivities. One such expression of a less disillusioned idealism is exemplified by the continuing efforts of jurists to import a loftier empirical meaning into the concept of justice. There is a parallel attempt, at the same time, to take into account the governing philosophy of the particular society. This is an abnormally difficult process because of the turbulent developments by which the current era is beset.

The whole question of justice is intimately intertwined with the predominant value system of a society. Indeed, justice is itself a mirror image of that system of values. When, therefore, we speak of justice, we are really asking to what complex of values do we subscribe? In its political aspect insofar as this country is concerned, we are accustomed to describe the system as a democracy—a

Paper presented at Carleton College, Northfield, Minnesota, October 29, 1976, a Symposium on Justice, Values and Education in Our Third Century.

term which itself would detain us much beyond the compass of this paper if we were going to embark upon its analysis.

In such a context, it would be essential for us to consider the distribution of wealth in the society and the right of suffrage, whether truly universal or so hedged about in its exercises as to constitute a substantial limitation of the right to vote. It would also be necessary to reflect upon the social function of property in its conferment of status and privilege. Of cardinal importance would be the question of freedom of thought and expression. A citizen must be completely free to pursue intellectual enquiry unconstrained by the governing group in possession of the state power.

Our forefathers sought to discover in the canons of Anglo-Saxon jurisprudence a means of constructing ideal norms of social equity. Consistently with this effort their philosophical professions were articulated in the organic law— the Constitution of the United States. This document asserts conventions that are the legal expression of the nation of justice. In its own terms this document is an instrument very like juristic perfection. Yet a perfection which must be regarded as existing within the confines of the age in which it was formulated. The point that I wish to stress is the importance of the evolutionary aspect of all ethical systems of which jurisprudence itself is merely a component. The further point I should like to stress at this stage is the presiding relationship of the value system to this social element of justice. But we still have not defined justice and I shall now therefore hazard the supposition that justice, if it is anything at all, must necessarily be reduced in its simplest terms to an equitable nexus between persons and between persons and between collectivities. This bond of mutual relationship must accord with the imperatives of civilized conscience.

We are confronting at this point of our discussion the still unresolved question of the precise nature of the value system. Without this, the whole concept of justice must necessarily remain meaningless and amorphous. For there can be no shape to justice, no social meaning of justice unless these two elements of that nexus are directly derived from our value system. What I am proposing then, is a definition of justice—not in academic terms—but as a living expression, a working model of that complex of ideas, customs and relationships which bind the society together as a philosophic entity. In the case of the United States—a democracy.

I am therefore postulating an inherently political meaning of justice. Yet I do not stop there. It would be a hollow pretense at exhausting all the implications of this concept if we did not consider with the most careful regard the pervasive demands of economics. Justice is a mere abstraction without social significance in the absence of a due consideration of the role that politics and economics play in its practical implementation. For what we are in fact contemplating when we speak of justice are the political professions of the state translated into social and economic relations among its citizens. How this is carried out, how it is effected is, in short, the empirical meaning of justice. To embrace this meaning in a verbal formula seems to me to be much less important than to apprehend that this is its essential nature. We shall revert to this theme presently, but for the moment, I should like to address myself to the companion and indeed predominant theme of values. Then . . . .I shall launch into a brief examination of government in order to construct finally an integrated view of our theme.

What are the values to which we subscribe in our society? This question involves certain schematic considerations. There are the values of the home and the family, of the larger community and the general society, of the state, church and marketplace. Each of these elements of the general system should, I urge, be considered in an evolutionary perspective. Clearly, the values to which our foreparents subscribed do not command the same allegiance today that they did in those bygone years. Quite visibly within our collective experience, there has been an ideological revolution of far-reaching import. Parental authority has been diminished almost to vanishing point—where it has not in many instances been entirely abrogated. That bond of mutual affection and respect, of caring and protecting, which once constituted the living core of the familial system is now largely, one fears, a relic of the past. It is the essence of the idea of social values that we ask ourselves whether this is a development, good or evil. I make this point in particular, because I would wish to remind you that when we speak of values we inevitably imply an indwelling ethical constituent. There are no values, the concept is meaningless, without a religious regard for its ethical inspiration. I mean religious in its broadest connotation. We customarily use the term to denote a compass of theological references. I desire, however, to effect a broader consideration and to include that range of social relationships to which theology is not always a part. Not that I would exclude the Church from our contemplation in this regard. I would unhesitatingly give the Church its due place. Yet I must not fail to invite your attention to what I earlier described as the marketplace, where, as perhaps we are all aware, the Church is often at polar opposites with the conventions prevailing in that arena. In short, God and Caesar do not often find it possible to reconcile their differences when they encounter each other in the marketplace. This conflict crucially influences the application in practice of those values we profess. The organic law, namely the Constitution of the United States, is constantly called upon to mediate this central conflict within our society. So that, in effect, there has emerged from this unresolved struggle, a dual system of ethics.

The distinguished sociologist, Max Weber, once posed the question which he answered in the affirmative—if there was not some correlation between protestantism and capitalism. The philosophical implications of this query extend, however, well beyond Weber's formulation. They encompass the whole value system of a given society. Nor is there any necessary reference to a particular religious conviction and practice or a given economic belief and its operation.

What we are contemplating at the moment is the dual system of ethics to which I earlier referred. Our public life, especially in certain of its recent manifestations bears witness to this dualism. We are therefore obliged to consider the effects of this ethical disjunction upon our national life. We are similarly obliged to consider whether our very system of jurisprudence itself has not been unduly determined in the application of its governing norms by this dualism. Neither must we omit to consider the extent to which this divergence between abstract profession and practical expression may have entered into our relations and to what purpose and how it has done so. I would emphasize again that our endeavor here must be to see justice and the values we enunciate as the reverse and obverse sides of the same coin. Bearing that in mind, we will now contemplate the role of the government as the third party to this uneasy relationship.

It is an uneasy relationship because the interests of the government, of any government for that matter, are not always themselves reflection of that philosophy which constitutes those ideals from which it derives its moral authority. It is unnecessary to remind you of certain lamentable incidents of the recent past. So when we speak of justice and values in government we are first of all assuming a national actuality for each of these terms. We thereby incur the risk of contradiction at some stage or stages for the very reasons that I pointed out at the beginning of my address. First, the difficulty of achieving conceptual precision in respect to any one of them, and the almost inevitable absence of semantic clarity. One is often tempted to say that justice in its practical application tends to be a figment of social idealism and that the values we so loosely delineate are themselves a case of ideals without a living content of idealism. They therefore remain mere verbal professions in a philosophical vacuum.

Since I have imported the third element, namely, government, into this stage of our discussion, it is necessary to demonstrate the part it plays in determining the nature of the social process of justice and of the operative factors of the value system. For government in a society which asserts itself as a government of laws is a government which by that fact assumes a critical responsibility. It takes upon itself the duty to invest the notion of justice with an inviolable sanctity and its generic system of values with unassailable sovereignty.

We might well remind ourselves at this point of the observation of Alexander Pope in his celebrated "Essay on Man": "For forms of government let fools contest; What ever is best administered is best."

That is an eminently practical view of the role of government which, according to Edmund Burke is "a contrivance of human wisdom to provide for human wants." You may indeed be of the opinion, however, that "that government is best which governs least." There are those who would construe this as a prescription for anarchy. But I am sure that their representatives are not at this moment in our midst. Perhaps the true balance is to be found in the "Common Sense" of Thomas Paine. "Government," he remarked, "even in its best state, is but a necessary evil; in its worst state, an intolerable one."

No individual should be restricted in their liberty to inquire, in their freedom of expression, in their right to be completely free within the law. But I do mean precisely that: *within the law*. Our system of values is never to be regarded as sacrosanct. Yet equally, it ought never to be viewed as a target for lawlessness. An abiding pervasive regard for law is a duty of citizenship. It is the prime function of government, to impose and to insure its observance. The government compromises its sovereign role whenever it defers to ethical dualisms. It brings into question its own respect for the underlying philosophy of the governing ideals from which it draws its moral mandate. Government should not excessively interfere—but government must firmly preside. It is obliged to do so in light of its own regard for the rule of law. Failing this, it compromises its title to legitimacy; worse yet, to the respect and obedience of its citizens. Have we, ladies and gentlemen, now reached such a stage in the course of these latter years of our Republic's luminous history?

This thematic triad—justice, values and government is clearly inextricably intertwined. They are, in a manner of speaking, the terms of a dialectic. Some perhaps less enchanged [*sic*] that I may believe that from time to time they even discern some persisting antitheses. I should hardly be in a position to deplore, let alone reject, this attitude if important regard were given to a number of current developments. Such events have made it plain that there may indeed be a sad necessity for the sense of repugnance experienced by a preponderant segment of the public in this connection. Too often has government failed in its responsibility to be the sovereign shrine of protection for those values which are the undying heritage bequeathed to us by our forefathers and from which justice derives its title to veneration in our society.

The interviewing of these strands of ideology and practice is the total society both in contemplation and action. Each is dependent upon the other for whatever virtue it may lay claim to. This interdependence breeds a contrariety, a variousness that is one of the most important factors in the life of our society. It is also a source of much of its surface turbulence. The youth rebellion of the 1960s exemplified an aspect of a rebellion against the traditional system of values. The political challenge on the part of disaffected minority groups to the legal system was also an instance of social revolt. The increasing tendency to call into question the right of government to exclude its citizens from the formulation of policy on all levels is again an example of this subversion of customary values. We must never forget that worlds are created out of chaos. Naturally, this cannot mean and never must mean that we view chaos as an indispensable precondition to the construction of a good society. The evils attendant upon chaos—legal arbitrariness, political tyranny, social dissolution and decay—are too well authenticated in the histories of societies who have yielded to this fatal circumstance. Yet when its prefigurings make their appearance, as from time to time they do on our national horizons, it would be the better part of wisdom and foresight if we were to regard such apparitions not only as harbingers of chaos but as heralds of opportunity for national reconstruction. At worst, they allow the possibility to reformulate our governing ideals. They create an opportunity to redesign the structure of our national life. They enable us to grasp with deeper appreciation the excellencies of the historic chance that led to the foundation of this society so rich in promise and by no means unfulfilled in many aspects of superlative achievement.

Regarded from this point of view, justice will achieve its true philosophic validity and also its highest practical utility as the instrument by which right is apportioned, wrong distributed and redress attained under the sovereign eye of government. In its turn, government vindicates itself by its own reverence for the historic inspiration articulated with such magnificent wisdom and foresight in the organic law—the Constitution of the United States.

Erosion of Civil Liberties

Barbara Charline Jordan

(1974)

*I*AM GOING TO TALK ABOUT civil liberties. Civil liberties—and if you write this subject, write civil liberties, colon, and then after that, write inoperative, and put a question mark; write inaudible, question mark; illegible, question mark; expletive deleted, question mark.

On the 30th day of April, the members of the Committee on the Judiciary received a document. That document purported to be the recorded conversations of the President of the United States. There are some omissions. One thousand six hundred seventy portions of conversations were marked either inaudible or illegible. One wonders what remains—what in the world remains—in terms of acts or in terms of deeds undiscovered because of some reason they could not be heard or could not be understood. Is it possible—I raise the rhetorical question—that individual liberties, that civil liberties, that individual freedoms, are somehow masked behind these little words: *inoperative, inaudible, unintelligible, expletive deleted;* if you answer those questions in the affirmative I would say that there is some justification for doing that in light of past and present events. Your Government has violated civil liberties. It admitted— the Government of the United States of America admitted—that it wiretapped its own employees 17 times. Newsmen, fearful that the First Amendment protections of freedom of the press are more rhetoric than fact, have come to the Congress and sought the passage of a Newsman's Shield Law. The politicization of the FBI has now become a matter of Congressional oversight. The President's right to suspend or alleged right to suspend the Fourth Amendment against unreasonable searches and seizures in the national security interests is somehow defended. The concept of Executive Privilege has been used rather "cavalierly" to disguise gross intrusions into the private life of the individual. You, the gradu-

---

Commencement Address, Howard University, May 11, 1974.

ate, will emerge from academia with the expectation, and with the hope, that you will be free to pursue your life as you define it, and you are going to hope that no one will interfere with your definition of your life. You have a basis for that presumption because there is something in the history of the United States which says that freedom, that liberty, is a part of what we are about. That history started in 1776, and now almost 200 years later those freedoms which were so painfully gained are threatened by erosion. That threat has become so serious that one can ask the question as to whether civil liberties is any longer an operative ideal in the United States of America.

Thomas Jefferson, a great President, in his first inaugural address, talked about civil liberties, talked about freedom, talked about justice and equality when he said equal and exact justice to all men of whatever persuasion; religious, political, peace, commerce, honest friendship with all Nations; entangling alliances with none; freedom of religion, freedom of the press; freedom of person; these are the principles, said Mr. Jefferson, which should guide the Republic; and then Jefferson went on to ask the question "Would the honest patriot, in the full tide of successful experiment, abandon a Government which has so far kept us firm and kept us free?" It is the "stuff" of America that its citizens want to be free of government intrusions into their private lives and into their personal affairs. This concept of freedom in America is etched into the Constitution of the United States; into the Bill of Rights. There are no gaps; there are no inexplicable "hums" in the Constitution of the United States. The language of that document flows well. The men who sought to get it passed, who sought to get it ratified, fought for it because they felt that they were constructing a Nation, the touchstone of which would be liberty and freedom and justice—they thought that—they felt that they were building—creating a new Nation with a system of government with checks and balances and separation of powers which would forever protect the citizens of the United States from gross abuses of power by public officials and by gross excesses of power by the government of the United States. The signers of that Constitution felt that we now had a government which would secure the blessings of liberty to ourselves and our posterity. We know that that liberty is shaky because modern technology now has invested the Government with the tools to invade private affairs through certain kinds of electronic mechanisms. Thomas Jefferson, again, warned us that the natural progress of things is for liberty to yield and government to gain ground—*liberty to yield and government to gain ground; the natural progress of things,* said Jefferson.

In recent years we have witnessed a willingness to accelerate the erosion of these guiding principles in American life. This erosion is very insidious because it didn't happen all at once but it happened one step at a time. It happened under the guise of the maintenance of national security; it happened, this erosion, under the guise of the legalisms of Executive Privilege. We know that an American President, we know that his top assistants believed that the First and Fourth Amendments of the Constitution of the United States could be suspended. The Amendments which say—that a person has a right not to be searched or to be seized unreasonably. We know that there have been attempts by the Government against political opponents to somehow prevent their exercise of free speech because somehow what they had to say did not meet government approval.

The Constitution and the Bill of Rights; a balance between the interests of the Government and interests of the governed. The history of individual liberty, particularly that of the right of privacy has been a history of resistance by the people of this country to governmental encroachments upon that which we hold private.

For example, in 1603 under English Common Law, this principle was stated which became incorporated in the Fourth Amendment of the Constitution. The principle was stated this way:

> In all cases where the King is party, the Sheriff, if the doors be not open, may break in the party's house, either to arrest him or to do other execution of the King's process, if otherwise he cannot get in, but before he breaks in [said the Law in 1603] he ought to signify the cause of his coming and make request to open the door.

In 1766 the sanctity of the individual's right to privacy in his home was again stated with great clarity by William Pitt. The Parliament of Great Britain was trying to impose a tax on cider, and people were resistant to paying the tax, and so the Parliament talked about passing a law that would allow the government to enter into a man's home, a man's cottage, and get the tax. This is what William Pitt said about that:

> The poorest man, the poorest man may, *in* his cottage, bid defiance to all the forces of the Crown. It, the cottage, may be frail, the roof may shake, the wind may blow through it, the storm may enter, the rain may enter, but the King of England cannot enter.

All of these forces—all of his forces dare not cross the threshold of that ruined tenement. Two hundred and eight years after that stirring declaration by William Pitt, what are we faced with? We are faced with state, federal and local authorities breaking into a man's home in a mistaken frenzy because they have uncorroborated tips that he is a suspect the Government needs; witness; the Collinsville, Illinois cases.

Last summer, John Erlichmann testified before the Senate Watergate Committee; Senator Talmadge, being familiar with the English Common Law principle as enunciated and affirmed by William Pitt, asked Mr. Erlichmann about that principle derived from English Law—that the King of England may not enter a man's home without his consent. How did Mr. Erlichmann reply? He said, "I am afraid that has been considerably eroded over the years." Eroded? Or inoperative, or inaudible, or illegible—any word you apply to it—which one is it? In addition to the continuing reality of smashed doors and actual physical invasion of private homes, we know that the Government has more sophisticated and more invidious tools—electronic tools. We also know that at least 50 federal agencies have substantial investigative and enforcement functions providing a core of some 20,000 investigators, working for such agencies as the FBI, National Intelligence, Post Office, Narcotics Bureau of the Justice Department, Securities and Exchange Commission, Internal Revenue Service, Food and Drug Administration, State Department, Civil Service Commission, and even the Department of Agriculture. They've all got their little policemen.

The events of the past several years have shown us, and reveal to us a very shocking pattern of disregard for Constitutional principles and for due process of law. It is apparent that the powerful tools of government spying and espionage against private citizens in pursuit of their lawful activities have become or have not kept within the legitimate bounds of self-restraint and self-discipline.

Justice Louis Brandeis enunciated the principle more clearly than many when he said this: "In a government of laws, existence of the government will be imperiled if the government fails to comply with the law."

Our Government is the potent, omnipresent teacher for good or for ill. It teaches the whole people by example. If the Government becomes a law-breaker, it breeds contempt for law and invites man to become a law in and of himself. If one thing is clear about the erosion of civil liberties, it is that there is no clear line between freedom and repression. Freedom is the fluid, intangible condition of our society. It thrives in some periods and it is beset in other periods. The events of the past few years and even the past few days have convinced us that it is possible for this country to stand on the edge of repression and tyranny and never know it. If the faith in the future is to be restored, if that which is good about the history of this country is to be regained, you must restore it; you must regain it. It would appear that this country is adrift right now; that the Ship of State is bobbing and weaving, and the words of Seneca come to mind: "If a man does not know to what port he sails, no wind is favorable." You ought to know where you are going; you ought to know to what port you sail, and perhaps the winds will favor your direction. *You* must *know* that. It is the confidence of your knowledge; it is the sureness of your knowledge which may perchance nudge this country in the right direction . . .

Remember how we began; Civil Liberties, colon; Inoperative, question mark? Inaudible? Illegible? Expletive deleted? Answer those questions in the negative. Affirm to everybody who will hear you that civil liberties *are* operative; that civil liberties *is* legible; that *no* expletive is intended and no expletive is necessary when you are discussing the freedoms and justice and liberty and foundation of this country. There are no brave new political worlds for you to discover out there. There are no new and innovative and creative structures for you to discover out there, but reaffirm what ought to be. Get back to the truth; that's old, but get back to it. Get back to what's honest; tell Government to do that. Affirm the civil liberties of the people of this country. Do that. And I suspect that you will have performed something in your day and generation which is worthy to be remembered.

Political Correctness: Professor Linda S. Greene vs. Robert Bork

Linda Sheryl Greene

(1993)

*B*ORK: POLITICAL CORRECTNESS, I think, is something that is widespread in this society, and it's part of a mood of radical egalitarianism which has taken hold. Of course, equality does not occur for all people without coercion. And I'm afraid that's what we're seeing. We're seeing it in affirmative action and quotas in the universities. And we're seeing it in the speech codes, which are judging speech not by what it objectively means, but by how somebody perceives it, over which the speaker has no control.

And I think this kind of leveling in speech and of rejection of the achievement principle for quotas isn't going to work. This kind of thing, I think, leads to hostility, a loss of civility and a rejection of the achievement principle upon which this society is really based.

Greene: P.C. is a menace, but perhaps for different reasons than the other side would say. It's a menace because it obscures the real problems and issues that we face as a society. It's a clever rhetorical phrase which turns a debate about racism and sexism into a debate about censorship.

If you can force us to discuss censorship instead of discussing racial epithets, censorship instead of discussing sexual harassment, censorship instead of discussing the question how we are going to transform our institutions into more diverse places, then you have set the terms of the debate and prevented a discussion of the real issues. And it seems to be a great cause of glee on the right, among conservatives, that they have been able to change this debate.

Let's stop attacking young people who come to college, whose parents send them to college with a reasonable expectation that they won't be the victims of racist, derogatory speech. Let's stop attacking the victims and start attacking the

---

The Next-to-Last Word on Political Correctness, New York Times, December 11, 1993, at 23.

problem of racism. P.C. labels prevent that. The P.C. charge prevents that, and that's why P.C. is a menace. Let's eliminate the phrase and get on with the unfinished business of transforming our society and transforming our educational institutions.

Bork: Professor Greene, do you think there is more racism in this society today than there was 30 or 40 years ago?

Greene: I think that racism has changed its character. I think that racism still exists but its character is different. I think we have two types of racism going on, or at least two. In one type we see the explicit racist remark or the explicit racial decision, sometimes because of an inadvertent slip. Other times we have a veiled racism, not necessarily the product of a person's specific intent, but an unconscious comfort which we have with the status quo.

What we need to do is not to focus on calling each other racist or sexist, but instead to try to understand how historical racism has affected our lives and consciousness and not make charges but try to understand how we all—white, black, men and women—have been affected by our past.

Bork: Professor Greene, I think none of us on this side of the table disagrees that people could be punished for making open racial or ethnic insults in a university. That is not the question in which this arises. This arises when students steal a student newspaper because they regard it as racist, although it's just conservative, or when a professor is put through sensitivity training for a remark that was not really offensive in the classroom, that's political correctness, and that's what we object to and it's happening. It's not just a question of forbidding talk about racism.

Greene: Well, is it political correctness because the university expresses a concern? It seems to me that if we eliminate the label of political correctness from our debate, we can talk more explicitly about what speech we want to empower people to engage in.

Let's stop talking about political correctness and instead talk frankly about what we want people to be able to say at the university. Are we saying that we want students to be able to say anything they wish to another person? Are we saying that we want faculty to be free to make remarks, however offensive or threatening to their students? Are we saying that we want professors to be able to make sexual remarks to their students?

I think that when you mention acts like the stealing of newspapers [at the University of Pennsylvania] or other acts of this nature, we all understand that these acts occur in a context. I don't think we want to continue to focus on these specific incidents. I think what we need to talk about is the way that the characterization of this debate prevents us from really discussing how much freedom a professor should [have]—we've both been professors. I'm a professor now. You've been a professor. You know how important it is to be free to speak and to not be misunderstood.

Bork: Nobody on this side of the table is saying we should not discuss racism or sexism and how to deal with it.

Greene: Judge Bork, don't you think that there is a great deal of hypocrisy in the free speech debate? We don't have an outcry over the regulation of speech in the context of stock offerings; we don't worry about regulating speech in the area of copyrights, plagiarism. Some of the conservatives are perfectly happy to suppress pornography and obscenity or other types of advertising. So how would you make the distinction between that speech which ought to be permitted and that speech which we ought to suppress?

Bork: At the core of the First Amendment—which I take it is the emblem of free speech in our society—there is concern for political speech, concern for speech about ideas, about social matters, and so forth. There is no concern about speech—at least there wasn't originally concern about speech which expresses no idea, but merely expresses hatred or obscenity or something of that sort.

If somebody says, for example, that Asian-American students turn out to be better at mathematics and physics than others, I take it a speech code might land them on that person. That's political correctness, and that's wrong. We've got to be free to discuss differences, abilities, and so forth. But when you get a code about a stock offering, you're merely saying don't sell somebody a product that you have lied about.

Greene: It seems that you're supporting the idea that we can regulate some hate speech—

Bork: In the university. In a university.

Greene: In the university. And hate speech which might be one person making a personally directed racial epithet at another person. Wouldn't you agree that that ought to be, if not punishable, certainly subject to some type of university discipline and correction?

Bork: There certainly ought to be. I remember there was an episode at Brown University not long ago in which a drunken student went out in the quadrangle and shrieked anti-Semitic remarks, and the dean had him in and I think he was suspended. I don't have much trouble with that.

Greene: How do you explain that there is so much intellectual and political firepower marshaled in favor of people who want to yell epithets and derogatory, hurtful language? How do we explain this marshaling of energy and intellect in support of people who want to act this way towards others?

Bork: I think nobody does.

Greene: Well, then, would you agree with me that what we need to do is talk about the real issues and stop hurling our charges at each other?

Bork: Oh, the charges are much more fun.

The United States Owes Reparations
to Its Black Citizens

Daisy G. Collins

(1970)

CURRENT DEMANDS HAVE BEEN MADE for reparations to black citizens. In 1968, the Republic of New Africa, a black nationalist government-in-exile, formally petitioned the United States State Department for five states—Georgia, Alabama, Mississippi, Louisiana and South Carolina—and for billions of dollars in reparations. In 1969, the National Black Economic Development Conference announced their plan to demand reparations from the United States Government and from the white churches. The Black Manifesto stated that "[t]he white Christian churches are another form of government in this country and they are used by the government of this country to exploit the people of Latin America, Asia and Africa . . ."[1]

Black's Law Dictionary[2] defines reparation as "the redress for an injury, amends for a wrong inflicted." According to *Words & Phrases*,[3] reparation as commonly understood carries with it the idea of making whole or giving equivalent or substitute of equal value; restitution is synonymous with reparation.

From the above definitions, it is apparent that there is a legal basis to black demands for reparations. A court can take judicial notice of the fact that black people have been discriminated against. It can also take judicial notice of the thirteenth and fourteenth amendments of the United States Constitution. The com-

16 How. L.J. 84 (1970) (some footnotes omitted). Twenty-five years after the Collins article was published, another black woman lawyer is a principal advocate for reparations. *See* Nkechi Taifa, *Reparations and Self-Determination,* in CHOKWE LUMUMBA, IMARI OBADELE, AND NKECHI TAIFA, Reparations Yes! 1 (Baton Rouge, The House of Songsay Commission and the Malcolm Generation, Inc. 1995). *See also* Michael Fletcher, *Reparations for Blacks Is No Laughing Matter,* THE BALTIMORE SUN, Oct. 13, 1994, at 17A; Richard America, *A New Rationale for Income Distribution,* 2 REVIEW OF BLACK POLITICAL ECONOMISTS 1 (1972).

1. National Black Economic Development Conference, Black Manifesto (1969).
2. BLACK'S LAW DICTIONARY (4th ed. 1951).
3. 36A WORDS & PHRASES, *Reparation* 786 (1962).

bination of the judicially noticed fact and law leads to the conclusion that the Government has failed in its obligation to its black citizens and is therefore liable to them for the payment of reparations. Merely because wrongs have been perpetuated against black people for a long time does not justify them, nor does it mitigate the liability. "There is no such thing as a vested right to do wrong."[4] . . .

Black Citizens to Whom Due.   All black citizens can claim reparations on the theory that the Government has the power to eliminate discrimination and that because it has not done so they are at an economic disadvantage with their fellow white citizens whose ancestors were slaves in this country because the Government failed to provide a means for the emancipated slaves to acquire property. Thus, it can be said that since they started behind their fellow white citizens who already had property at the time the black people became citizens, it is a logical conclusion that black citizens of today who have exerted the same amount of effort as white citizens of today do not have as much as the white citizens because the white citizens have inherited property from their ancestors who had property at the time when black men became citizens without property. Furthermore, the failure of Congress to enact appropriate legislation to make meaningful the abolition of slavery and involuntary servitude and the citizenship of the freedman has further widened the gap between the property held by whites and that held by blacks.

As a matter of fact, the great majority of the black population was born in the United States. And since the free men of color constituted a small percentage of the total black population during the time of slavery, the conclusion is that most of the black citizens of the United States are descendants of persons who were slaves in the United States.[5]

Mechanics for Obtaining Reparations.   A class action should be brought, pursuant to Rule 23[6] of the Federal Rules of Civil Procedure, to obtain reparations. The class should consist of black people from all economic levels, i.e. from the welfare recipient to the millionaire.

The computation for each person should consist of two elements: one element would be a comparison of his annual earnings for every year which he has worked with the average earnings for comparably educated whites for the appropriate year and award him the cumulative differences; the second element would be to compare the present value of his net worth to the present value of the average net worth of comparably educated whites and award him the dif-

---

4. Johannessen v. United States, 225 U.S. 227, 242 (1912).

5. *See* H. PLOSKI & R. BROWN, THE NEGRO ALMANAC 219 (1967).

6. 60 Stat. 1050 (1946).

ference. (The present value comparison would necessarily take into consideration life expectancies.) For most black persons, both elements would be applicable: for some only one element would apply. In the event that a black citizen
comes up with a negative figure, he will not have to pay the Government since
this would be contrary to the purpose of the suit.

In order to make the computations for all black citizens making claims and
to facilitate the payments to them, a Black Claims Commission, similar to the
Indian Claims Commission pursuant to 60 Stat. 1049 (1946), should be established. The Act creating the Indian Claims Commission empowered the Commission to hear specified classes of claims against the United States on behalf of
any Indian tribe; one class was claims based upon fair and honorable dealings
that are not recognized by any existing rule of law or equity. . . . The Act also
provided that no statute of limitations or laches would be available as defenses
. . . There were also Congressional enactments to provide for Japanese-Ameri-
can evacuation claims resulting from the evacuation or exclusion of Japanese
Americans from certain areas on or after December 7, 1941.[7] . . .

Factual Comparisons of Black Citizens with White Citizens.   The right to work
for a living in the common occupations of the community is of the very essence
of the personal freedom and opportunity that it was the purpose of the fourteenth amendment to secure.[8] It is undoubtedly the right of every citizen of the
United States to follow any lawful calling, business, or profession he may choose,
subject only to such restrictions as are imposed upon all persons of like age, sex,
and condition.[9] The late President John F. Kennedy said on February 28, 1963 in
his special message on civil rights that "the harmful, wasteful and wrongful results of racial discrimination and segregation still appear in virtually every aspect of national life, in virtually every part of the Nation."[10]

The following facts support that statement. According to the Bureau of the
Census publication, We the Black People of the United States,[11] the average
black family earns less than the average white family although the average black
family is larger. Nine percent of the families in the United States are black, but
they receive only 5% of the national income.[12] Negro median income was 59%
of the median income for white families in 1967, the highest percentage ever.
This percent remained the same in 1968.[13] About two of every five black men

---

7. 62 Stat. 1231 (1948); 70 Stat. 513 (1956).

8. Truax v. Raich, 239 U.S. 33 (1915).

9. Dent v. West Virginia, 129 U.S. 114 (1889).

10. Johnson Publishing Co., The Negro Handbook 7 (1966).

11. U.S. Department of Commerce, Bureau of the Census (1969).

12. Estimated United States population as of July 1, 1968 was 175,505,000 white; 22,229,000
black (11.1% of total); and 2,126,000 other. U.S. Bureau of the Census, Statistical Abstract of the
United States 23 (1969).

13. WASH. POST, Nov. 9, 1969.

and more than half of all black women who work are service workers, laborers, or farm workers. Black men represent 10% of the employed males in this country, but only 2% of the doctors, 2.5% of the dentists, 15% of the electricians, and 0.5% of the engineers. Black women represent 13% of the employed women but only 2.4% of the lawyers, 5.6% of the professional nurses, 6.5% of the medical technicians, 2.4% of the telephone operators, 1.5% of the secretaries, and 8.8% of elementary teachers. In 1963, 7.3% of black available workers were without jobs, while only 3.3% of available white workers were unemployed.

Following is a percent distribution comparison of the years of school completed in 1968 by the persons who were 14 years old and over as of March 1968.[14]

Years of School Completed	Total	Negro
Elementary School		
Less than 5 years	4.6%	12.9%
5–7 years	9.4	17.1
8 years	13.9	12.5
High School		
1–3 years	22.1	27.5
4 years or more	30.7	20.7
College		
1–3 years	10.6	5.8
4 years or more	8.7	3.5
	100.0%	100.0%
Median School Years Completed	12.0	9.8

In 1968, the median annual income of white households was $8,062; that of black households was $4,755, i.e. 59% of the white amount.

The following comparison supports the statement that black citizens generally have less income than white citizens with comparable education.

Years of School Completed By Head of Family	Family Median Income White	Non-White[15]
Less than 8 years	$ 4,932	$ 3,670
8 years	6,608	4,897
1–3 years high school	7,971	5,083

14. U.S. Bureau of the Census, Statistical Abstract of the United States 325 (1969).
15. Black population is about 94% of the non-white population, *supra* note 12, at 237.

4 years high school	8,962	6,665
1–3 years college	10,277	8,189
4 years college	12,770	10,485

For families whose head had completed four years of college, 36.7% of the whites earned $15,000 or over while only 24.6% of the blacks earned $15,000 or over.

Another indication of the black citizen's deprivation of property is that in 1960, 64.4% of white-occupied housing units were owner-occupied (and 35.6% renter-occupied) while in the same year only 38.4% of non-white-occupied housing units were owner-occupied (and 61.6% renter-occupied).

A 1968 publication of the National Committee Against Discrimination in Housing entitled How the Federal Government Builds Ghettos states that nearly 67% of the dwelling units occupied by black families in urban areas are substandard compared to less than 20% of the units occupied by whites. In many cities the incidence of overcrowding among black citizens runs eight or nine times higher than that of whites.[16] . . . The Federal Housing Administration has not effectively used the two major opportunities which it has to encourage desegregation, i.e. in the housing it insures and in the housing it acquires through mortgage foreclosures.[17] It is high time that the Government stop repeating its good intentions and find ways to enforce them. . . .[18]

Some Examples of the Government's Failure to Fulfill Its Obligation. An article . . . entitled "Government is cause for slow progress," which appeared in the December 20, 1969 *Washington Afro-American,* began with the following statement: "The Southern Regional Council charged last Saturday [that] there has 'seemed to be a deliberate effort' on the part of the federal government to reverse progress in school desegregation." This statement pretty well illustrates the general attitude of the United States Government, as far as the rights of its black citizens are concerned.

Mr. Justice Harlan, dissenting in the Civil Rights Cases,[19] said that prior to the thirteenth, fourteenth, and fifteenth amendments "Congress, with the sanction of this court, passed the most stringent laws—operating directly and primarily upon States and their officers and agents, as well as upon individuals— in vindication of the right of the master, [and it was somewhat anomalous that the Supreme Court decided that Congress] . . . may not now, by legislation of a like primary and direct character, guard, protect and secure the freedom established, and the most essential right of the citizenship granted, by the constitu-

---

16. National Committee Against Discrimination in Housing, How the Federal Government Builds Ghettos 21 (1968).

17. *Id.* at 27.

18. *Id.* at 28.

19. Civil Rights Cases, 109 U.S. 3 (1883).

tional amendments."[20] It seems proper to say that the Supreme Court "bears a considerable measure of responsibility" for the vestiges of slavery which still exist today . . . [21]

Since the United States Government has deprived its black citizens of property without due process of law, it owes reparations to them.

---

20. *Id.* at 53.

21. Erwin N. Griswold, Lawyers in the United States 11 (Cambridge, Harvard University Press 1965).

Freedom

Give Colored Women the Right to Vote

Mary Ann Shadd Carey

(1870s)

*M*R. CHAIRMAN, AND GENTLEMEN of the Judiciary Committee:
In respectfully appearing before you, to solicit in concert with these ladies, your good offices, in securing to the women of the United States, and particularly, to the women of the District of Columbia, the right to vote, a right exercised by a portion of American women, at one period, in . . . the country, I am not vain enough to suppose, for one moment, that words of mine could add one iota of weight to the arguments from these learned and earnest women, nor that I could bring out material facts not heretofore used by them in one stage or another of this advocacy. But, as a colored woman, a resident of the District, a taxpayer the same as . . . the male colored voters [and] claiming affiliation with two and half million of the same sex, in the country at large, including in the provisions of recent constitutional amendments, and not least by virtue of a decision of the Supreme Court of this District a citizen, my presence at this time, and on an errand so important, may not—must not—be without significance.

The crowning glory of American citizenship is that it may be shared equally by people of every nationality, complexion and sex—should they be of foreign birth . . . [M]illions of citizens of every complexion, and embracing both sexes are born upon the soil. I want to be particularly clear upon this point. By the provisions of the 14th and 15th amendments to the Constitution of the United States, a logical sequence of which is the representation by colored men of time-honored commonwealths in both houses of Congress, millions of colored women today share with colored men the responsibilities of freedom from chattel slavery. From the introduction of African slavery to its extinction, a period

---

This rare testimony, discovered in the Moorland-Spingarn Research Center, at Howard University, was reconstructed by the editor from handwritten notes of Ms. Shadd and addressed to or presented before a U.S. Senate Judiciary Committee circa 1870–71.

of more than two hundred years, they, equally with their fathers, brothers—women everywhere throughout the land [have been] denied the right to vote . . . The colored women of this country though heretofore silent in great measure . . . have neither been indifferent to their own just claims under the amendments, in common with colored men, nor to the demand for political recognition so justly made by the women suffering of the country for women everywhere throughout the land.

The strength and glory of a free nation is not so much in the size and equipment of its armies, as in the loyal hearts and willing hands of its *men* and *women;* and this fact has been illustrated in an eminent degree by well-known events in the history of the United States. To the women of the nation co-jointly with the men, is it indebted for arduous and dangerous personal service, and generous expenditure of time, wealth and counsel, so indispensable to the success in its hour of danger. The colored *women* though humble in sphere, and unendowed with worldly goods, yet, led as by inspiration, not only fed and sheltered and guided in safely the . . . soldiers of the Union when escaping from the enemy, or the soldier who was compelled to risk life itself in the struggle to break the backbone of [the] rebellion.

[The colored women] gave their sons and brothers to the armies of the Nation and their prayers to high Heaven for the success of Right. The surges of fratricidal war have shaped, we hope, never to return, the premonitions of the future—peace and good will—these blessings, so greatly to be desired, can only be made permanent in responsible government . . . by giving to both sexes practically the equal powers conferred in the provisions of the Constitution as amended. In the District of Columbia, the women in common with women of the states and territories, feel keenly the discrimination against them in the retention of the word *male* in the organic act . . . [T]hey sincerely hope that the word may be stricken. Taxed and governed in other respects—without their consent—they respectfully demand that the principles of the founders of the government may not [be] disregarded in their case; but, as there are laws by which they are tried, with penalties attached thereto, that they may be invested with the right to vote as do men; that thus as in all Republics indeed, they may in [the] future be governed by their own consent. . . .

The Necessity of Universal Suffrage

Georgia Huston Jones Ellis

(1932)

*T*HE TENDENCY TOWARD UNIVERSAL SUFFRAGE has been gathering force through the years until immediately following the World War it swept in irresistible waves over practically the entire civilized world. We note that since 1918, the gathering forces of self-determination have expressed themselves in unmistakable terms in Europe, Africa and Asia, until today there exists but one absolute Monarchy on the face of the Earth—The Black Kingdom of Abyssinia.

The British Empire on whose vast possessions the Sun never sets, has maintained the Monarchial Form largely because it has heeded the call of its people for a voice in its government and its many Colonies and provinces are self-governing except certain portions of India on whose struggle for complete autonomy the entire world has its attention focused.

Germany became a Republic in 1918, as did Austria, Czechoslovakia, Lithuania, following by a year the establishment of the Union of Soviet Socialist Republics of Russia. Estonia is an independent autonomous Republic in which the state power is in the hands of the people. Finland was proclaimed an independent Republic in 1917, and Universal Suffrage prevailed (men and women). France, of course, is a well established Republic with its legislative authority vested in the Chamber of Deputies and the Senate—all of its Colonies in Asia, Africa and America being represented therein. Greece is an independent Republic and Italy, though a nominal Kingdom has its actual power vested in Prime Minister, and a Fasnal Council. Poland is a Republic in which legislative power is vested in a National Assembly of two Houses and Universal Suffrage prevails—and so I might cover practically the entire world, even the troubled

Georgia Huston Jones Ellis delivered this paper before and is in the ANNUAL CONVENTION OF THE NATIONAL BAR ASSOCIATION PROCEEDINGS OF THE EIGHTH ANNUAL CONVENTION, Indianapolis, Indiana, August, 1932, at 97.

countries of China and Japan have felt the urge of self-determination. China having a President and Executive Council and Japan being a nominal Kingdom with its legislative power vested in the Emperor, Privy Council and the Imperial Diet, consisting of a House of Peers and a House of Representatives.

In the United States, the year, of 1776, is an appropriate date from which to trace the development of suffrage in as much as that date marks the beginning of this country as an independent nation. The American people have boldly proclaimed that all men are created equal. That they are endowed by their Creator with certain inalienable rights; that among these are life, liberty and the pursuit of happiness; that to secure these rights Governments are instituted among men, deriving their just powers from the consent of the governed. They have set forth in that great document of human rights known as the "American Declaration of Independence," that the underlying principle of democratic government is that the "power vested in the government" is derived from the consent of those governed. This is the basis of all self-government.

Political autonomy can only be maintained by full participation of all of the governed in some method or manner giving expression to the will of the people. Out of this general expression of the desires of its governed, grew the Elective Franchise.

The tendency toward general and universal suffrage seems to be deep rooted in the mind of men. We can only account for it by a deep seated, firm though more or less unreasoning conviction, that all men should bear the burdens of government, hence, should have a voice in determining what those burdens should be.

Alexander Hamilton, that wizard of finance, who "smote the Rock of National Resources and Streams of Revenue gushed forth," once said that "the right which is exercised by the citizens at large in voting at elections is one of the most important rights, and in a Republic ought to stand foremost in the estimation of the law." It is a right by which we exist as a free people.

Elective Franchise means the right of choice—and having emancipated from the people it would seem to be an all inclusive term. However, from the moment it was heralded to the world as a blazing torch, lighting the way for a people henceforth free and untrammelled, its very authors have besought by every human effort to limit the power of expression to the favored few. It would seem then that from the very moment of our new freedom, restrictive limitations were placed upon the voting power of the people. One of the earliest qualifications of the voter was the land-universal requirement for the exercise of suffrage—but this concept was not so consistently applied as to grant suffrage to minors, women and certain others who were not considered fit to exercise the Franchise. The theory seemed fairly well fixed, though, that a man's property entitled him to vote, and for almost two hundred years the idea prevailed that a man owning property was a qualified voter.

Suffrage limitations were largely determined by the social and economic conditions of the community, and gradually each of the States formulated its own code for the exercise of suffrage. Thus in rural Virginia the freehold requirement of fifty acres excluded very few of the best type of men—but such a requirement in an urban community would have been intolerable. Moral qualifications were restricted almost entirely to New England, and it was often necessary to prove one's good character before being allowed to vote.

In the State of Georgia, residence in the State six months was a pre-requisite to voting and throughout the South there were restrictions against men of certain race. New York excluded Jews and Catholics, Rhode Island excluded Catholics and New Hampshire required ownership of property in the district where the voter cast his vote. Virginia had more restrictions on suffrage rights than any of the Colonies, excluding free Negroes, mulattoes, Indians, women, minors and Catholics from any direct participation in the governmental affairs.

South Carolina required payment of taxes, residence of one year and adherence to the Protestant religion. As other States came into the Union, the property test gradually gave way to newer requirements, the chief ones being citizenship.

In recent years, legislatures have levied poll taxes and imposed literacy tests as a pre-requisite to voting, and disfranchisement for infamous crime has long been a suffrage limitation. Restrictive limitation of suffrage has become more or less fixed throughout the United States to apply to residence and citizenship requirements, still excluding women and Negroes until the conclusion of the Civil War and the passage of the 13th, 14th and 15th Amendments. Then came the greatest struggle for suffrage rights since this country freed itself from British rule—that of full and equal suffrage for Negro Americans. Hand in hand with the battle for the Negro suffrage went the fight for women suffrage, which upon the passage of the 19th Amendment in 1920, left this country battling with the question of the Negro's right to full and equal suffrage. It will be noted that all the machinery of the government has been directed toward limiting the suffrage of certain groups—which has, since the passage of the 19th Amendment, been the Negro-American. Since the history making *Dred Scott* decision announced to the world that the Negro had no rights which the white man was bound to respect, there have been enacted by the various legislatures of the several States every piece of legislation in restriction of Negro suffrage that it was possible for the mind of man to devise. Most of this legislation, such as the Grandfather Clause and laws restricting alienation of property, was of course, declared unconstitutional, but the fact remains that more than 90 per cent of the citizens of color of all the States South of the Mason and Dixon line are denied their suffrage rights. As a result, their property rights are denied, their civil liberties are restricted, their economic status is lowered and their right to justice in the courts of the land is seriously impaired.

The admonition to secure property is farcical when, having acquired it, the Negro has no means of protecting his wealth or even his person against unlawful search and seizure by any white mob which sees fit to constitute itself the law. This National Association of Lawyers could devise no more effective program, could consecrate themselves to no higher duty than to dedicate their organized effort to the end that every piece of legislation in restriction of the suffrage of any citizen should be erased from the statute books of every State in the Union where it now obtains, that this might, indeed, be the land of the free.

The necessity for universal suffrage is self-evident. Any group of people denied the full and equal right to participate in the enactment of laws by which, of course, all governmental policies are fixed, must necessarily suffer. He must obey the law which he has no voice in making. He must pay taxes which he takes no part in fixing, he must shoulder arms in defense of his country, yet, he shall not say when that country shall resort to war.

In order to maintain a government of the people, for the people, by the people, there must be no restrictive limitations placed upon the suffrage right of any normal citizen having attained a legal voting age. When every citizen of every country shall have learned to exercise freely and intelligently his suffrage rights, when every citizen of every country shall have recognized the right of each to participate fully and freely in his government's affairs, when no man's right to vote shall be predicated upon the number of acres he owns or upon the amount of taxes he pays, when no man's suffrage shall be determined by his race or religion, then indeed, shall we have a parliament of man, a federation of the world.

The Role of Law in Effecting Social Change

CONSTANCE BAKER MOTLEY

(1978)

*T*HIS VISIT TO CHARLESTON HAS given me the occasion to recall the mo-
mentous civil rights events of the 1950's and early 1960's in which I participated . . .

The process of desegregation continues not only in education but in employment and housing. The process has required that we use all of our American ingenuity, pick our best brains, and cast some of the burden of undoing the
effects of past discrimination on the white community . . . [O]ur goal as a nation is still equality of opportunity and in achieving this goal the white community must recognize that just as the black community has been called upon
to continue to bear the burdens of past discrimination during this troublesome
transition period the white community must share these burdens. If during this
period of transition some desegregation plans result in some incidental discrimination against whites as a group, it must be remembered that discrimination in the past was directed at blacks as a group. All blacks, for example, were
barred from Clemson College in 1960, qualified or not.

The official ending of segregation in the nation has meant the beginning
of the dynamic new social, political, and economic era which we see today. There
have been many factors which have contributed to the creation of this new day
since 1954, but the single most important factor has been the law. The role of law
in effecting social change in America is best illustrated by the transition which
has occurred here in South Carolina in the past quarter-century. No community in this nation can better demonstrate how the law and our legal institutions
can be used to effect change. The struggle to rid the South and the rest of this
country of official segregation put our commitment to the rule of law to the test
of the century. Our commitment prevailed. However, it is once again being chal-

CRISIS, January, 1978, at 24.

lenged by those who believe that the function of law in society is more restricted and should not be used as an instrument of social change.

The opponents of the use of law and the court as an alternative to other methods for achieving social change have recently made a number of proposals for limiting access to the Federal courts and restricting the use of Federal civil rights statutes. Such proposals are not new. They are perennially put forth in the guise of proposals to lessen the burden on the Federal courts without acknowledging that the burden would then be cast upon the even more overburdened state courts. They are often proposed without recognition of the fact that it was the specific design of the Reconstruction Congress to provide a Federal forum for the redress of grievances which result in the denial of rights guaranteed by the newly amended Constitution and newly enacted civil rights legislation. They are almost invariably proposed without an acknowledgement that it was the intent of the framers of the national Constitution, as set forth in the preamble, that it be forever the responsibility of the national government to establish justice in this nation . . .

There is now a whole new world of Federal civil rights jurisprudence. And, as might be expected, all of this activity has resulted in a staggering increase in the number of civil rights cases being filed in the Federal courts today. There is truly cause for alarm since this increase in civil rights litigation has been accompanied by increases in litigation in other areas of traditional Federal concern. Consequently, many of the proponents of these limitations on access to the Federal courts are proceeding in good faith. However, as I see it, the issue is not the good faith or bad faith of the proponents of limited Federal court access. The issue is whether the right of unfettered resort to the Federal courts, which the Congress long ago sought to secure, for the redress of grievances arising out of violations of Federal constitutional and statutory rights is to be preserved as an alternative to other methods of achieving social change in the American community.

I am not one of those who believes that the courts are equipped to or should deal with every conceivable societal problem. And frivolous constitutional claims should manifestly be barred. What I believe is that this alternative for vindicating Federal constitutional and statutory rights—affecting minorities—should remain forever free of encumbrances. I perceive this unfettered access to the Federal courts to be a necessary precondition to the viability of our ever expanding, increasingly complex, and amazingly diverse society. The history of America's transition from a segregated society to a desegregated society in the past quarter-century amply demonstrates this fact . . .

The black community has . . . developed a core of lawyers who have become proficient in the Federal court system. As the years have gone by these lawyers have continued their practice in the Federal courts dealing with such issues as Federal court abstention, exhaustion of administrative remedies, First

Amendment rights, and class actions. Most significantly, these black lawyers have continued to participate in the development of new legal theories which go beyond the rights of the black community and involve the constitution and Federal statutory rights of Americans generally.

Since 1964 Congress has enacted many new civil rights statutes affecting rights in the area of housing, employment, and places of public accommodation, giving black lawyers further opportunities for gaining skills as lawyers and insight into the development of Federal legislative remedies for dealing with complex social issues. Black lawyers who participated in the civil rights movement regularly have been consulted by lawyers serving other public interest groups. They are viewed in the public interest field as the real experts in Federal procedure and Federal jurisprudence.

This core of black lawyers includes several who started here in South Carolina and similar communities across the South back in the early 1950s. They have had such spectacular success in Federal court practice that they have over the years inspired other young black Americans to seek law as a profession. The number of black students in law schools today has increased tremendously during the past two decades. Law, legal institutions, and the legal profession are now important to black communities throughout America. This development is manifestly important to the future of this country. Not too many years ago, the law, the courts, and lawyers were viewed as enemies by many blacks. I recall that during my early days as a member of the staff of the NAACP Legal Defense and Educational Fund many blacks rejected the notion that the courts could be fair. As we look back now we can see that the most enduring changes have been enshrined in law. This fact has not been lost on the black community . . .

The fact that the law has been successfully invoked as the instrument of vast social changes in our society should also be viewed as a welcome development. This development has served to strengthen the rule of law. It should, therefore, be encouraged and all efforts to restrict access to legal education for qualified blacks and to the Federal courts for the resolution of Federal constitutional and statutory issues should be defeated. As long as the Federal courts are open for the redress of these rights, my experience with the law tells me that we need have no fear for our future as a nation.

Just as the litigants and the lawyers before the Federal courts have changed, reflecting a new day in the life of this nation, the composition of the Federal courts themselves, must now change. Presently, there are about 600 Federal judges, about 18 of whom are black and six of whom are women. No system can call itself fair if major groups which that system purports to serve have not been included. There are whole areas of this country in which there is not a single black Federal judge, but where blacks are a major portion of the population. There has never been a black Federal judge in the South. The 18 blacks who are now serving as Federal judges are scattered in the East, the Midwest, and on the West Coast.

The fact that there are only six women serving as Federal judges when women are the majority group in the population is simply indefensible. The present paucity of blacks and women speaks louder than words. The idea that women should be better represented in the Federal judiciary is an idea whose time has come. I have often said to women's law groups around the country, "It would be great to have a woman on the Supreme Court, but it would be equally as great to have women serving as Federal trial judges and Federal appeals court judges." Federal trial judges are among the most powerful Federal officials in the country. Yet this fact is hidden under a bushel.

The issue, therefore, is not whether the system should include blacks and women and members of other groups not previously included as an acknowledgement of the existence of these groups, but whether power shall be shared with these groups. The issue of access to the Federal courts thus includes the question of whether black lawyers and women lawyers aspiring to be judges can be appointed to the Federal bench. If there is no access by blacks and women to the Federal bench, then the system is in trouble. Blacks and other minority litigants, as well as women litigants, must be convinced that the system is fair in the sense that all segments of the legal profession are represented. . . .

New Civil Rights Demands: White Resistance

Frankie Muse Freeman

(1969)

*I*T WOULD BE PRESUMPTUOUS FOR anyone to attempt to lecture the people in this room on the importance of securing equal rights for all Americans, or to suggest that they should make a commitment to work to secure these rights . . . The euphoria that attended the early 1960s, when break-throughs were being made on many fronts, has long since vanished to be replaced with the realization that the tortuous climb to the top of the mountain becomes more difficult as the distance to the summit decreases.

This change in attitude, however, has not been all negative in effect. It has stripped away many illusions that actually stood in the way of bringing about meaningful changes in this society. As long as we believed, as many of us did, that the mere passage of laws would correct the basic racial injustices of this system, then we could not see that the injustices were so firmly imbedded that laws alone could not root them out. It was almost as if we were playing the shell game; while our attention was diverted in one direction, the main part of the game was going on in another direction.

The passage of the various civil rights laws were, of course, of monumental importance, but they were not the end of the struggle, only one more step along the road. Laws alone could not solve the matter of poverty, of people crippled by inferior education, of all the by-products of this nation's most deadly sin. The problems faced by Blacks and other minority groups were so complicated, so interwoven one with the other, that simple solutions were just not possible.

Once this was realized a disillusionment set in among a number of our allies who retreated from the struggle, unwilling to have their hands soiled with

---

This article appeared in the Extension of Remarks, 116 CONG. REC. E2482 (1970). It is from a speech Commissioner Freeman made at the 1969 NAACP Freedom Fund Dinner in Milwaukee, Wisconsin. She was a member of the U.S. Civil Rights Commission.

the real and unglamorous nitty-gritty problems of Black people. Some of our own people also went through a traumatic shock, becoming convinced that the problems were so deep-rooted that they could not be solved in the present social context, and the only answer was racial separation.

What all this has meant, is that the Civil Rights Movement, as it has been known, has been fractured, perhaps beyond repair. While it was in existence it did perform many useful acts in bringing this country to the point where segregation and discrimination are no longer legally supported, and where there is widespread concern for civil rights. Having done this, it is in the nature of historical progression that the Movement would be replaced by some other type of structure more capable of dealing with a different set of problems . . .

A new type of Movement is developing, that even more than the old, reaches out to involve all segments of the community. This type of constituency gives the new Movement more power than the old Civil Rights Movement which was basically middle-class oriented and middle-class developed and so limited in concept and effectiveness.

One of the weaknesses of the old Civil Rights Movement was this middle-class mindness. It was never able to develop, except in a few instances, and these most notably in the South, a broad based community involvement. The usual pattern was for the Civil Rights Movement to depend upon white liberals and middle-class Blacks for both financial support and direction, while the great mass of Black people remained untouched.

While the majority of Blacks could share vicariously in the achievements of the Movement, its goals were so far removed from their basic concern, as to be to a large degree, irrelevant. The Movement, however, did achieve its greatest victories coincidental with a period in which the Black community, through the rapid improvement in communications, was becoming more aware that it was not sharing equitably in the good life.

Black fathers, struggling to keep a family together on sub-par wages, looked at television and saw White America relaxing in California, flying to Europe, driving the latest automobiles from Detroit, and asked themselves—why can't that be me. The golden apple of success was dangled just beyond the reach of Black people, and they wanted the fruit. The old excuse—time will take care of everything—was no longer acceptable and spurred on by what had been done on the legal level, the demand for fundamental changes in the White-constructed and White-dominated society began to be heard.

These demands have changed the character of the Civil Rights Movement, they have created a new ordering of priorities, and because they cannot be answered without basic changes in this society, they have produced resistance on the part of many Whites who aren't concerned with whether Blacks vote in Mississippi, but are concerned when Blacks seek homes in all-White sections of Milwaukee.

If the public opinion polls are correct, and if such studies as *Newsweek* magazine recently made of the mood of White America are to be believed, the issue of civil rights has become a source of irritation to many Americans who feel that too many demands are being made by too many people who have already received too much.

The truth is that not enough demands have been met or made, for there to be any relaxation of efforts to bring the scales into balance.

Rather than to face up to the bitter truth that the system has not responded to the need for change, a large number of Whites believe that if only enough repressive pressure is applied, if only attention can be diverted from the racial problems, then this nation can return to the past and the headache she now experiences will go away. It is difficult to imagine a more dangerous game than this, for all it accomplishes is to under evaluate the seriousness of the problem and to over evaluate the ability of force and repression to stifle ideas.

On every hand we see a growing insensitivity to this most critical domestic problem. While Blacks fall further and further behind Whites in income the anti-poverty program is being dismantled. While Black Panthers are being killed or thrown in jail as part of the law and order campaign, the Attorney General of the United States is not sure that he can enforce desegregation rulings. While cities sink deeper into their own filth, billions are poured into an unwinnable war, thousands of miles away from this country. While millions are available for the construction of supersonic transport to carry the well-off to far flung corners of the world, people are being thrown off farms and our Congress quibbles over food programs.

Something is wrong, something is very wrong. . . .

Dynamics of Change

Marian Wright Edelman

(1970)

ONE PROBLEM CIVIL RIGHTS LEADERS have had is a tendency to preoccupy themselves periodically with passage of big laws. Civil rights groups got together and pressed for the Civil Rights Act of 1964 and the Voting Rights Act of 1965. And they were crucial steps forward. Then we forgot about them. The lack of attention to the enforcement of laws that were intended for Blacks and for poor people has been a serious gap in our efforts for change.

What we don't realize is that often the guidelines that are written by administrative agencies are as important, or more important, to the ultimate impact of the law as the law itself. Everybody who is against our interests is in there trying to make sure civil rights laws are weakened, i.e. that the guidelines leave loopholes for evasions; that appropriations are so slim that little staff can be hired to carry out the law's mandate. As a result, Blacks and poor people are often harmed by the absence of representatives at this crucial stage. This administrative enforcement vacuum is beginning to be corrected slowly. But much more remains to be done.

Sometimes I feel we don't need any more laws. All we need is adequate enforcement of existing laws. We need to seek enforcement mechanisms to bring about the promise of legislative changes. Poor and Black people would improve by half if the laws that were intended for them were actually used in their behalf. But these laws are generally watered down, or weakly enforced or not enforced at all. There has been no commitment and no systematic outside pressure to force lawmakers to do more than what they have done. There has to be more attention to administrative enforcement of the laws if they are to mean anything.

AFRO-AMERICAN STUDIES SERIES, NO. 1, AFRO-AMERICAN STUDIES PROGRAM, Boston University, at 7 (1970).

A second problem of civil rights groups is that Black and poor people's representatives always come in complaining too little and too late. We don't know what is happening until after it has happened. We don't have any effective early alert system as many other special interest groups have. Many agencies wouldn't dare think of changing the laws or regulations or otherwise making major decisions which affect the labor movement without consulting with them beforehand. Very seldom do they do that with Black or poor folk. For all the weaknesses and shortcomings of the Poor People's Campaign, it did establish one principle: that poor people have some right to input and consultation in the administrative process before vital decisions affecting them are made. Not that [relevant federal agencies and departments do] what we always want them to do. But at least they now call up and tell us what they are going to do and we can have a little time to fight against them if we disagree. This is not enough. But it is a beginning handle. For example, NWRO (The Negro Welfare Rights Organization) meets every month with the Department of Health, Education and Welfare (HEW) on rule changes that affect welfare recipients. They don't always win, but at least they know what is going on and can try to protect their interests.

An early alert system which has a strong informational flow out to the right groups is a very important thing. In effect, one of the operations of our office in Washington is simply to know what policy makers are thinking about doing before they do it. An example is the early [President Richard M.] Nixon attempt to completely water down the school desegregation guidelines. We happened to find out about it beforehand by obtaining a key memorandum prepared by HEW General Counsel proposing the policy changes. With that kind of information, you can alert civil rights groups, Senators or Congressmen, and the press, and apply pressure against those who want to undercut Black progress. Of course, policy makers lie. They often deny any impending changes. HEW denied for weeks and weeks that any policy changes were being considered while we were getting new drafts at the same time. Each draft was a little better. Eventually they came out with a new policy. It was bad and weakened the desegregation effort but it was considerably better than the initially proposed policy.

School desegregation policy is much better than it would have been had there not been someone in there applying pressure and building up a counter-reaction from the other side. That kind of thing has to be done on many issues on behalf of the poor and Blacks if they are to begin to get any kind of fair shake. The government and its policy makers are going to do nothing for you unless you make them . . .

We must learn how to begin to take the initiative on behalf of our clients and our communities and to stop reacting to the decisions of other people. I don't think poor and Black people have understood how decisions are made in this country. I think that is true at the administrative and at the legislative level.

I don't care how you feel about the system—you have to know it to do anything about it. Today, we still see civil rights leaders engaging in "symbolic" visits with the President or with the secretaries of HEW or Labor to talk about schools or to talk about welfare.

And then nothing happens . . . You have to inject yourself into the process at all levels as well as at the top. It's a slow, hard, tedious, persistent undertaking. Unfortunately, too few people who are on our side understand how tough it is to change things or have the patience to stick with it. The same thing is true of the legislative process. You can leave nothing to chance . . . Blacks and the poor have an undeveloped legislative lobby that must be strengthened. We must begin to think through what our own strategies and program goals are . . .

Finally, I want to talk about what's going to be needed from Black lawyers. We're going to have to give Black and poor people the kind of leadership they need. That means getting involved in something broader than providing case-by-case help. Economic development is now a big issue in the Black community. In part that's because government agencies are becoming less responsible. And we are recognizing albeit late that nobody else is going to take care of us if we don't. One of the things we haven't done is to think about real economic development on a broad scale. Nor have we examined all the potential mechanisms to exploit. For instance, how to use federal programs like Southern Whites use federal programs, like everybody uses federal programs, to finance and push their own interests . . .

We have to stop thinking in narrow terms if we're going to give Black and poor people genuinely good services. We're going to have to begin to prepare ourselves with more sophistication. It has not always been done in the past. We work, and with poor and minority representation who are also going to stick with it and not flit from issue to issue. That can only come by having some private mechanism for training young Blacks and young minority people and others interested in lobbying techniques. Few major lobbying groups in Washington have Black staff lobbyists.

Also, we have to learn the techniques of good advocacy, how to identify those few issues which are "winnable" and important, which can convince people that they can make a difference. And they can. We must also begin to generate communication with local clients and people. It doesn't do any good if we do all this lobbying in Washington and change laws and those in Mississippi or Alabama are not aware of it or don't want or need what we're lobbying about . . .

Once we get the laws passed, good lawyers and good lobbyists must stay with an issue. We must police the administrative process, disseminate information about new occurrences to local communities and provide them the necessary assistance to take advantage of new ideas and regulations. It will be necessary to help local people write applications and process them through the bureaucracy . . .

In all my work, the most instructive examples have been the ability of many Black women, particularly sharecropper women in Mississippi who have survived all those years against the hardest odds and have never lost a sense of dignity, a sense of commitment, a sense of purpose for their children or their future. I always feel terribly inadequate next to them. It seems to me that those of us who are "narrowly educated" must have a broader sense of what educational goals are for. We must try both to give something in a way of technical skill to the Black community which has not had the opportunities for education we have had. We must also try to learn something from those who from wider leadership and persistence, have survived.

Minority Coalitions to Secure Civil Rights

Margaret Bush Wilson

(1972)

*I*T IS IMPERATIVE . . . FOR Americans of African descent to be not just aware of but agitated about any retreat from and denial of their fundamentally guaranteed rights. In my view this is a survival technique not just a social action tactic. The quest for political, economic and social equality by black America has no chance for success in a national climate of repression and restriction . . .

If this new jeopardy to equal protection of the law for minorities were an isolated phenomenon, there could be less cause for concern. But, the detail and documentation is provided almost daily in the news signaling potential retreat across the board. The rights of a free press have been under attack; there have been infringements on the rights of privacy; detention without warrant has been advocated; and the rights of dissent and association are being questioned. The decade of the 1960's, with its array of civil rights laws, seems to have an uncanny parallel to a century ago and the 1860's. In short shrift the gains which blacks had won—Emancipation, the fourteenth and fifteenth amendments and the Civil Rights Act of 1875—collapsed. They had no economic base to undergird their freedom . . .

Coalition politics, with an economic agenda aimed at poverty and unemployment, is an urgent strategy. It can mean survival for black Americans and a new and humane society for all Americans. Without political power the changes of basic reforms are slim. But the politics and political action which conceivably are necessary are much too important to be left to politicians.

One of the perplexing anomalies which exists in the black experience is the almost proud and stubborn way most of the organizations of stature in the black community eschew politics and political action. But, we are deep in political ac-

DONALD W. WYATT, ED., PROGRESS IN AFRICA AND AMERICA 109 (New Orleans, Dillard University 1972).

228

tion whether we want to be or not—that's what the civil rights movement is all about. And there are ways to function politically, that rise above the distasteful connotation which the word politics holds for some.

Three very recent developments offer exciting possibilities for political action. They can be the basis for mutually productive alliances for blacks and others with overlapping self-interests.

The first is the rise of black political office holders in the South. This is the unfinished business of Reconstruction, of course, and I hope it continues apace. Encouraging, too, is the fact that these black office holders have lines of communication open among themselves and to potential friends and allies.

The second emerging force has the potential for the most significant new thrust for black liberation in this half of the twentieth century. This force is the Congressional Black Caucus, composed of thirteen members of Congress from urban centers with an estimated constituency of over five million people. The fact that these constituencies are concentrated in a half dozen or more urban centers of America has political significance which should not be overlooked.

Last month, at the invitation of the Congressional Black Caucus, the Institute of Politics at Harvard and four distinguished newspapers—more than 300 concerned persons—met in Cambridge and debated for three days "What Our National Priorities Should Be." The process can be described in another way as "doing the homework"—a tedious but necessary chore which black Americans cannot ignore. From that session and others like it, the caucus hoped to generate an agenda for legislative action in Congress behind which blacks and their allies can rally.

And that brings me to the third event of great significance which occurred recently—not so much in what it did, but in what it was. This event took place in Gary, Indiana, in March and was, of course, the Black political convention called to hammer out an agenda with which to challenge both major political parties which meet later in this presidential year.

Some people were disappointed in Gary. Others were frustrated, and still others were disgusted. There may have been some basis for each of these reactions. But what went on in Gary was, in my view, not nearly as significant as what it represented. Several thousand people from all walks of life in black America felt strongly about effecting institutional change to meet collectively to deal with the subject of their exercise of political power. They were expressing a concern that relates to twenty million black people whose contributing share to this nation's gross national product exceeds 45 billion dollars. That is more than the gross national product of some entire nations of the earth. Ours is reported to be the richest aggregations of black people in the world. It is high time we practice with serious purpose the politics and economics of equality . . .

It is high time we do this, not just for our own survival but because this nation desperately needs some emerging new moral leadership. Almost daily we are confronted with news of corruption on all levels that suggests America is splitting its moral seams. The most recent and astonishing of these news reports was that involving the transgressions of an institution whose business it is to review and pass judgment on the honesty, integrity and credibility of the rest of us. I speak, of course, of Dun and Bradstreet.

Black people have a history of suffering that should generate a sensitive compassion. They face now the challenge of commitment and service at a time when this nation sorely needs great doses of both. In a few years, several great cities in America will have black populations in such numbers that control of the machinery of government must shift. Competent leadership, instead of demagogues and self-serving hacks, can come from the black community. Effort and energy can be directed toward improving the lot of the group and the community rather than seeking petty privilege. If ever there was a people that by experience and suffering ought to view the use of power with enlightenment, it ought to be those of us in America of African descent. . . .

Freedom of Gay Citizens
from Discrimination

Julia Cooper Mack

(1987)

Our society is built upon a heterosexual model. We are met at the outset with centuries of attitudinal thinking, often colored by sincerely held religious beliefs, that has obscured scientific appraisal and stunted the growth of legal theories protecting homosexual persons from invidious discrimination. We know one basic fact—that homosexual and bisexual citizens have been part of society from time immemorial. These orientations, like that of heterosexuals, have cut across all diverse classifications—race, sex, national origin, and religion, to name but a few. After careful reflection, we cannot conclude that one's sexual orientation is a characteristic reflecting upon individual merit.

Modern research on sexual orientation began with the investigation of Alfred C. Kinsey and his associates into human sexual behavior. From his study of twelve thousand white males, still the largest of its kind, Kinsey reports that only 50% had neither overt nor psychic homosexual experiences after the onset of adolescence.[1] Another 37% had at least some overt homosexual experience to the point of orgasm between adolescence and old age, while the remaining 13% reacted erotically to other males without having physical contacts. Almost half of his sample had both heterosexual and homosexual experiences at some point during their lives.[2] Kinsey's findings challenged the popular assumption that the vast majority of people are either exclusively heterosexual or exclusively homosexual and suggested that instead individual responses and behavior fall somewhere between these extremes for some 46% of the population.[3] While stress-

---

Excerpt from Judge Julia Cooper Mack's majority opinion in Gay Rights Coalition v. Georgetown University, 536 A.2d 1, 33–36 (D.C. App. 1987) (some footnotes omitted).

    1. Alfred C. Kinsey, Wardell B. Pomeroy & Clyde E. Martin, Sexual Behavior in the Human Male 650–51 (Philadelphia, W.B. Saunders 1948).

    2. *Id.*

    3. *Id.*

ing the existence of a continuum, for convenience Kinsey adopted a seven-point scale, with zero denoting the exclusively homosexual and six the exclusively heterosexual.[4] The Kinsey scale continues to be relied upon today. . . . At a minimum, Kinsey's research revealed the complexity and diversity of human sexual orientations and prompted considerable further inquiry.

As yet, there is no scientific agreement as to the origins of heterosexual, bisexual or homosexual orientation. Although various biological, psychoanalytic and social learning theories have been advanced, none has won common acceptance.[5] On the other hand, several popular theories have been disproved.[6] Some researchers posit that sexual orientation may have multiple roots.[7] It is generally agreed, however, that individual sexual orientation develops at least by adolescence.

It was found in one study of almost fifteen hundred heterosexual and homosexual men and women that homosexual adults had typically experienced sexual feelings in that direction about three years before engaging in intimate homosexual activity.[8] There is no reliable evidence that adult homosexual orientation—the attempt is never made in the opposite direction—can be "cured."[9] The Alfred C. Kinsey Institute for Sex Research has concluded from its empirical studies that

> [H]omosexuality is as deeply ingrained as heterosexuality. . . . [E]xclusive homosexuality probably is so deeply ingrained that one should not attempt or expect to change it. Rather, it would probably make far more sense simply to recognize it as a basic component of a person's core identity. . . . Neither homosexuals nor heterosexuals are what they are by design. Homosexuals, in particular, cannot be dismissed as persons who simply refuse to conform. There is no reason to think it would be any easier for homosexual men or women to reverse their sexual orientation than it would be for heterosexual readers to become predominately or exclusively homosexual . . . [10]

Just as it is impossible to typecast heterosexuality oriented persons (or, for that matter, members of racial minorities or women), gay people cannot be neatly

---

4. *Id.* at 636–50.

5. *See generally* JOHN MONEY & ANKE A. EHRHARDT, MAN AND WOMAN, BOY AND GIRL: THE DIFFERENTIATION AND DIMORPHISM OF GENDER IDENTITY FROM CONCEPTION TO MATURITY (Baltimore, John Hopkins University Press 1972) (other citations omitted).

6. ALAN P. BELL, MARTIN S. WEINBERG & SUE K. HAMMERSMITH, SEXUAL PREFERENCE—ITS DEVELOPMENT IN MEN AND WOMEN 210–11 (Bloomington, Indiana University Press 1981).

7. *Id.*

8. SEXUAL PREFERENCE, *supra* note 6, at 187–88.

9. *Id.* at 217.

10. *Id.* at 190, 211, 222.

pigeonholed into any recognizable category. A homosexual orientation tells nothing reliable about abilities or commitments in work, religion, politics, personal and social relationships, or social activities, except to the extent that in many areas the lives of gay people are frequently conditioned by the attitudes of others.[11] It is often forgotten that "homosexuality encompasses far more than people's sexual proclivities. Too often homosexuals have been viewed simply with reference to their sexual interests and activity. Usually the social context and psychological correlates of homosexual experience are largely ignored, making for a highly constricted image of the persons involved . . ."[12]

Despite its irrelevance to individual merit, a homosexual or bisexual orientation invites ongoing prejudice in all walks of life, ranging from employment to education, and for most of which there is currently no judicial remedy outside the District of Columbia or the State of Wisconsin . . .[13]

Such discrimination has persisted throughout most of history. . . .

---

11. Alan Bell & Martin S. Weinberg, Homosexualities—A Study of Diversity among Men and Women 195–216 (New York, Simon and Schuster 1978).

12. *Id.* at 24–25.

13. *See generally* Rhonda R. Rivera, *Queer Law: Sexual Orientation Law in the Mid-Eighties* (Part II), 11 Dayton L. Rev. 275 (1986).

PART 6

Crime and Criminal Justice

The plight of black women incarcerated in the nation's prison system is growing at an alarming rate, especially among black female inmates with children. In 1994, the female inmate population was 64,403 accounting for 6.1 percent of all prisoners in the United States.[1] While not all states have large female inmate populations, enough do to cause persons to inquire about the impact that incarceration has on society, both in and outside prison walls.[2]

The first article in this part is authored by a black female U.S. District Court judge. She brings attention to the plight of young and older women in American prisons and their needs for special attention and particular accommodation. The article is one of the all-too-few expositions on the subject of female inmates written by one of the all-too-few black women sitting on the federal courts.

The second article addresses the concern of a leading civil rights lawyer on the stubborn increase in violent crimes in the black population and the corresponding increase of black citizens in prison, male and female. In 1995, the Department of Justice reported that the number of state and federal prison inmates grew by 89,707 during the twelve months ending the month of June, 1995, the largest one-year

---

1. *See* Allen J. Beck and Darrell K. Gilliard, *Prisoners in 1994*, Bureau of Justice Statistics (DOJ) 5, Aug., 1995.

2. *See* Earl Ofari Hutchinson, *Black Women Overpopulate Jails, Too*, THE HILLTOP, Feb. 23, 1996, at A9. Hutchinson states: "Many children of imprisoned women drift into delinquency, gangs and drug use. This perpetuates the vicious cycle of poverty, crime and violence." *Id. See also* Reginald Stuart, *Behind Bars*, EMERGE 43 (March 1997) (regarding the number of Black women in prisons); Verna M. Keith and Garry L. Rolison, *Race, Gender and the Timing of Justice, in* CEDERIC HERRING, ED., AFRICAN AMERICANS AND THE PUBLIC AGENDA: THE PARADOXES OF PUBLIC POLICY (Thousand Oaks, Sage Publications 1997) (regarding age at first arrest and incarceration of African American women). New issues related to women inmates are being litigated. *Women's Prisons in 2 States Targeted by Federal Lawsuit*, WASHINGTON POST, March 11, 1997, at A5 (Justice Department alleges civil rights abuses).

population increase in history. In mid-1995, state prisons had an inmate population of 1,004,608 and federal prisons held 99,466. The proportion of black females incarcerated was eight times that of white women; 6.8 percent of all black male adults were either in jail or prison compared to less than 1 percent of white male adults.[3]

Statistics such as these and the public response that more prisons and incarceration of black people is the solution to the crime problem prompt the second author in this part to conclude that the nation's response to violent crime and drug policies is conceived out of fear and politics. She warns that the nation's policy of constructing more prisons as the solution to a societal problem of poverty and diminishing opportunity will soon confront and haunt it.

---

3. *Prisoners in 1994, supra,* note 1.

The Female Inmate

Consuelo Bland Marshall

(1993)

I THOUGHT IT MIGHT BE INTERESTING for you to know more about the person that we're talking about, this female inmate. She is normally a single parent. She lived alone with one to three children before she went into the institution. She comes from a single-parent home, or a broken home. She is generally a runaway, or was a runaway in her teenage years. She is generally the victim of sexual abuse.[1] She has alcohol and drug history, prior arrests and convictions; she is a high school dropout. Her previous work experience was in sales, services, or clerical work, and her earnings were between $3.36 to $6.50 per hour.

In the federal system, not every state has an institution. This is one of the reasons . . . for the very serious problems faced by the institutionalized woman who has children. Many of these women are placed long distances from their home. Their families do not visit them, for economic reasons—they just don't have the money for transportation. Some of the facilities are located in very remote areas, like one of the female facilities in West Virginia, Alderson, a female camp. I spoke with one of the former wardens of that facility, and I think it was the first time that I gave much thought to the difference between the woman in prison and the man in prison, in terms of what life is like. The warden explained that most of these women have children that they leave behind when they go to prison and . . . it is not the male in her life that takes care of the children; it is her mother, her sisters, the other female supporters in her life. Because those people are caring for her children, they're not able to come visit her, so the female inmate does not get as many visits as the male inmate. Some authors have suggested that when the male goes to prison, he just loses his freedom, but when

Symposium on Women and the Law, 20 PEPPERDINE LAW REVIEW 1197 (1993).

1. *See, e.g.,* Steven A. Holmes, *With More Women in Prison, Sexual Abuse by Guards Becomes a Troubling Trend,* N.Y. TIMES, Dec. 27, 1996.

a female goes to prison, she loses not only her freedom, but her family . . . What is typically said is that the male who goes to prison still has the female support-ing him. She visits him, she often moves to a location closer to the prison facil-ity so that she and children can visit with him. When a female goes to prison, the male in her life often is no longer in her life. He does not visit her and does not continue to support her. Therefore, one of the problems obviously is loca-tion of the facility and the inability for visitation.

Some facilities house both males and females. One such facility is the Met-ropolitan Correctional Center in New York. Males have the privilege of leaving their units with passes, or reporting to a daily work detail, while females must be escorted and their movement is limited. Males can be transferred to another facility, such as Otisville in New York, which, as prisons go, is a very nice-look-ing place. The woman often has no other place to be transferred, so she stays in that facility until she is sentenced. The result of this is greater restlessness, agi-tation, and depression. The woman lives an average of 160 miles away from her family, so that presents the transportation problem that I addressed. Also, fe-males often complain about lack of supplies in the institution. They never have enough underwear; uniforms do not fit properly. The same uniform is given to a pregnant female that is given to a non-pregnant female. If you visited the courtroom you'd see that this woman must be uncomfortable because her body is in a dress that is simply too small. The commissary doesn't sell specific female items, and child care is a problem . . . Staff members who have worked in insti-tutions with females said it takes about five to ten minutes to handle the prob-lem of a male inmate, and thirty to forty minutes to work out a problem for a female inmate, just because of the nature of the problem. Medical complaints, of course, are different from the medical complaints of men. The prisons are be-ginning to try to staff them so that women are provided with better prenatal care and receiving the medical care they need, but that's been a problem for a long time.

The pregnant female is a serious problem in an institutional setting. The question is not only what happens to those children she left in the community, but what happens to the infant born while she is in prison? There is not a large number of these women, but it is large enough to cause concern and to cause us to examine what should we do with that female and the baby born when she is in custody.

On my calendar recently I had a brother and sister from Ghana, Africa, who were caught carrying drugs into this country. The woman left two children in Ghana and was pregnant when she left there. She entered our facility two months pregnant in May 1992 and we just tried her case about two weeks ago. The jury found her not guilty. Frankly, I was very happy because I was very re-lieved. She would have faced a ten-year mandatory minimum sentence, and I don't think there would have been any basis for departing. I saw it as at least a ten-year sentence for her. The quantity of drugs was large; there was no question. Her defense? Knowledge. She said that she did not know that the drugs were in the suitcase she was carrying. They were concealed behind a lining and customs discovered them. When I called our facility to find out what happened to the woman, where she had delivered her child, I was told—and this is typical of what I've heard from wardens—that the woman stayed in the institution until she was ready to deliver. The female inmate in labor goes to the contract facility for twenty-four-hour period. If she has medical problems she might stay in the hospital a bit longer. Generally, arrangements have already been made for the care of her child. If she has family in the area, the child will go to them, or social services intervention and the child is placed, or the child might be given up for adoption if that's what the woman decides. She now has a child who is a United States citizen. I don't have a background in immigration law, but on my staff we were all discussing what happens to the child if the woman is deported and returns to her country. Would the child be left here, would the child be taken back to Africa? Since that child was born in the United States, is it easy for that child to just come back to this country at a later time in the child's life? I was told by those who have immigration knowledge that if a child like this goes with his mother to Africa and grows up there, that child must reapply for citizenship. He does not automatically retain U.S. citizenship.

Let's return to the story of the woman herself. After giving birth, she returns to the Metropolitan detention facility to await trial. Since she was found not guilty, she is now facing the deportation process. That's another interesting question for those of you taking immigration law; this is something that should really be examined closer. It is not uncommon for us to receive writs of habeas corpus from inmates asking us to order immigration officials to start the deportation process before these people complete their sentences. What generally happens is that the process is not started, and those inmates who have to serve sentences complete those sentences, and then immigration begins deportation. I spoke to a warden at Lexington, one of the female institutions, and she said that they normally keep the women there for another month just waiting for the immigration process to commence so that they can then place her someplace else. Apparently no federal facility exists for the detainment of these persons who have been held in federal prisons and are now going through the immigration process. I asked someone on my staff to find out what happened to this woman who was found not guilty. She is still in the community . . . She . . . will now be detained until the deportation process can be completed and then eventually—I am told the process will take four to six months—I am sure she will voluntarily deport . . .

The other woman in prison that we are concerned about is the older female offender. You might ask, "How old is 'older'?" I have to smile because she's defined as a woman who is fifty-five or older, "elder" is defined as sixty-five or older, and "aged" is seventy-five to eighty-five. There are women this old in institutions.

The older woman says that she is concerned about younger women inmates rushing through the hallways that might knock her down and cause her to hurt herself or break a bone. She is confused by the noise and all the instructions she receives. She is humiliated by strip searches. She is also concerned about the sores that she receives from having to sleep on a thin prison mattress. She doesn't understand the reprimands she is receiving. She worries most about dying in a friendless place.

The older woman in the institution of course has many other medical problems: menopause, breast cancer, osteoporosis; she needs intervention. There are also terminally ill people in institutions. Many hospice workers volunteer to help these women who are terminally ill. You might think that these are people we wouldn't send to prison, but sometimes with the Sentencing Guidelines we're not able to exercise that discretion. Judges have lost that discretion with these Guidelines; therefore, these people are still being institutionalized.

A very large number of inmates are HIV-positive . . . According to the study based on the testing of nearly 11,000 inmates entering ten prisons' hospitals between 1988 and mid-1989, the study found that 2.1 to 7.6 percent of male inmates were infected, and 2.5 to 14.7 percent of females were infected. At nine of the ten correctional facilities, women had higher rates of HIV infection than men; the difference was greatest among prisoners under twenty-five years of age, with 5.2 percent of women in that age group testing positively, compared with 2.3 percent of men. Minority groups also ranked higher: 4.8 percent overall, compared with 2.5 percent of white inmates. In April of 1992, twelve percent of the HIV-positive inmates in the Federal Bureau of Prisons were women. However, the rate of infection among women was higher: 1.52 percent versus .9 percent for males.

I don't want to leave you feeling too discouraged . . . [T]here are places in the world, other countries, specifically, that have decided that the answer to the problem of the woman who is pregnant when she enters prison, or the woman who has young children, is to allow the child to stay in the institution with the woman. This is quite a controversial subject. Canada has a task force recommending that such a woman be permitted to keep her baby in the institution at least until age two. There was a time in this country, at Alderson, that women gave birth at the institution and kept their children. Around the 1960s, social workers decided that prison was no place for children and they tried to come up with another solution. California, New York, and a few other states have adopted legislation that permits the woman who is pregnant when she enters an institution to actually go to a community facility if her sentence is six years or less. She will then serve her sentence in the community; her children are able to join her there. They do require that these women participate in parenting skills programs and educational programs that benefit them once they serve their sentences. This is certainly one solution.

It seems to me that it costs less for us to have the woman in a community placement or facility with her children, rather than to have the children cared for by someone else, with social welfare probably paying that cost. It not only solves some of the problems of placement, but it also helps with the bonding and the relationship between the woman and her child.

Our Present Violent Crime and Drug
Policies Conceived out of Fear
and Politics

ELAINE RUTH JONES

(1994)

*I*AM VERY GRATEFUL FOR THE opportunity to testify today concerning two matters of great concern to the country: how should we reduce violence and violent crime while also restoring fairness to the criminal justice system.

During the past decade, Congress has enacted a series of increasingly "tough" crime bills. This legislation, similar to that enacted in some states, has brought us, *inter alia,* guideline sentencing, mandatory minimum sentencing for a significant number of nonviolent offenses and a renewed federal death penalty. It has also sanctioned, and even encouraged, the so-called "war on drugs."

Despite these efforts, the only certain result thus far is the unprecedented explosion in the prison population. With no close competitor in sight, we have by far the highest incarceration rates and corrections budgets in the free world. Moreover, enormous problems confront us still. While the rate for some nonviolent crimes has leveled off, the rate for violent crimes has stubbornly increased. It is these crimes that frighten Americans most and which have the most destructive impact in the poorer and minority communities . . .

At present, many of our fellow citizens live lives governed increasingly by the fear of being victimized by violent crime. Evening trips to the mall are decreasing; more are now made in the daylight hours. Jogging alone in the nearby park is out; running is increasingly a group activity. And these reports come from suburban communities least affected by crime.

In any isolated and impoverished urban neighborhoods, fear of being the next victim of a violent crime is a frightening constant, and increases every time anyone—young or old—leaves their home. Like the children of Sarajevo, our

---

Statement submitted to the Subcommittee on Crime and Criminal Justice of the Committee on the Judiciary, U.S. House of Representatives on H.R. 3315 (1994).

inner city youth must take "safe" routes, pass through metal detectors and walk by armed security staff to arrive at their classrooms unharmed. Some churches have moved evening services to afternoon hours so that worshipers can attend and return home before dark.

Just as more and more citizens have come to perceive our country as a far more dangerous place than a decade ago, our public debate over what to do about crime has itself become dominated by fear. Legislative debates of recent time have been highly politicized, as each party has jockeyed to claim the high ground as being the "toughest" on crime. Instead of enlivened, informed, searching discussion, our dialogue on this stubbornly complex issue has descended into a cyclical monotonous clamor of competing simplistic soundbites. Former Deputy Attorney General Philip B. Heymann's recent candid remark that "this whole area is so much a matter of political debate that there is no room for reasoned debate" is right on the mark.[1]

It is no wonder then that policies forged from political heat rather than good common sense have delivered so few positive returns. Indeed, it is becoming increasingly clear that not only are our present "get tough" policies having little ameliorative effect upon the crime that concerns us most, they are extorting an enormous and increasing share from state and federal treasuries.

While those concerns should be sufficiently troubling to warrant a change in direction, we know of yet another consequence. Some of the more punitive measures—for example, mandatory minimum sentencing and the "war on drugs"—are themselves harming many minority communities with their large scale removal and incarceration of nonviolent offenders. A brief review of one such policy—the "war on drugs"—shows that this punitive tool has done little to remove drugs from the community, and has been levied almost exclusively at communities of color . . .

When the "war on drugs" was conceived, government data showed that the overwhelming number of persons who consumed illegal drugs in this country were white. In 1989, former Drug Czar William Bennett described the typical cocaine user as "white, male, high school graduate, employed full time and living in a small metropolitan area or suburb."[2] A survey conducted by the Parents Resource Institute for Drug Education, Inc., that same year found that "white high school seniors are more apt to use cocaine than black seniors."[3] Another survey, conducted by the National Institute on Drug Abuse, found that blacks made up "about 12 percent of the people who use drugs regularly, and about 16 percent

---

1. David Johnson, *Ex Official Attacks Crime Bill Backed by Clinton*, N.Y. TIMES, Feb. 16, 1994, at A-16.

2. Sam Meddis, *Whites, Not Blacks, At the Core of the Drug Crisis*, USA TODAY, Dec. 20, 1989, at 11A.

3. *Id.*

of people who use cocaine regularly."[4] These data accordingly debunk the widely held perception that drugs are primarily a minority community problem, and support law enforcement experts like current Police Foundation director Hubert Williams, who assert that it is "ludicrous . . . to think of this problem as a minority problem, as a black problem. . . ."[5]

Because drug abuse is centered largely in the white community, it is not surprising that "from 1968 to 1981, the per capita arrest rate for black juveniles lagged behind that of whites for drug violations, according to FBI statistics."[6] In the mid-1980's, however, with the advent of the drug war, the arrest rates changed dramatically.

> In 1985, the numbers just exploded: arrests of black youths for drug-related offenses skyrocketed. Paradoxically, white youth arrest rates during the same period fell significantly—22%—even though federal agencies reported that the drug use rate by white teenagers was actually higher than for black youths.[7]

Dramatic changes in arrest rates were seen throughout the country. In Baltimore, while 15 white juveniles and 86 African American juveniles had been arrested in 1981 for selling drugs, in 1991, two less whites were arrested while 1,304 blacks were arrested.[8] Indeed, for adults in Baltimore, "of the 12,956 arrests for 'drug abuse violations' in 1991, 11,107 (86%) were African Americans."[9]

> In Columbus, Ohio, where African American males make up only 8% of the population, they comprised almost 90% of the drug arrests. In Jacksonville, Florida, 87% of those arrested on drug charges were African American males even though they made up only 12% of the county's population. In New York, 92% of the drug arrests were of African Americans and Hispanics. These patterns were repeated across the nation and were soon reflected in incarceration rates.[10]

Media examination of the impact of the "war on drugs" has confirmed these observations. "The typical target of that enduring drug war symbol—the

---

4. *Id.*

5. *Id.*

6. Ron Harris, *Hand of Punishment Falls Heavily on Black Youths*, LA TIMES, Aug. 24, 1993, at 7.

7. *Id.*

8. Jerome G. Miller, *Search and Destroy: The Plight of African American Males in the Criminal Justice System*, Sept., 1992, at 23 (National Center on Institutions and Alternatives) (hereinafter *Search and Destroy*).

9. *Id.* at 14.

10. *Id.*

kick-down-the-door drug raid—is a Black or Hispanic male. Yet the government's own figures show that three times as many whites are regular buyers and users of drugs."[11] In Philadelphia, 93% of those prosecuted on drug offenses in 1990 were minorities; that city is 54% white. In Atlanta, 94% of those charged with possession to distribute illegal drugs in 1990 were African American; nearly half of Fulton County, where Atlanta is located, is white.[12] In Sacramento, while African Americans comprise only 12.9% of the population, they made up nearly 70% of those convicted of the most common drug felonies in 1989.[13]

Largely because of the war on drugs, "the color of teenagers kept in locked detention centers across the country [has grown] decidedly darker."[14] Eight years ago, more [incarcerated juveniles nationwide] were white. Now, most are black . . ."[15] Indeed "a one day survey in Georgia found that every juvenile (110) detained in the Youth Development Center for drug offenses was black . . ."[16]

The impact of the "war on drugs" becomes even more alarming when placed in the context of history and as we look toward the future. At the height of the Jim Crow era, African American males comprised only 5% of the general population but an alarming 21% of the prison population. Those were the good old days. In 1991, while black males had inched up to 6% of the nation's population, they comprised almost half (49%) of the prison population.[17] This extraordinary incarceration rate for African Americans in the United States is four times higher than for blacks in South Africa.[18]

Compelling evidence strongly suggests that unless we move away from the policies of today, these numbers will continue to grow. A 1992 survey of African American males aged 15–35 in Washington, D.C., showed that while 42% were presently under the supervision of the criminal justice system on any given day, the lifetime risk rose to between 80% and 90%.[19] Similar results are projected for African American males in Baltimore, Jacksonville and elsewhere.[20] These numbers alarm even "get tough" prison officials. Recently, a Georgia corrections

---

11. David Zucchino, *Racial Imbalance Seen in War on Drugs,* PHIL. INQUIRER, Nov. 1, 1992, at A1.

12. Trisha Rinaud, *Drug Sentencing Law Comes Under Attack,* FULTON COUNTY DAILY REPORT, Nov. 27, 1991, at 1.

13. Michael Wagner et al., *Most Drug Abusers Are White—But Blacks Fill Jail Cells Here,* SACRAMENTO BEE, Dec. 10, 1990, at 1.

14. *Search and Destroy, supra* note 8, at 23.

15. Harris, *supra* note 6.

16. *Study: All Drug Offenders in YDC's are Black,* MILLEDGEVILLE UNION RECORDER, June 22, 1990, at 1.

17. *Search and Destroy, supra* note 8, at 6.

18. Marc Mauer, *Americans Behind Bars: A Comparison of International Rates of Incarceration, The Sentencing Project,* January, 1991, at 3 ("Black males in the United States are incarcerated at a rate of four times that of Black males in South Africa, 3,109 per 100,000 to 729 per 100,000").

19. *Search and Destroy, supra* note 8, at 4.

20. *Id.*

spokesman expressed candid and grave concern that the state's "lock-em-up" policies of the past decade—resulting in the prison population changing from less than 40% to nearly 70% black—were a subtle form of genocide. He wrote:

> As you walk through our prisons, it is frightfully apparent that there is a crisis of immeasurable magnitude occurring in our black community. If not reversed, it is a tragedy that will reach Holocaust proportions.[21]

While there are considerable problems in inner-city communities of color, the real tragedy is that our current urban and crime policies fail to address them. If we have learned anything from the past ten years, it is that Americans will not become more secure as long as we ignore social problems that foster violent crime. Still longer prison sentences and more prison beds will not reclaim our communities.

We can wait no longer to take steps aimed at reducing the level of crime, particularly violent crime, while at the same time insuring that our prison beds—precious resources[22]—are occupied not by every three-time loser or failed two-bit drug user, but by those who harm us the most . . .

The time has come for us to rise above the fear of seeming "soft" on crime and to search honestly for solutions that lessen crime.

---

21. Andy Bowen, *Faces of Criminals: Society Must Solve Prison Overcrowding,* ATLANTA CONSTITUTION/JOURNAL, Dec. 10, 1991, at 23.

22. Prison space does not come cheaply. The average annual cost is $23,000 per inmate. The average cost per bed in maximum security is three times as great. Ann Blackman et al., *Lock Them Up and Throw Away the Key,* TIME, Feb. 7, 1994, at 56.

PART 7

International Concerns

In 1957, Jeane L. Noble, who is not a lawyer, issued a study on "Negro Women To-day and Their Education."[1] In her study, Noble concludes that black women have been shortchanged for international understanding and cooperation. International studies was identified "as one of the least important values to get out of college and over 52 percent of [black female graduates] felt their colleges had no particular effect or a negative effect on their education in this area."[2]

In this part, three of the five black women lawyers (Barbara Mae Watson, Edith Spurlock Sampson, and Goler Teal Butcher) are acknowledged experts in international law and policy.[3] The other two lawyers (Arnette R. Hubbard and Althea T. L. Simmons), acknowledged bar leaders and civil rights advocates, apply their expertise in international concerns on civil and human rights.

The first two articles, by Watson, and the third article, by Sampson, are historically important because they are statements reportedly by the first black women in the history of the country to serve in high posts at the Department of State.[4] The Sampson article is rare because it is one of the few documents published by the first black woman to serve as a U.S. representative to the United Nations.[5] The state-

---

1. Jeane L. Noble, *Negro Women Today and Their Education*, 26 J. NEGRO ED. 15, 19 (1957).

2. *Id.*

3. *See, e.g.*, J. Clay Smith Jr., *The Foreign Policy of Goler Teal Butcher*, 37 How. L.J. 139 (1994); HANES WALTON JR., BLACK WOMEN AT THE UNITED NATIONS: THE POLITICS, A THEORETICAL MODEL, AND DOCUMENTS 12, Tab. 1 (San Bernardino, The Borgo Press 1995) (listing black women at the United Nations—1950–1990) (regarding Sampson). *Id.* at 24 (Tab. 2).

4. The groundbreaking roles that these and other black women have played in the history of the nation's foreign policy must be credited for laying the foundation for the naming of Madeleine K. Albright as the first woman Secretary of State. *See* Alison Mitchell, *Albright to Head State Dept.; Republican in Top Defense Job*, N.Y. TIMES, Dec. 6, 1996, at 1; Michael Dobbs and John M. Goshko, *Albright's Personal Odyssey Shaped Foreign Policy Beliefs*, WASH. POST, Dec. 6, 1996, at A25.

5. In 1947, black women lawyers such as Eunice Hunton Carter and H. Elsie Austin served as

ment of the third author (Hubbard) has dual importance because it is the first public statement by the first woman president of the National Bar Association.

The last two statements by Butcher and Simmons make strong appeals for the inclusion of more minority women in international law and against racial discrimination toward the Buraku people in Japan, respectively.

---

delegates of the National Council of Negro Women to the first General Conference of International Organizations called by the United Nations. Elsie Austin, *Emphasis on United Nations*, AFRAAMER-ICAN WOMEN'S J. 12 (Summer/Fall 1947).

Pioneer at the Department of State

Barbara Mae Watson

(1968)

*I*T WAS NOT UNTIL 1968, nearly 180 years after the establishment of the United States Department of State in 1789, that the first woman to be appointed with the rank of assistant secretary of state was sworn in. I was that woman.[1] The secretary of state, Dean Rusk (a former Rhodes scholar), noted on that occasion that some changes would have to be made. The statute which created this post specifically described the duties as calling for performance by a male person. "He" shall do thus and so. It perhaps stemmed from the days of Thomas Jefferson, our first secretary of state, who later became president. He said: "The appointment of a woman to office is an innovation for which the public is not prepared and neither am I." Secretary Rusk sought advice from Webster's Dictionary and found that, among other things, a "He" is a person whose sex is immaterial. The federal statutes were no more help. They said that the masculine gender shall include the feminine and the neuter. Secretary Rusk then announced firmly that such an appointment was one for which not only he was ready but, more importantly, so was the president.

If this unprecedented development might be endowed with greater significance, it would derive from that fact that I am also black. It was thus in its terms a dual achievement. Yet the fact is both sad and deplorable that we were obliged

---

"Female Liberation and Human Survival," before World Convention Speech, Eminent Women International Women's Year, Grahamstown, South Africa, December 2, 1975.

1. Barbara Mae Watson's confirmation hearings indicate that she was nominated to be Administrator, Bureau of Security and Consular Affairs, at the Department of State. This record is silent on the rank of the Administrator. Transcript of Hearings before the Committee on Foreign Relations, U.S. Senate, 89th Cong., 2d Sess. 1–10 (1968). However, at the Department of State, Consular Affairs officers held the rank of Assistant Secretary of State. *See* Principal Officers of the Department of State and the United States Chiefs of Mission, 1778–1988, at 11 (listing Watson as Assistant Secretary of State, Aug. 12, 1968).

to celebrate as a triumph what should otherwise have been an unremarked incident. On the contrary, however, the traditional relationships between men and women in our world culture dictated a certain sensationalism. Indeed, the presence of women in the Department of State at all was remarkable only for the fact that as a rule they occupied positions of little consequence. Was it that they had been proven incompetent, because of their sex, to hold superior posts in the department? The obvious answer is that they had never been afforded an opportunity to demonstrate whether this might be so or not. We were simply excluded more or less as a whole. There is, in fact, abundant historical evidence that, if anything, the position of women has declined in the circumstances of the modern world by comparison, for example, with the prerogatives enjoyed by the women of Sparta in the ancient Greek civilization.

My position in the Department of State offered me a stimulating intellectual challenge which required me to deal with the entrenched male bureaucracy as well as with members of Congress in the course of congressional hearings. That august legislative body was predominantly male whose traditions have been constricted according to social forms, from which women, by definition, were excluded. The challenge was an educational one and I am happy to say I survived and, with all due modesty, succeeded in some degree in raising the somewhat restricted view of the male insofar as female competence is concerned. . . .

Human Rights and Social Relations

Barbara Mae Watson

(1968)

TWENTY YEARS AGO, ON December 10, 1948, the United Nations General Assembly, meeting in Paris, adopted the Universal Declaration of Human Rights. The adoption of the Universal Declaration, by a unanimous vote, with eight abstentions, was a landmark in mankind's progress toward freedom. This was the first time in history that the world community had agreed upon a statement of goals and standards concerning human rights. That document reflects the best in the American tradition.

The essence of the Universal Declaration is contained in its first article: "All human beings are born free and equal in dignity and rights." Thus, for the first time the principle of human equality—defined by philosophers, preached by religious leaders, acknowledged by statesmen—was defined in detail in an international document.

What are these human rights? The United Nations defines human rights as " . . . those rights which everyone is entitled to enjoy by virtue of the fact that he or she is a human being . . . Nothing alters the existence of human rights, or causes them to disappear. Because all human beings are born equal in dignity, the rights of each are precisely equal. Therefore no State, institution, group, or individual shall make any discrimination whatsoever in matters of human rights on the ground of race, color, sex, language, religion, political or other opinion, national or social origin, property, birth, or the status of the country or territory to which a human being belongs."

We have now before us this international proclamation. But what does it mean to you and me and each person in the world, this country, our community in practical terms? It has to do with the very essence of our everyday lives. That is, our social relationships with one another.

Speech to an unidentified group, November 26, 1968. The author made this speech in her capacity as Assistant Secretary of State, Administrator, Bureau of Security and Consular Affairs, Department of State.

Surely our material well-being is of great importance. Today we live in an age of dizzying economic and technological progress. Scientific accomplishments which have been realized in recent years are fantastic to contemplate. Our own parents can recall a day when speed was something with two wheels. Scientific development means a great deal to our well-being and progress.

However, we know that real happiness is not determined by the size of one's house, the fineness of one's clothes, or the status of one's neighborhood. The level of happiness and joy of all of us is dependent upon our relationships with one another. Our lives are full and rich only when our relationships with other people reflect goodwill, mutual respect, and love. When these are lacking—however satisfactory our economic position may be—there is friction, discord, and unhappiness.

This is a time of unparalleled social ferment in this country and, in fact, all over the world. It is a time of social revolution. At the core of all this ferment, as we well know, is the problem of racial disharmony. The struggle of the black American to achieve his full rights as a human being and as an American is more strenuous and more widespread than ever heretofore. All of you, all of us here, all Americans—black or white—will be and are being drawn into this social struggle in some fashion. None of us can entirely escape its demands. We can see that all the world too will suffer or gain according to the success we have in eliminating the flaw of racial discord from our society.

I do not suggest here that because tension and strife are today at a higher pitch that race relations have deteriorated. This is not the case. In a sense it is *because* race relations are getting better. The pressures and tensions of today—the marches, the sit-ins—are evidence that however bad race relations may be, they have at least improved and progressed to the point where there is an exchange of ideas.

I have no doubt that our country will prove that it has the greatness to solve the injustice of this great social problem.

In his opening address, Mr. Roy Wilkins, chairman of the United States delegation to the International Conference on Human Rights at Tehran,[1] described with the utmost frankness what he called "the tortuous path by which the United States has corrected its past myopia about human rights, often by pain and once by a Civil War." He concluded his description of the "tortuous path" with these moving words:

"There is not the slightest doubt in my mind about my country's glittering future for all Americans—black men and white, Indians, Protestants, Catholics, Jews, and nonbelievers. Such a statement is justified by the confidence that the President of the Nation, its court system, and belatedly its National Legislature, are fully committed toward this ideal—and the country will surely follow."

---

1. Wilkins was also the Executive Director of the NAACP.

Citation for Persons Killed in Service
of the United Nations

Edith Spurlock Sampson

(1952)

*I*T IS WITH REVERENCE that I speak now, on behalf of the United States, supporting the resolution presented to this Assembly by the delegation of France. It is indeed fitting that tribute to those who have died for the United Nations should be proposed by the great French Republic, whose traditions of liberty and human progress are renowned throughout the world.

The resolution now before us would confer a mark of honor on those who have lost their lives in the cause of the United Nations and in the cause of peace. In thinking of this proposal, our minds and hearts turn to Korea. It was there that the United Nations met the challenge of aggression, in the first collective action in history by an international organization.

The Republic of Korea is the child of the United Nations. This organization gave it life. When that Republic was wantonly attacked by Communist forces, bent on crushing out the beginnings of liberty with the iron heel of totalitarianism, the United Nations had to make a decision. Would it resist? Or would it yield to the plans of those who had calculated on easy conquest?

The answer has been impressive. Fifty-three states joined in the decision to defend the Republic of Korea. Under resolutions of the Security Council and the General Assembly, 16 members of the United Nations have sent units of their armed forces to repel the attack in Korea. The aggression was turned back, and it has been made clear to the aggressors "that armed force shall not be used, save in the common interest."

The cost has been heavy. In adopting the resolution proposed by the delegation of France, we do not wipe out the debt owed to those who have sacrificed their lives that there may be peace in the world. We only acknowledge the debt.

---

27 U.S. State Department Bull. 997 (Dec. 22, 1952). In 1952, Edith Spurlock Sampson was serving her second term as an alternate U.S. Representative to the General Assembly of the United Nations.

We need to do more. In defining that "something more," I can think of no better words than those of the great American President who spoke in the midst of our own Civil War.

He, too, wished to honor men who had given their lives. And he wished to tell his countrymen how they, the living, could begin to pay their debt to these men. "It is," he said, "rather for us to be here dedicated to the great task remaining before us—that from these honored dead we take increased devotion to the cause for which they gave the last full measure of devotion—that we here highly resolve that these dead shall not have died in vain."

For the General Assembly, this should be a day of rededication to the ideals set down in the Charter of the United Nations. With the will to accomplish, the nations can move forward in the achievement of the Charter goals. As peoples gain confidence in collective security for attaining world peace, the human energies of all nations can be directed ever increasingly to the realization of man's creative possibilities.

Speaking Out against Duplicity
in Foreign Policy

ARNETTE RHINEHART HUBBARD

(1981)

BEING THE FIRST WOMAN President of the National Bar Association, to be sure, is an awesome responsibility which has, in my first month in office, taken its toll on me.[1] Nevertheless, it is a job which is rewarding and which poses daily challenges not only nationally but internationally.

Our plight, as a people and as Black lawyers, is inextricably tied to Black people around the world. When one considers the history of racism in this country, the recent veto by the U.S. of the United Nations' resolution condemning South Africa's invasion of Angola was predictable.

South Africa is a nation of $27\frac{1}{2}$ million people. For over 30 years, the majority population of 22 million Blacks have been forced to inhabit only 13 percent of the country's land—remote infertile wastelands—designated, ironically, as homelands. According to Dr. Margaret Nash, an Anglican Church worker, the mass relocation of Black South Africans to tribal reserves "is a system of deliberate impoverishment which generates wealth for the employer group and assures the permanent servitude and sanctions debilitation of the black community. For the five years that the Sullivan Principles have been in effect, they have made no differences in Apartheid or in the lives of the black masses."[2]

In our testimony before the House subcommittee on Africa in May of 1980, the NBA emphasized that only economic sanctions, not the Sullivan Principles, can bring about change in South Africa. We called upon the United States to introduce a resolution in the United Nations imposing economic sanctions against South Africa.

---

13 THE NATIONAL BAR BULLETIN 2 (Sept.–Nov., 1981).

1. Ms. Hubbard became president of the National Bar Association in August, 1981, its first woman president since the founding of NBA in 1925.

2. *See* David Beaty & Drew Harari, *South Africa: White Managers, Black Voices,* 65 HARV. BUS. REV. 98 (July–Aug., 1987) (contains outline of Sullivan Principles which outline fair employment practice and guidelines to seeking political changes in South Africa).

Needless to say, nothing was done. But when Russia invaded Afghanistan, the U.S. was furious and led the international fight condemning Russia's invasion. Yet, a few months ago, when South Africa illegally invaded Angola (a Black nation), the U.S. became the only nation in the world to veto a simple resolution in the United Nations condemning this action. The United States' concern for human rights and its policy against international terrorism seem to disappear when a black nation's rights or black people's rights are at stake. Despite uncontradicted evidence that South Africa is the world's most racist and terrorist government, the United States continues to provide economic (17% of the foreign investment in South Africa comes from the U.S.) and political comfort to that disgraceful government. We can not remain silent while this obvious duplicity in foreign policy is being employed against Black people.

As Black lawyers, it is our responsibility to point out contradictions in American policy regardless of whether they involve domestic or foreign affairs. As long as the U.S. remains in bed with South Africa giving warmth and protection to apartheid, freedom and equality for Blacks in America will continue to be a dream rather than a reality. For we are perceived no differently than our Black sisters and brothers in Africa.

Let me assure each of you, that during my tenure as President of this great organization, the voices of black lawyers will ring throughout the nation and the world on all matters impacting Black people. As we travel through the year, we will examine the immigration policy that the Administration has instituted against Haitians. We will scrutinize the Attorney General's Task Force on violent crime recommendations, and we will examine other matters that are crushing our souls right here within the borders of America.

Our voices will be heard, and they will make a difference.

Women and Minorities
in International Law

GOLER TEAL BUTCHER

(1987)

$\mathcal{F}$IRST, A MAJOR FOCUS OF THIS project is on substantive concerns arising out of the exclusion and underrepresentation of women and minorities in the variety of professional international law institutions. Second, the study looks both to the meaning women and minorities give as to their exclusion or under-representation and to the significance or meaning of this exclusion and under-representation to the development of international law itself and to international legal institutions. We will assess the meaning, under international law, of the concept of underrepresentation. Furthermore, we will consider the meaning of equitable representation of women and minorities in international legal institutions and the international law process.

In analogy to a court case, there first must be a focus on preliminary or threshold issues. Without addressing these, we do not get into the merits of the substantive issues, or we do so in a limited framework. We must get the facts, insofar as possible, on what is the present picture of representation of women and minorities in international law, and their entry and experiences. In so doing, we must look at common experiences and problems and then focus on each group. So, we start off by looking at statistics on representation of women and minorities in international law . . .

At what levels do you find women and minorities? . . . [I]n what kind of jobs do you find women and minorities? For example, if we look at the Legal Adviser's Office (in the Department of State) and the attorney advisers in the geographical offices where they work on different issues, on particular foreign policy problems, are these women in offices that do not concentrate on foreign

PROCEEDINGS OF THE AMERICAN SOCIETY OF INTERNATIONAL LAW 520–21, 523–24, 528–29, 532, 540 (1987).

policy issues? It's critical if we are to understand what the facts are as to under-representation and their meaning . . .

While I appreciate the value of numbers, I am impatient with them. I studied international law in 1958, during that time and since my experiences tell me there is significant underrepresentation and exclusion, and we must look at it in terms of those in international law and those who wanted to get in but could not. To what extent does underrepresentation relate to nonprofessional factors? Based on my experience, when women and minorities come in it is not just professional concerns that provide the basis for the hiring decision . . .

I worked in international law for more than 10 years before I started working on African affairs. I think it is important that we look at blacks in the whole area of international law . . . With respect to the question of whether or not minority women are included, the answer is not at all, and yet we do have definite problems as women. When I first worked in the State Department, I had tremendous difficulty getting to see my clients because the secretaries were primed not to allow a woman to see the male Foreign Service officers. So we do have problems as women, and when women's problems are addressed, we as black women have to be included . . . This project, however, should look at women across the board. Not surprisingly, there is amazing insularity. We get so preoccupied in focusing on our own problems that although we have these problems, because we as a group are segmented, we tend to segment ourselves as well.

My observation has been that the most exclusive area in international law is human rights and yet the observation of white women is that it is not. We can testify, however, to the fact that it has been primarily minorities, and minority women, who have blazed the trail for human rights and human rights litigation in U.S. courts. We did it for a decade before others, although I am aware that absolutes are wrong for the most part. But blacks in this country did, to a significant extent, propel the human rights movement. What is astonishing, however, in spite of the great interest of black women with regard to the human rights field, is the absence of black women on various panels concerning human rights and international law within the Society. We therefore do have problems, and I hope that they will be considered seriously . . .

It has been my experience that women are much more prone to speak out than are men. We need to look at the impact of women and minorities on the willingness of international lawyers to confront the intersection of existing international law norms and human values, human needs as indicated in evolving norms. How will women and minorities affect this by calling for decisions that reflect what the law should be if it is to reflect principles of justice and equity? What would be the impact on the need for prioritization of certain critical issues in international law (e.g., the law of war and of individual responsibility)? What would be the impact on the critical issues of underdevelopment and poverty? How will women and minorities broaden our understanding of new approaches to the issue of whether foreign policies are or should be influenced by international law? How would women and minorities broaden our understanding of the impact of particular norms of international law on peoples and countries throughout the world, particularly the non-European countries, which form the majority of the world? How would women and minorities affect our perspectives of international law as an ever-evolving process by broadening our perspectives on international legal issues and thus enabling us to reflect a greater understanding of public and private international law and lessen the tendency toward paralysis in the international law development process?

We are most fortunate in our country. This is a pluralistic society with people of all countries and all cultures, and it would be, and it is, a tremendous loss to our country that we do not take advantage of this treasure that we have. Today, in a multiethnic domestic society and a truly global international community, the input of the international law issues to all facets of our country is critical to a better comprehension of what is referred to as the changing realities of modern international life and therefore, to the possibility of an increased measure of wisdom in our quest to secure the underpinnings of a system of world order.

The Japanese Buraku Problem: A Foreigner's Perspective

ALTHEA T. L. SIMMONS

(1982)

I BRING YOU GREETINGS FOR a fruitful Conference from the oldest largest most effective civil rights association in the United States of America. Civil rights advocacy has been central to my adult life. First as a volunteer member of the National Association for the Advancement of Colored People, and then for the past 21 years as a professional civil rights advocate employed by the same organization.

In the past few weeks I have been an avid reader of documents, papers, and books which describe the plight of the Buraku.[1] I have noted the differences in the kind of discrimination experienced by members of the Buraku in Japan and members of my own black race in the United States of America.[2] The *commonality* is discrimination. The dissimilarity lies in the fact that we are a highly visible minority.

America has no "top secret" listing of its 26 million black Americans. We are a "visible" minority identifiable by skin color and, in some instances, by where we live within a community; identity by place of residence is occasioned

---

Remarks before the First International Conference Against Discrimination Sponsored by the Buraku Liberation Research Institute and the Buraku Liberation League, Osaka, Japan, Dec. 4, 1982.

1. James Kirkup writes, "In Japan . . . there exist a minority group, the burakumin, established at three million outcast people existing in some 6,000 communities scattered over the whole land and comprising over 2 percent of the Japanese population. One of the various names for them is hinin, literally 'non-humans'." James Kirkup, *Obituary: Sue Sumii*, THE INDEPENDENT, June 23, 1997, at 16.

2. *See* Nicholas D. Kristof, *Japan's Invisible Minority: Better Off Than in Past, But Still Outcast*, N.Y. TIMES, Nov. 30, 1995, at A18, which states, "Some Japanese say the reason that their country has made progress with the burakumin is not broad-mindedness, but rather the inability to figure out who is a burakumin." *Id.* However, the burakumin, years after Simmons's speech remain "occupational outcasts." *Id. See also* FRANK K. UPHAM, LAW AND SOCIAL CHANGE IN POSTWAR JAPAN 78 (Cambridge, Harvard University Press 1987).

by discrimination in housing. However, America has no law or tradition that says members of a minority race must live in certain enclaves as is the case of the Buraku. Blacks who can financially afford to rent or purchase housing in all-white neighborhoods have long used intermediaries to aid them in securing these premises. Some have sought legal redress in an effort to break the invisible barriers of housing discrimination.

Marriage discrimination as a government matter became a thing of the past after a court decision found invalid a state law prohibiting racial intermarriage.

Employment discrimination still exists in the United States and has its basis in race, sex, religion, and national origin. The series of Civil Rights Acts enacted since 1957 provided for legal redress, including back pay when discrimination is proved. Legal redress is not available in Japan to the Buraku who suffer severe discrimination. Also, since 1966 American citizens have been able to secure unclassified government documents under the Freedom of Information Act.

However, I note many similarities between discrimination practiced against the Burakumin and that practiced against black Americans and other minorities in the United States of America.

The 1867 Emancipation Proclamation freeing black Americans was official recognition by the government that a separate class status for a group of citizens was illegal. This can be compared with the 1969 Law on Special Measures for Dowa Projects in Japan. Black Americans, like the Buraku, are still forced to live in ghettos as a direct result of income or lack thereof, but there is no governmental limitation on the type of occupation they can pursue.

Some black Americans, unlike the Buraku, have been able to move from the "invisible visible" that was an accepted part of American culture after Reconstruction through the early 1950s. Then came the mid-1960s. This era brought a strong forward push for full equality—socially, economically, and educationally—for black Americans. Blacks and whites engaged in protest marches or demonstrations for equality with the result that many more black Americans have access to education, job promotions, and newly opened well-paying career opportunities. Through civil protest—sometimes marred by violence—the legal process, and affirmative action, blacks, unlike the Buraku, became more mobile.

A word about the Buraku lists. If such lists existed in the United States of America, my organization, the National Association for the Advancement of Colored People, would mount a nationwide campaign, using the print and electronic media, protest marches, and demonstrations on a sustained basis. On a second level, we would draft legislation to make illegal the despicable practice, and find legislative sponsors to introduce and support the measure. Thirdly, we would seek to bring the issue before the Supreme Court, the highest legal body in our country seeking redress . . .

The NAACP was the moving force, through one of its principal spokesman, Dr. W. E. B. Du Bois, in identifying the fundamental links between the problems of racism in America and colonialism and human exploitation in Africa, the Caribbean, and Asia. In directing world attention to these pervasive problems, the Association led in the creation of the Pan African Congresses, the first of which was held in Paris in 1919. These Congresses brought together black leaders from around the world and helped to foster and crystalize human liberation thought and ideology. Thirty-five years ago, Dr. Du Bois presented to the United Nations a 155-page petition entitled *An Appeal to the World,* which was a compilation of five papers by leading American scholars documenting the denial of human rights in the United States.

What I see at this point—excepting a country's unique history and style—are the common elements in *all* forms of discrimination. These are, among others, housing, living standards, gainful employment, and education.

It may appear presumptuous for a foreigner to offer suggestions regarding the domestic problems of another country. There is, however, some merit in taking a look at problems of discrimination in other countries and examining with a critical eye the methods and strategies used in trying to overcome the twin evils of segregation and discrimination.

As we approach the 35th Anniversary of the World Declaration of Human Rights, it is certainly timely that we gather here today in the international spirit of equality for all . . . Yesterday, I had an opportunity to inspect Buraku district of Izumi, to walk through the community, to note the harshness of discrimination which has resulted in inferior housing, lack of running water and congestion. These are certainly tragic conditions. I have gained an appreciation of the plight of the Burakumin that could never be achieved through the written word alone. Discrimination is demoralizing, whether it is because of race, religion, sex, occupation or tradition or a feudal system.

The people of Japan can no more afford the luxury of discrimination than we can in my country, the United States of America. We are both leaders in the world arena and, as such, we have a responsibility to serve as role models for the world. We *must* banish discrimination now.

I believe that the Buraku of Japan, as well as people in other countries where discrimination is politically manipulated, can certainly learn from each other.

Without doubt, positive social change can be effected by an educational program, legislative thrust, and resort to judicial remedies. Great strides appear to have been made by the Buraku in spotlighting the problem. They raised their nation's consciousness to the injustice of the pattern and practice of discrimination. This public information campaign, coupled with an unrelenting legislative thrust to have laws enacted making unlawful discrimination in education, housing, and employment, would provide the legal framework for significant change.

A much harder change to effect is social—that of marriage. I have no magic formula for this change. I can point out that in the United States of America, we sought repeal of laws against intermarriage on the statute books, lobbied, that is to say we worked through our government and our legislators, to prevent the enactment of other such laws, and sought and successfully won an appeal to the High Court to overturn statutes that made it illegal for persons of different races, i.e., black and white, to intermarry. It was an arduous process, but the prohibition no longer exists as a governmental edict.

Because of the nature of the NAACP's objectives, it is obvious that our main focus is on the elimination of all forms of racial discrimination, on the national level and, of course, internationally. If somehow the ideas of this International Conference were adopted and literally and fully implemented, the reason for the NAACP's existence would terminate, *and we would gladly cease to exist.* Unfortunately, we cannot predict that result in the foreseeable future. Therefore, this conference assumes significance as one means of reaching this goal.

I do believe that if this 1982 International Conference Against Discrimination strengthens solidarity among we who are struggling to eliminate discrimination, it can hone the mood for peace and human rights.

Appendixes

Appendix A

The First Black Women's Legal Sorority:
The Epsilon Sigma Iota Sorority Select
Minutes 1939–1945

In October, 1886, "[t]he first association of women lawyers" was organized.[1] It was called the Equity Club. The club was organized by women law students and graduates of the Law Department of Michigan University School of Law. The stated purpose of the club was "the exchange of encouragement and friendly counsel between women law students and practitioners."[2] In 1888 a second organization called the "Women's International Bar Association" was formed. The stated purpose of the association was "1. To open law schools to women 2. To remove all disabilities to admission of women to the bar, and to secure their eligibility to the bench 3. To disseminate knowledge concerning women's legal status 4. To secure better legal conditions for women."[3] No black women students or lawyers were involved in these groups.

The first law sorority for women was founded at Chicago-Kent Law School in 1908. The membership of the sorority was described as "small." One of its members stated that the sorority rarely met and was created because "[t]he men had fraternities, so we had to have a sorority."[4] No black women students are known to have been members of this sorority.

On November 4, 1920, eight black "lady students of the Senior and Middle classes [at Howard University School of Law made] an application" to the "Gen-

---

1. Ada M. Bittenbender, *Women in Law, in* ANNIE NATHAN MEYER, WOMAN'S WORK IN AMERICA 218, 243 (New York, Henry Holt & Company 1891).

2. *Id.*

3. *Id.*

4. RONALD CHESTER, UNEQUAL ACCESS: WOMEN LAWYERS IN A CHANGING AMERICA 98 (Massachusetts, Bergin and Garvey Publishers, Inc. 1985), quoting Blanche Aronin Lippitz. There is evidence of other women's law societies that existed before 1908. For example, a Women's Legal Education Society existed at New York University in 1900. Isabella Mary Pettus, *The Legal Education of Women,* 61 ALBANY L.J. 325, 326 (1900).

tlemen" of the faculty of law to "establish a sorority with the view to their mutual improvement, the lifting of the standard of scholarship and the promotion of the feeling of loyalty to the school."[5] On November 6, 1920, by unanimous vote, the faculty granted permission to the "lady students" to establish a legal sorority.[6]

On June 17, 1921, the legal sorority was incorporated under the name of *Epsilon Sigma Iota* by Ollie May Cooper, Bertha C. McNeill, and Gladys E. Tignor.[7] For at least twenty-five years the sorority functioned as the only social and legal group for black women law students and black women lawyers.

There were important black women's clubs and organizations that black women lawyers joined, but the legal sorority was a new experiment in the development of black professional women. Like the Equity Club, *Epsilon Sigma Iota* "provided women lawyers and law students with a way . . . to build a community of women with similar professional interests and concerns."[8]

What follows is select minutes of *Epsilon Sigma Iota* Sorority between 1939 and 1945:

Washington, D.C.
January 16, 1939

The *Epsilon Sigma Iota* Sorority met on the above date at the residence of Soror [Etta B.] Lisemby, at 1609 1st St., N.W., at 8PM.

Present: Sorors [Gladys] Peterson (Chief Justice), [Etta B.] Lisemby (Attorney General) [Isadora Augusta Jackson] Letcher, [Pearl] Cox (Marshal), [Alma S.] Cornish, [Ollie May] Cooper (Clerk).

The meeting was opened with the Lord's prayer. The Minutes of the last meeting were read and approved.

The letter to Miss Geneva Davis of Dec. 22, 1938 granting the extension requested by the Pledge Club of the Robert H. Terrell Law School was read and discussed. The Clerk reported that no payment has been received by her according to the agreed terms, neither had she received any further word from Miss Davis concerning the same.

The Clerk was authorized to write Miss Davis and remind her that the first installment was overdue.

Letter to Miss Florrie [L.] Willis (Blackwell) read. Matter of affiliation

---

5. The application is contained in the Faculty Minutes, November 6, 1920. The application is signed by: Margaret DuBose, Chr., May Corinne Martin, Willie H. Blount, Zephyr A. Moore, Pearl Beldon, Bertha McNeill, Ollie May Cooper, and Gladys E. Tignor, Secretary.

6. *Id.*

7. District of Columbia Certificate of Incorporation, Liber 37, Folio 78, File No. 16192.

8. Virginia G. Drachman, Women Lawyers and the Origins of Professional Identity in America: The Letters of the Equity Club, 1887–1890, at 2 (Ann Arbor, University of Michigan Press 1993).

of practicing attorneys postponed to a later date. Report on pins made by Soror Lisemby. It was properly moved, seconded and carried that the original pen design be used, letters proportionate sized, with pearls in letter "I" in proportion to its size, guard and pin, not to exceed $11.00.

The pin committee to have actual cost of such pen at next meeting.

The Clerk was directed to purchase a new minute book and voted that the necessary cost thereof stand appropriated. Dues collected as follows:

Peterson	$1.00
Letcher	1.00
Cornish	1.00
Lisemby	1.00
Cooper	1.00
Total	6.00
On hand	10.40
Total	16.40
Minute book	1.50
Balance	14.90

A delicious menu was served by our hostess.
Adjourned.

G.T. Peterson, C.J.
O.M. Cooper, Clerk

Washington, D.C.
February 20, 1939

The *Epsilon Sigma Iota* Sorority met on the above date at the residence of Soror Letcher, 1635 5th St., N.W., at 8pm.

Present: Sorors Peterson, Letcher, Cornish, [A.R.] Smootz, Cox and Cooper.

The meeting was opened with a prayer by the Chief Justice [Gladys T. Peterson]. The minutes of the last meeting were read and approved. The letter to Miss Davis dated Jan. 14, 1939 was read. As nothing further has been heard from the Pledge Club it was properly moved, seconded and voted that the matter of setting up a chapter at the Terrell Law School was closed.

The matter of action on the affiliation of practicing attorneys was again postponed until Soror [Lavinia Marian] Poe can be present and enlighten the members on what she has in mind.

In the absence of Soror Lisemby on account of her husband's illness, Soror Letcher of the Pin Committee reported that the jeweler was also ill and estimate on pin was not available.

The nature of the spring project was considered. After discussing several propositions, it was finally moved, seconded and voted that we have a tea and members wear cellophane dresses (if such dresses are not too expensive); that the tea be held the first Sunday in May at the residence of Soror Letcher . . .

Our hostess catered to both our sense of taste and sense of sight, because the menu was delicious and the table decoration beautiful with Geo. Washington Cherry Trees and hatchets.

Adjourned.

G.T. Peterson, C.J.
O.M. Cooper, Clerk

Washington, D.C.
March 20, 1939

The *Epsilon Sigma Iota* Sorority met on the above date at the residence of Soror [A.R.] Smootz, at 1010 Park Road, N.W.

Present: Sorors Peterson, Lisemby, Letcher, Cox, Smootz and Cooper.

The meeting opened with the Lord's prayer repeated in concert. The minutes of the last meeting were read and approved.

As a check for $20.00 had been received by the Clerk from Miss [Betty B.] Briggs as the initial payment of five prospective pledges of the Terrell Law School, it was properly moved, seconded and voted that the issue (setting up a Chapter at Terrell) which was closed at the February meeting, be reopened since the Clerk had received a letter from Miss Davis, dated Mar. 18, 1939, in which she stated that the number had been reduced to four who planned to join at this time, that Miss Lucia [T.] Thomas, one of the persons who paid $5.00 on her fees desires the return of this sum and plans to come in next fall.

The remaining prospects are Miss Betty B. Briggs (who has paid nothing), Mrs. Bessie S. Chase, Miss Geneva E. Davis and Miss Gladys Mc-Gaffey.

After a careful consideration of the matter, it was properly moved, seconded and voted that the Sorority regretted that the request of Miss Davis could not be granted because the number is too small to form a chapter, as it would consist of officers only with no lay members. It is absolutely necessary to have at least seven persons. That we still hope that a sufficient number of ladies may be interested to bring the Pledge Club up to the required minimum. Also that the $5.00 be returned to Miss Lucia [T.] Thomas . . .

In connection with the Cellophane Tea to be given May 7th, Soror Letcher was requested to contact Mrs. Alma J. Scott for permission to use the name of the Southwest Settlement House for which the tea is given. The following colors were selected for the cellophane dresses: Letcher (Red), Peterson (Pink), Lisemby (Green), Cox (White), Cooper (Blue), Smootz (Yellow) . . .

After a wonderful repast by our hostess, the meeting adjourned.

G.T. Peterson, C.J.
O.M. Cooper, Clerk

Baltimore, Maryland
April 21, 1939

The *Epsilon Sigma Iota Sorority* met on the above date at the residence of Soror [Mrs. Jesse W.?] Redden, 436 W. Biddle St., Baltimore, Md.

Present: Sorors Peterson, Lisemby, Letcher, Cornish, Cox, Redden, Smootz and Cooper.

The meeting opened with the Lord's Prayer repeated in concert. Minutes of last meeting read and approved.

The Clerk read letter sent to Miss Davis of the Terrell Law School stating inability of the Sorority to set up Chapter at this time because of small number who have made initial payment. Letter dated Mar. 27, 1939. As no answer had been received from Miss Davis, the Clerk was instructed to again write her asking what disposition is to be made of the amt. paid in and what success she had made in securing the minimum number of pledges. Ask for an immediate reply.

The matter of planning for the tea was taken up with the following results.

Mrs. Lisemby to secure services of a woman for Saturday and Sunday to help with the cleaning, dish washing and serving. Mrs Letcher to purchase chickens for salad, ham and other things for salad and punch along with Mrs. Lisemby. Punch Bricks & Flowers . . .

This meeting was enjoyed by all not because of the bounteous menu but because it was the first time a meeting had been held out of the city of Wash[ington D.C.].
Adjourned

G.T. Peterson, C.J.
O.M. Cooper, Clerk

Washington, D.C.
February 19, 1940

The *Epsilon Sigma Iota* Sorority met on the above date, 8 P.M. at the residence of Soror Cornish, 138 R. St., N.W.

Present: G.T. Peterson, I.A. Letcher, A.S. Cornish, Pearl Cox, O.M. Cooper.

The minutes of the last meeting were read and approved. It was decided to have a "Gay Nineties Tea" for the annual Tea to be given May 5, 1940. The project for which the tea is to be given was left to be decided later.

The Committee appointed to investigate the necessary steps to be taken in order to accept the Terrell law graduates and students reported that the matter has been taken up with the Dean of Women, who had asked for a written statement of the organization, purpose and work of the Sorority and the reasons for requesting permission to take in members from law schools other than Howard, particularly Terrell. The statement, addressed to the President & Board of Trustees was submitted approved, signed by the Chief Justice and the Clerk, and the Clerk was directed to transmit the same to Dean [Susie G.] Elliott, with a cover letter . . .

G.T. Peterson, C.J.
O.M. Cooper, Clerk

Washington, D.C.
March 18, 1940

The *Epsilon Sigma Iota* Sorority met on the above date at the home of Soror Lisemby, 1609 First St., N.W., at 8 P.M.

Present: G.T. Peterson, C.J., E.B. Lisemby, I.A. Letcher, A.R. Smootz, A.S. Cornish, Pearl Cox, O.M. Cooper.

The meeting opened with the Lord's prayer. Minutes of the last meeting read, corrected and approved.

The projects for which the tea might be given—Settlement House Building Fund, Lobbying-non partisan and [Benjamin] Leighton [ex-Dean of the Howard University School of Law] Loan Fund for Howard Law students were discussed, and it was duly motioned by Soror Lisemby, seconded by Soror Letcher that special effort be [made] to raise money for the student loan fund at Howard University and a small percent of the proceeds be retained in the treasury for expenses. Carried . . .
Adjourned

G.T. Peterson, C.J.
O.M. Cooper, Clerk

Washington, D.C.
May 27, 1940

The *Epsilon Sigma Iota* Sorority met on the above date at the residence of Soror Smootz, 1815 S. St., N.W., 8 P.M.

Present Sorors Peterson, Lisemby, Letcher, Cox, Smootz, Cooper.

The meeting opened with the Lord's prayer. The minutes of the last meeting were read and adopted. The Chief Justice stated the purpose of the meeting to be to elect officers and decide whether or not to dissolve the present organization and reorganize under a different set-up.

After a full discussion of these questions it was decided, first to delay the election until the second question is finally acted upon; and in view of the fact that no answer has been received from [Howard University] President [Mordecai Wyatt] Johnson to the Sorority's letter of Feb. 15, asking permission to admit students from the Terrell Law School and other law schools, it was voted that a letter be written to [Howard's law] Dean [William Henry] Hastie (to whom the matter has been referred by the President) giving him the background of the situation, and requesting a reply by June 10. The Clerk was directed to write such letter.

After the service of a tasty repass, the meeting adjourned.

G.T. Peterson, C.J.
O.M. Cooper, Clerk

Washington, D.C.
November 12, 1944

The *Epsilon Sigma Iota* Sorority met on the above date, pursuant to notice, at the residence of the Chief Justice, Gladys T. Peterson, 1002 Kenyon St., N.W., at 6 P.M. to discuss plans for reviving the Sorority by taking in those female students in the School of Law who are not eligible for membership. This included members of the 2nd and 3d Yr evening classes. After a full discussion of the eligibility of the prospective candidates, it was moved, properly seconded and voted that an invitation be extended to the following persons: Miss Grace C. Rowe, 3d Yr. Eve. Cl; Miss Ena M. St Louis, 2d Yr. Eve. Cl; Miss Helene F. Southern, 2d Yr. Eve. Cl . . . .
Adjourned

G.T. Peterson, C.J.
O.M. Cooper, Clerk

Washington, D.C.
Sunday, Dec. 10, 1944

The *Epsilon Sigma Iota* Sorority met on the above date, 6:30 P.M., at the home of the Chief Justice, 1002 Kenyon St., N.W. for the purpose of initiating the three candidates for membership into the Sorority. Present: G.T. Peterson, [Chief Justice], E.B. Lisemby [Attorney General], A.S. Cornish, E.T. Jefferson, M.R. Young, P.B. Cox, Lillian Skinker Malone, Z.C. Hart, O.M. Cooper, Clerk.

The candidates appeared, were examined and after meeting all the requirements, were initiated and received as full members of the Sorority. They were welcomed. . . .

G.T. Peterson, C.J.
O.M. Cooper, Clerk

Washington, D.C.
Sunday, Feb. 25, 1945

The *Epsilon Sigma Iota* Sorority met on the above date at 6:00 P.M. at the residence of the Chief Justices . . . Present: Lisemby, Letcher, Cornish, Cox, Rowe, St. Louis, Hart, Jefferson, Southern, Cooper, Young.

The Chief Justice explained the main purpose of the matter of extending invitations to the female students of the first year class, [Howard University] School of Law. The clerk presented the list of ten names all of whom had a "C" average or above for the first semester of 1944–45. The question of eligibility as to scholarship and character was discussed. Because the members do not come in contact with these students, do not know them and have no way of passing upon their qualifications, it was decided to invite the following to a get together or fellowship meeting. It was moved by Soror Rowe, seconded by Soror Lisemby—that we plan some entertainment by which we might meet the persons above referred to, namely: Ruth J. Anderson, Frankie [Muse] Freeman, Margaret E. Gill, Mabel D. Haden, Edna W. McClellan, Gloria C. Oden, Charlotte R. Pinkett, Juanita [Kidd] Stout, Veva I. Young. . . .

It was voted that the election of officers be the main business of the April meeting and the discussion of candidates for membership into the Sorority. . . .

G.T. Peterson, C.J.
O.M. Cooper, Clerk

Washington, D.C.
March 17, 1945

The *Epsilon Sigma Iota* Sorority met on the above date . . . for a get together meeting with the female members of the first year class who had been invited to be present. Of those invited all but two came. Present were: Ruth J. Anderson, Frankie [Muse] Freeman, Mabel D. Haden, Edna W. McClellan, Charlotte R. Pinkett, Juanita [Kidd] Stout, Veva I. Young.

Cards, games and music furnished entertainment followed by a collation. A pleasant evening was enjoyed. . . .

Gladys T. Peterson, C.J.
Ollie M. Cooper, Clerk

Washington, D.C.
April 22, 1945

The *Epsilon Sigma Iota* Sorority met on the above date at 6 P.M. . . . Present G.T. Peterson, I.A. Letcher, Grace C. Rowe, Helen F. Southern, Meta R. Young, Etta B. Lisemby, Pearl Cox, Ollie May Cooper . . .

The matter of extending an invitation to all the members of the group who were invited to the get together meeting or those who actually attended, to become pledgees, was discussed, Moved by Soror Southern, seconded by Soror Lisemby, that all the girls be invited to become pledgees, carried. The Chief Justice voted "no" . . . [T]hat a fee of $1 be assessed each pledge carried . . .

The election of officers was held. Soror Peterson was re-elected Chief Justice, Soror Rowe unanimously elected Associate Justice. It was moved, seconded and carried that the Sorority have a Recording and a Correspondence Clerk, and that the present Clerk (Soror Cooper) will be the Recording Clerk and that Soror Southern will be Corresponding Clerk. Soror Cox was reelected Marshal . . . Also dues from all except the three new members will be due in the amount of $2.50 for the year . . .

G.T. Peterson, C.J.
O.M. Cooper, Clerk

Washington, D.C.
Sunday, May 22, 1945

The *Epsilon Sigma Iota* Sorority met . . . Present: G.T. Peterson, P. B. Cox, G.E. Rowe, L.S. Malone, H.F. Southern, I.A. Letcher, O.M. Cooper . . . Upon motion of Soror Letcher . . . the Pledge Club were accepted and Monday, June 11, 1945, at 9 P.M. was set for the induction of members into the Pledge Club as the Lex Club.

Soror Southern was named as sponsor for the Club to be assisted by Soror [Lillian S.] Malone. These Sorors were instructed to work out and submit plans and instructions for the pledgees over the vacation period. Soror Malone and Soror Rowe were named as a committee to investigate and purchase, if available, some type of Pin with the letter "Σ" to be worn by the pledgees during this period. It was decided that the night of the induction the pledgees should . . . wear black dresses and a flower. [Pledgees Freeman, Anderson, Gill, Pinkett, Haden, McClellan Stout and Young each paid a $1 pledge fee.]

G.T. Peterson, C.J.
O.M. Cooper, Clerk

Washington, D.C.
June 11, 1945

Meeting of the *Epsilon Sigma Iota* Sorority on the above date at the residence of the Chief Justice for the purpose of formally inducting the applicants into the Lex Pledge Club: Present—Cox, Lisemby, St. Louis, Malone, Rowe, Cannady, Southern, Cornish, Cooper, Jefferson. The Chief Justice asked each applicant whether or not she desired to become a pledgee, and receiving an affirmative reply, explained some of the purposes of the organization and then received their signed pledges. Soror Lisemby told about the history of the organization and its members.

The Lex Club was then formed with the following officers and members: Frankie [Muse] Freeman, Pres., Ruth J. Anderson, Vice Pres., Charlotte J. Pinkett, Treas., Margaret Gill, Secy., Edna W. McClellan, Ch. Social Com., Mabel D. Haden and Veva I. Young.

It was decided that Mrs. Juanita [Kidd] Stout, who was absent because of personal illness and had gone to her home in Texas be taken into the Club by the officers and the president was so instructed . . .

G.T. Peterson, C.J.
O.M. Cooper, Clerk

Appendix B

Pioneering Facts about Black Women Lawyers and Law Teachers

First Black Woman Lawyer

Name	Law School	Location	Year
Charlotte E. Ray	Howard	Washington, D.C.	1872

First Black Women to Teach Law: Black Law Schools

Professor Lutie A. Lytle is the groundbreaker for all women now teaching in organized law schools in the country. The contributions, conceptions about law, and the role of black women in law teaching have been lost or ignored.[1] The year indicates when these women started to teach.

Name	Law School	Location	Year
Lutie A. Lytle	Central Tennessee	Nashville, Tennessee	1897
Ollie May Cooper	Howard	Washington, D.C.	1925

---

1. *See* J. CLAY SMITH JR., EMANCIPATION: THE MAKING OF THE BLACK LAWYER, 1844–1944, at 365, n.225 (Philadelphia, University of Pennsylvania Press 1993) (Lutie A. Lytle); *Id.* at 86, n.228; *Id.* at 91, n.302 (Ollie May Cooper); *see also Ollie Cooper, 94, Dies; Taught Law at Howard U.,* WASH. POST, Apr. 17, 1981, at B5; Telephone interview with H. Elsie Austin, Oct. 12, 1995; Lucia T. Thomas, *Biographical Bits about Terrell Teachers,* 1 THE BARRISTER 9, 13–14 (May 2, 1941); Telephone interview, Marjorie Lawson, Sept. 29, 1995; TEACHERS' DIRECTORY, ASSOCIATION OF AMERICAN LAW SCHOOLS 146 (1955) (Lula Morgan Howard); Telephone interview, Margaret Haywood, Oct. 5, 1995; TEACHERS' DIRECTORY, ASSOCIATION OF AMERICAN LAW SCHOOLS 194 (1951) (Jane M. Lucas); North Carolina College at Durham, THE SCHOOL OF LAW: BULL. OF INFORMATION 2 (1952) (Sybil Marie Jones Dedmond; Telephone interview with Sybil Marie Jones Dedmond, Oct. 12, 1995; DIRECTORY OF LAW TEACHERS IN AMERICAN BAR ASSOCIATION APPROVED SCHOOLS 324 (1961) (Cynthia Straker); *Id.* at 161 (1966) (Patricia R. Harris); DIRECTORY OF LAW TEACHERS 1967–1968, at 24 (1968); *Id.* at 79 (Jean Camper Cahn).

Name	Law School	Location	Year
H. Elsie Austin	Terrell	Washington, D.C.	1941
Marjorie Lawson	Terrell	Washington, D.C.	1943
Lula Morgan Howard	Lincoln	Jefferson City, Missouri	1945
Margaret A. Haywood	Terrell	Washington, D.C.	1946
Jane M. Lucas	Howard	Washington, D.C.	1946
Cassandra Maxwell	South Carolina	Orangeburg, South Carolina	1947
Sybil Jones Dedmond	North Carolina Central	Durham, North Carolina	1951
Cynthia Straker	Howard	Washington, D.C.	1956
Patricia R. Harris	Howard	Washington, D.C.	1961
Jean Camper Cahn	Howard	Washington, D.C.	1967

The list indicates only the starting date of teaching because in most cases no more is known about the duration these women taught or what they taught. The following information survives:

Lutie A. Lytle taught for about four years. She taught the following courses: Domestic Relations, Evidence, and Criminal Procedure.

Between 1925 and 1930, Ollie May Cooper taught a one-hour course (unidentified) without pay and recognition. The exact year(s) that she taught this course is unknown.

H. Elsie Austin taught Agency and Administrative Law. She taught for three years.

Marjorie Lawson taught Labor Law for one year.

Lula Morgan Howard taught from 1945 until the mid-1950s. Her subjects included Bills and Notes, Legal Bibliography, Wills, and Taxation.

Margaret Haywood taught from 1946 until 1951. Her subjects included Personal Property, Wills & Administration, and Insurance Law.

Jane M. Lucas taught from 1946 until 1951. Her subjects included Contracts, Bills and Notes, and Legal Bibliography.

Cassandra Maxwell taught Contracts, Legal Bibliography, and Bills and Notes between 1947 and 1966.

Sybil Marie Jones Dedmond taught from 1951 until 1964. Her subjects included Property, Future Interests, and Criminal Law.

Cynthia Straker was a Law Librarian and Instructor from 1956 until the mid-1960s. She taught Legal Bibliography and Insurance.

Patricia Roberts Harris taught from 1963 until 1966, and 1969. Her subjects included Torts, International Law, Constitutional Law, Appellate Practice, and Government Regulation of Business.

Jean Camper Cahn taught for one year. Her subjects included Jurisprudence, International Law, and Constitutional Law.

First Black Women to Teach Law: White Law Schools

Name	Law School	Location	Year
Jean Camper Cahn	George Washington	Washington, D.C.	1968
Joyce Anne Hughes	University of Minnesota	Minneapolis, Minnesota	1971

Jean Camper Cahn appears to be the first black woman to teach at a white law school in the nation's history at George Washington University School of Law. She was a visiting professor during the time she spent at the law school. She was the Director of the Urban Law Institute at George Washington's law school from 1968 to 1971. She taught the following courses at the law school: Law and Poverty, Jurisprudence, International Law, Federal Programs, Police in the Community, and Community Organization.[2] She was "never offered a teaching position on tenure track at George Washington's law school, and that is why she left the law school."[3]

Joyce Anne Hughes is the first black woman to teach in the nation on tenure track at a white law school. In 1971, Professor Hughes joined the faculty at the University of Minnesota Law School, after clerking for U.S. District Judge Earl R. Larson, and working in a major law firm in Minneapolis. She is the first black woman to graduate (1965) from and to teach at the University of Minnesota's law school. She taught Practice, Modern Real Estate, and The Legal Profession.[4] Hughes taught at the University of Minnesota until 1975, when she joined the law faculty at Northwestern University, where she has taught Banking, Evidence, Immigration, and Real Estate Transactions.[5]

First Black Woman Founder of an American Law School

Name	Law School	Location	Year
Jean Camper Cahn	Antioch	Washington, D.C.	1972[6]

---

2. DIRECTORY OF LAW TEACHERS ASSOCIATION OF AMERICAN LAW SCHOOLS 120 (1970).

3. Telephone conversation with Dean Jack H. Friedenthal, Nov. 28, 1995. In 1971 the student newspaper of the George Washington Law Center carried several protest articles pro and con about the closing of the poverty law program run by Professor Cahn. Most were critical of Dean Kramer's decision to close the Urban Law Institute, which would also end Cahn's professorship. *See* Jean Cahn, *Jean Cahn Fights Decision,* THE ADVOCATE, March 1, 1971, at 1; Jerome Duncan, *BALSA: Kramer's Act 'Racist,'* THE ADVOCATE, March 1, 1971, at 3. (One of the grounds asserted by the Black American Law School Association in opposition to the Dean's action was that "[Professor Cahn] is the only black professor on the Law School Faculty.")

4. *Id.* at 275 (1971) and *Id.* at 315 (1972) (ties down starting date of 1971); *At the University of Minnesota Law School: A 'Together' Prof,* EBONY 39, May 1972.

5. *See* THE AALS DIRECTORY OF LAW TEACHERS, 1994–1995, at 504 (1995).

6. J. Y. Smith, *Jean Camper Cahn Dies at 55; Founded Antioch Law School,* WASH. POST, Jan.

First Black Women Deans of American Law Schools

Name	Law School	Location	Year
Patricia R. Harris	Howard	Washington, D.C.	1969
Jean Camper Cahn	Antioch	Washington, D.C.	1972
Marilyn V. Yarbrough	University of Tennessee	Knoxville, Tennessee	1987
Maya L. Harris	Lincoln	San Jose, Calif.	1996
Alice G. Bullock	Howard	Washington, D.C.	1997[7]

First Black Women Editors-in-Chief of a Law Review

Name	Law School	Location	Year
Clara Burrill Bruce	Boston University	Boston, Massachusetts	1925[8]
Goler Teal Butcher	Howard	Washington, D.C.	1956[9]

5, 1991, at B6. Edgar S. Cahn, Jean Camper Cahn's husband was a cofounder of Antioch Law School. Jacqueline Trescott, *Pros and Cahns: Triumph and Turmoil the Constant Companions of Antioch's Rebels,* WASH. POST, Jan. 19, 1980, at D1. Both of the Cahns were 33 years old when the law school was founded. Courtland Milloy, *A Passion for Justice that Never Waned,* WASH. POST, Feb. 17, 1991, at B3. Antioch Law School closed in 1988. Adam Sommers, *Antioch Law School Holds Last Graduation,* WASH. TIMES, May 23, 1988, at B1. After Antioch closed, Dean Cahn was retained by the governing board of the D.C. Law School to select its first faculty, librarian, and student body, thus stamping her imprimatur on a successor law school. Telephone interview with Edgar S. Cahn, Oct. 14, 1995. The D.C. Law School was founded in 1986, but did not become operational until 1988. The D.C. Law School presently carries on the Antioch tradition. William L. Robinson, *Unlike Other Law Schools,* WASH. POST, Nov. 6, 1988, at C8; Saundra Torry, *D.C. Law Makes History With 1st Graduating Class,* May 19, 1991, at B3.

7. *See* J. Clay Smith Jr., *Patricia Roberts Harris: A Champion in Pursuit of Excellence,* 29 How. L.J. 437 (1986); *Jean Camper Cahn Dies at 55, supra* note 6. The appointment of Dean Marilyn Virginia Yarbrough as the first black woman dean in the South appears to have escaped the major press sources. However, her appointment was covered by THE CHRONICLE OF HIGHER EDUCATION. *See* Michelle N.-K. Collison, *The South's First Black Woman Law Dean,* THE CHRONICLE OF HIGHER ED., Feb. 24, 1988, at A3. Even her departure as dean of the University of Tennessee Law School at Knoxville received meager press coverage. *See The Southeast; Romer May Switch to GOP,* THE ATLANTA J. AND CONSTITUTION, Feb. 5, 1991, at 2A.

Regarding Maya L. Harris, half black, half East Indian, she is the Dean of a free standing law school and at age 29 may be the youngest woman ever to head a law school in the country. *See* Ken Meyers, *The Dean is Young, Gifted, Black and Trying to Right Rocky Ship,* NAT'L L.J., Aug. 5, 1996, at A16.

Regarding Alice G. Bullock, *see Alice Gresham Bullock Named Dean of Law School,* 18 CAPSTONE 2, Aug. 16, 1997.

8. EMANCIPATION, *supra* note 1, at 39.

9. J. Clay Smith Jr., *United States Foreign Policy and Goler Teal Butcher,* 37 How. L.J. 139, 147 (1994).

First Black Women on Law Review

Name	Law School	Location	Year
Clara Burrill Bruce	Boston University	Boston	1925
Sadie T. M. Alexander	University of Pennsylvania	Philadelphia	1926
H. Elsie Austin	University of Colorado	Boulder	1928
Juanita Mitchell	University of Maryland	Baltimore	1948
Harriet W. Batipps	Howard	Washington, D.C.	1955[10]
Patricia Harris	George Washington	Washington, D.C.	1959
Joyce Anne Hughes	University of Minnesota	Minneapolis	1964[11]

First Black Woman Lawyer to Publish in an Academic Law Review

Name	Law School	Location	Year
Pauli Murray	UCLA	Los Angeles	1948[12]

First Black Women Lawyers/Law Professors to Publish in Bar Journal

Name	Law School	Location	Year
Sadie T. M. Alexander	University of Pennsylvania	Philadelphia	1941[13]
Lula Morgan Howard	Lincoln University	Jefferson City, Missouri	1949[14]

---

10. Harriet Batipps was the first woman to hold the title of editor of the HOWARD LAW JOURNAL, a rank just below editor-in-chief. *Id.* 147, n.38 (1994).

11. EMANCIPATION, *supra* note 1, at 39 (Burrill and Alexander), 39–40, n.77 (Austin) (listing law review articles). Austin's achievements at the University of Colorado made the press. *Elsie Austin Wins Honor,* THE NEW HERALD, 1928, clipping in author's files; *Elsie Austin Wins Praise at Colorado U.*, (1928), clipping in author's files, which states: "Miss Austin came to Colorado . . . because we believed a year in the West would broaden her. She will return to [the University of Cincinnati Law School] next year to complete her law course and claim the honor of being the first girl of her race to graduate from the law school there." It is likely that a black woman made law review at some other white law school before the 1960s, but the identity of such a person, if she exists, is not known by this author. Only one name has surfaced: Joyce Anne Hughes, who was on the MINNESOTA LAW REVIEW in 1964. *See* 48 MINN. L.REV. (1964).

12. *Id.* at 490, n.69 (EMANCIPATION) (listing article).

13. Sadie Tanner Mossell Alexander, *Women as Practitioners of Law in the United States*, 1 NAT'L BAR J. 56 (1941).

14. Lula Morgan Howard, *Recent Tax Court Decisions in Section 22(k) Cases*, 7 NAT'L BAR J.

First Black Woman Lawyer to Head the National Bar Association

Name	Law School	Location	Year
Arnette R. Hubbard	John Marshall	Chicago	1981[15]

First Black Woman Lawyer to Head a State Bar Group
(Iowa Colored Bar Association)

Name	Law School	Location	Year
Gertrude E. D. Rush	Read Law	Des Moines	1921[16]

First Black Lawyer to Head AALS and SALT

Name	Law School	Location	Year
Emma C. Jordan	Howard	Washington, D.C.	1992[17]

First Black Woman Lawyer Admitted to U.S. Supreme Court

Name	Law School	Location	Year
Violette N. Anderson	Chicago Law School	Chicago	1926[18]

First Black Woman Judge

Name	Law School	Location	Year
Jane Matilda Bolin	Yale	New York	1939[19]

---

398 (1949). In 1949, Lula Morgan Howard was a Professor on the law faculty of Lincoln University School of Law.

15. Alex Poinsett, *After 56 Years the President is a Lady: Chicago Attorney Arnette Hubbard Heads National Bar Association,* EBONY 137 (Oct. 1981).

16. EMANCIPATION, *supra* note 1, at 574. Gertrude Elzora Durden Rush is the first woman lawyer in the nation to cofound a national bar group composed of men and women. In 1925, Ms. Rush was a cofounder of the National Bar Association. *Id.* at 556.

17. Professor Jordan is the only black lawyer to head two academic law professors' groups: The Association of American Law Schools (AALS—1992) and The Society of American Law Teachers, 1986–88 (SALT). At the time of these two achievements, Professor Jordan was and is presently on the law faculty of Georgetown University.

18. Ms. Anderson was admitted to practice to U.S. Supreme Court on motion of Judge James A. Cobb, a black judge on the local court of the District of Columbia. EMANCIPATION, *supra* note 1, at 432, n.140.

19. Ms. Bolin became a judge at the age of thirty-one. She was appointed to the Domestic Relations Court of the City of New York by Mayor Fiorello La Guardia. Ms. Bolin also has the distinc-

First Two Black Women on Local High Courts

Name	*Law School*	*Location*	*Year*
Julia Cooper Mack	Howard	Washington, D.C.	1975
Juanita Kidd Stout	Indiana— Bloomington	Indiana	1988[20]

First Black Federal Woman Judge

Name	*Law School*	*Location*	*Year*
Constance Baker Motley	Columbia	New York	1966[21]

First Black Woman to Try Case

Name	*Law School*	*Location*	*Year*
Charlotte E. Ray	Howard	Washington, D.C.	1875[22]

---

tion of being the first black woman graduate of Yale Law School in 1931. *See* JESSIE CARNEY SMITH, ed., NOTABLE BLACK AMERICAN WOMEN 94 (Detroit, Gale Research Inc. 1991).

20. Judge Mack was appointed to the D.C. Court of Appeals, the court of last resort in the District of Columbia, by President Gerald Ford in September 1975. Justice Stout was appointed to the Supreme Court of Pennsylvania by Governor Robert P. Casey in January 1988. *See* Lawrence Feinberg, *D.C. Black Lawyer Named for Judgeship*, WASH. POST, July 5, 1975, at C1 (Mack); NOTABLE BLACK WOMEN, *supra* note 19, at 1087 (Stout).

21. Judge Motley was appointed to the United States District Court of the Southern District of New York.

22. Godling v. Godling, Case No. 4278, Supreme Court of the District of Columbia (In Equity) (1875). This was a divorce case. Ray is listed as "complainants solicitor." Courtesy of Jill Norgreen.

Appendix C

U.S. Census: The Number of Women Lawyers by Race and Nationality in Each State/Select Territories and the Combined Total of Male Lawyers (all races), 1950–90

1950 Census

The information regarding women and male lawyers is found in *Table 77*, titled, "Race and Class of Worker of Employed Persons, by Occupation and Sex, for the State and for Standard Metropolitan Areas of 100,000 or More: 1950." *Table 77* is found in various bound Parts by individual states of the *U.S. Census of the Population: 1950, Vol. II, Characteristics of the Population* (Washington, D.C., U.S. Government Printing Office 1952).

The data relevant to lawyers and judges in Hawaii is found in *Table 52*, titled, "Detailed Occupation of the Experienced Civilian Labor Force and Employed Persons, by Sex, for Hawaii and for the Honolulu Standard Metropolitan Area: 1950." Vol. II, *id.*, Parts 51–54, published in 1953 by the Government Printing Office.

The data relevant to lawyers and judges in Alaska is found in *Table 56*, titled, "Detailed Occupation of the Experienced Civilian Labor Force and of Employed Persons, by Sex, for Alaska: 1950" and is marked by asterisk (*) in chart 1. Except for white women, neither *Table 52* (Hawaii) nor *Table 56* (Alaska) provides a racial breakdown of female lawyers and judges.

As constructed, the chart includes only women by race as identified in the chart totaled by state. The total number of male lawyers combines all races and is not broken out as the data on women is. The total for male lawyers in the population of individual states is race cumulative.

Below, in all charts, the information in brackets identifies the [volume-page] of census data submitted by each state on legal occupations for the relevant decade.

CHART C1. 1950 Census

	White Female Lawyers	Negro Female Lawyers	Other Races Female Lawyers	Total Female Lawyers	Total Male Lawyers
Alabama [2-214]	37	1	—	38	1772 [2-212]
Alaska [51-59]				5	89 *
Arizona [3-109]	23	—	—	23	687 [3-107]
Arkansas [4-185]	23	—	—	23	1318 [4-183]
California [5-349]	546	5	3	554	11947 [5-347]
Colorado [6-147]	65	—	—	65	1683 [6-145]
Connecticut [7-164]	67	—	—	67	2512 [7-162]
Delaware [8-98]	5	—	—	5	295 [8-96]
D.C. [9-75]	564	10	1	575	4163 [9-73]
Florida [10-237]	104	—	—	104	3435 [10-235]
Georgia [11-302]	112	1	—	113	2827 [11-300]
Hawaii [52-99]				10	256 *
Idaho [12-120]	17	—	—	17	509 [12-118]
Illinois [13-287]	391	13	—	404	12289 [13-285]
Indiana [14-239]	80	—	—	80	3399 [14-237]
Iowa [15-201]	70	1	—	71	2497 [15-199]
Kansas [16-193]	57	—	—	57	1879 [16-191]
Kentucky [17-223]	42	1	—	43	2476 [17-221]
Louisiana [18-206]	57	—	—	57	2198 [18-204]
Maine [19-109]	19	—	—	19	712 [19-107]
Maryland [20-143]	159	—	—	159	4340 [20-141]
Massachusetts [21-222]	375	1	—	376	6770 [21-220]
Michigan [22-269]	178	6	—	184	5278 [22-267]
Minnesota [23-206]	58	1	1	60	2870 [23-204]
Mississippi [24-182]	32	—	—	32	1346 [24-180]
Missouri [25-249]	139	5	—	144	4594 [25-247]
Montana [26-124]	12	—	—	12	645 [26-122]
Nebraska [27-165]	27	1	—	28	1496 [27-163]
Nevada [28-84]	10	—	—	10	221 [28-82]
New Hampshire [29-87]	11	—	—	11	426 [29-85]
New Jersey [30-226]	177	3	—	180	7430 [30-224]
New Mexico [31-115]	15	—	—	15	499 [31-113]
New York [32-328]	1254	19	2	1275	31707 [32-326]
North Carolina [33-243]	30	3	—	33	2279 [33-241]
North Dakota [34-120]	12	—	—	12	477 [34-118]
Ohio [35-368]	287	5	—	292	8855 [35-366]
Oklahoma [36-205]	94	—	—	94	2923 [36-203]
Oregon [37-140]	51	—	—	51	1544 [37-138]
Pennsylvania [38-387]	198	2	—	200	8186 [38-385]
Rhode Island [39-98]	11	—	—	11	759 [39-96]
South Carolina [40-170]	37	—	—	37	1273 [40-168]
South Dakota [41-135]	17	—	—	17	565 [41-133]
Tennessee [42-258]	67	—	—	67	2600 [42-256]

continued

CHART C1.   Continued

	White Female Lawyers	Negro Female Lawyers	Other Races Female Lawyers	Total Female Lawyers	Total Male Lawyers
Texas [43-499]	224	2	—	226	7856 [43-497]
Utah [44-119]	10	—	—	10	633 [44-117]
Vermont [45-84]	17	—	—	17	309 [45-82]
Virginia [46-255]	197	3	—	200	4198 [46-253]
Washington [47-185]	64	—	—	64	2,404 [47-183]
West Virginia [48-178]	27	—	—	27	1372 [48-176]
Wisconsin [49-188]	86	—	1	87	3465 [49-186]
Wyoming [50-96]	10	—	—	10	287 [50-94]
TOTALS	6,165	83	8	6,271	174,550

1960 Census

The information regarding women and male lawyers is found in *Table 122*, titled "Occupation of the Civilian Labor Forces by Color, of the Employed by Race and Class of Worker, and of Persons Not in Labor Force with Work Experience, by Sex, for the State, and for the Standard Metropolitan Statistical Areas of 250,000 or More: 1960." *Table 122* is found in various bound *Parts* by individual states of the *U.S. Census of the Population: 1960, Vol. I, Characteristics of the Population* (U.S. Government: Printing Office, Washington, D.C.: 1963. The number of male and female lawyers is found on separate pages, but in the same table (*Table 122*). Below, in chart 2, the first and second bracketed numbers, such as [2-381] following the name of the state Alabama, mean that the "characteristic of the population" of women and male lawyers is located at Part 2-Page 381 of Vol. I. As constructed, the chart includes only women by race as identified in the chart totaled by state. The total number of male lawyers combines all races and is not broken out as the data on women is. The total for male lawyers in the population of individual states is race cumulative.

The employment statistics collected by the census in 1960 varied from the other years used in this study. In 1960, the census tracked the number of persons in the civilian workforce, including both those employed and unemployed persons with work experience. To be consistent with the data used in other years, the number of employed female and male lawyers is reported in the table below. The total number of female and male lawyers is actually higher because the number of unemployed lawyers is not included.

The author cannot explain why the number of lawyers dropped so dramatically in California during the 1950–60 decade.

CHART C2. 1960 Census

	Negro Women Lawyers	Other Non-white Lawyers	White Female Lawyers	Total Female Lawyers	Total Male Lawyers
Alabama [2-381]	—	—	62	62	2256 [2-379]
Alaska [3-186]	—	—	24	24	214 [3-184]
Arizona [4-226]	—	—	8	8	266 [4-224]
Arkansas [5-343]	—	—	26	26	1261 [5-341]
California [6-722]	—	—	29	29	619 [6-720]
Colorado [7-298]	—	—	98	98	2328 [7-296]
Connecticut [8-289]	—	—	57	57	3517 [8-287]
Delaware [9-194]	—	—	7	7	486 [9-192]
D.C. [10-123]	19	—	476	495	3415 [10-121]
Florida [11-471]	—	—	180	180	5754 [11-469]
Georgia [12-530]	—	—	166	166	3045 [12-528]
Hawaii [13-197]	—	4	7	11	458 [13-195]
Idaho [14-218]	—	—	24	24	623 [14-216]
Illinois [15-609]	8	—	426	434	13232 [15-607]
Indiana [16-439]	4	—	85	89	3527 [16-437]
Iowa [17-404]	—	—	42	42	2635 [17-402]
Kansas [18-392]	—	—	91	91	2427 [18-390]
Kentucky [19-406]	—	—	48	48	2454 [19-404]
Louisiana [20-380]	5	—	93	98	2929 [20-378]
Maine [21-206]	—	—	4	4	773 [21-204]
Maryland [22-295]	—	—	193	193	6143 [22-293]
Massachusetts [23-387]	4	—	362	366	7395 [23-385]
Michigan [24-506]	15	4	203	222	6172 [24-504]
Minnesota [25-437]	—	—	74	74	3398 [25-435]
Mississippi [26-335]	—	—	28	28	1363 [26-333]
Missouri [27-476]	4	—	201	205	4633 [27-474]
Montana [28-238]	—	—	78	78	699 [28-236]
Nebraska [29-362]	5	—	28	33	1512 [29-360]
Nevada [30-178]	—	—	27	27	372 [30-176]
New Hampshire [31-170]	—	—	24	24	402 [31-168]
New Jersey [32-510]	16	—	170	186	8022 [32-508]
New Mexico [33-229]	—	—	12	12	768 [33-227]
New York [34-641]	26	6	1418	1450	36182 [34-639]
North Carolina [35-445]	3	—	38	41	2758 [35-443]
North Dakota [36-271]	—	—	20	20	517 [36-269]
Ohio [37-673]	21	—	304	325	9765 [37-671]
Oklahoma [38-397]	4	—	115	119	2968 [38-395]
Oregon [39-260]	—	—	72	72	2035 [39-258]
Pennsylvania [40-733]	4	—	241	245	9637 [40-731]
Rhode Island [41-185]	—	—	24	24	815 [41-183]
South Carolina [42-306]	—	—	47	47	1601 [42-304]
South Dakota [43-296]	—	—	12	12	556 [43-294]
Tennessee [44-431]	—	—	79	79	2957 [44-429]

continued

CHART C2.   Continued

	Negro Women Lawyers	Other Non-white Lawyers	White Female Lawyers	Total Female Lawyers	Total Male Lawyers
Texas [45-871]	4	—	318	322	10041 [45-869]
Utah [46-224]	—	—	24	24	767 [46-222]
Vermont [47-170]	—	—	21	21	361 [47-168]
Virginia [48-449]	—	—	158	158	5442 [48-447]
Washington [49-301]	—	—	91	91	3005 [49-299]
West Virginia [50-302]	—	—	8	8	1227 [50-300]
Wisconsin [51-400]	—	—	122	122	4002 [51-398]
Wyoming [52-182]	—	—	11	11	315 [52-182]
TOTALS	142	14	6,476	6,632	188,049

1970 Census

The information regarding women and male lawyers is found in *Table 171,* titled, "Detailed Occupations of Employed Persons by Residence, Race, and Sex: 1970." *Table 171* is found in the various bound *Parts* of the *U.S. Census of Population, Vol. I, Characteristics of the Population* (Washington, D.C., U.S. Government Printing Office 1973).

Below, in chart 3, the first and second bracketed numbers, such as [2-600] following the name of the state Alabama, mean that the "characteristic of the population" of women and male lawyers is located at Part 2-Page 600 of Vol. I. As constructed, the chart includes only women by race as identified in the chart totaled by state.

Table 171 lists a Hispanic category of persons of Spanish language or Spanish surname as reported by Arizona, California, Colorado, New Mexico, and Texas (shown by **). New York, New Jersey, and Pennsylvania list a Hispanic category for "persons of Puerto Rican birth or parentage" (shown by *).

The "total" of white female lawyers was formulated by subtracting the number of female lawyers of Spanish language and Negro female lawyers from the total females. The total number of male lawyers combines all races and is not broken out as the data on women is. The total for male lawyers in the population of individual states is race cumulative.

The four non-white women lawyers identified in the 1960 census for Hawaii cannot be accounted for in the 1970 census, probably because the racial categories are different.

CHART C3.   1970 Census

	Negro Female Lawyers	Female Lawyers of Spanish Language	White Female Lawyers	Total Female Lawyers	Total Male Lawyers
Alabama [2-600]	7	—	107	114	2366
Alaska [3-299]	—	—	9	9	281
Arizona [4-397]	—	—**	44	44	1962
Arkansas [5-583]	—	—	23	23	1337
California [6-1539]	53	56**	1391	1500	25252
Colorado [7-481]	5	—**	148	153	3130
Connecticut [8-602]	—	—	182	182	4597
Delaware [9-300]	—	—	32	32	665
D.C. [10-265]	70	6	388	464	3558
Florida [11-826]	6	13	356	375	7835
Georgia [12-824]	4	—	209	213	3889
Hawaii [13-302]	—	—	47	47	554
Idaho [14-359]	—	—	26	26	642
Illinois [15-1004]	44	—	683	727	15292
Indiana [16-789]	7	—	205	212	4244
Iowa [17-646]	—	—	114	114	2481
Kansas [18-618]	5	—	89	94	2782
Kentucky [19-688]	—	—	127	127	2612
Louisiana [20-593]	4	12	117	133	3678
Maine [21-351]	—	—	30	30	704
Maryland [22-543]	44	5	449	498	8636
Massachusetts [23-782]	5	—	560	565	8419
Michigan [24-831]	35	—	317	352	8209
Minnesota [25-631]	—	—	179	179	4103
Mississippi [26-512]	10	—	92	102	1825
Missouri [27-695]	11	17	172	200	5013
Montana [28-362]	—	—	14	14	743
Nebraska [29-521]	—	—	36	36	1773
Nevada [30-311]	—	—	32	32	501
New Hampshire [31-331]	—	—	26	26	529
New Jersey [32-839]	15	—*	430	445	10519
New Mexico [33-389]	—	34**	43	77	964
New York [34-906]	60	19*	1898	1977	39061
North Carolina [35-672]	6	—	110	116	3139
North Dakota [36-367]	—	—	21	21	467
Ohio [37-1136]	14	10	581	605	11212
Oklahoma [38-563]	5	7	126	138	3107
Oregon [39-410]	—	—	111	111	2356
Pennsylvania [40-972]	19	—*	566	585	10797
Rhode Island [41-367]	—	—	29	29	1087
South Carolina [42-509]	—	—	42	42	1707
South Dakota [43-407]	—	—	15	15	599
Tennessee [44-629]	—	—	111	111	3248

continued

CHART C3.   Continued

	Negro Female Lawyers	Female Lawyers of Spanish Language	White Female Lawyers	Total Female Lawyers	Total Male Lawyers
Texas [45-1578]	7	22**	571	600	12775
Utah [46-383]	—	—	35	35	1065
Vermont [47-282]	—	—	29	29	370
Virginia [48-765]	10	—	390	400	8021
Washington [49-489]	—	—	148	148	3643
West Virginia [50-476]	—	—	45	45	1273
Wisconsin [51-641]	—	—	146	146	4501
Wyoming [52-282]	—	—	13	13	318
TOTALS	446	201	11,664	12,311	247,841

1980 Census

The information regarding women and male lawyers is found in *Table 218,* titled "Detailed Occupation of the Experienced Civilian Labor Force by Sex, Race, and Spanish Origin: 1980." *Table 218* is found in various bound *Parts* by individual States of the *U.S. Census of the Population: 1980, Vol. I, Characteristics of the Population* (Washington, D.C., U.S. Government Printing Office 1983).

Below, in chart 4, the first and second bracketed numbers, such as [2-252] following the name of the state Alabama, mean that the "characteristic of the population" of women and male lawyers is located at Part 2-Page 252 of Vol. I. As constructed, the chart includes only women by race as identified in the chart totaled by state. The total of males combines all races and is not broken out as the data on women is. The total for male lawyers in the population of individual states is race cumulative.

This census was the first time the Spanish Origin category was used. In some instances where Spanish Origin was indicated, the total of all racial categories exceeded the total number of female lawyers. For example, in Rhode Island, the total number of female lawyers is 126. This total includes 120 white females, 6 black females and 10 Spanish Origin females. It is assumed that in these instances some respondents indicated more than one racial category.

CHART C4. 1980 Census

	White Female Lawyers	Black Female Lawyers	American Indian, Eskimo or Aleut Female Lawyers	Asian or Pacific Islander Female Lawyers	Spanish Origin Female Lawyers	Total Female Lawyers	Total Male Lawyers
Alabama [2-252]	377	27	—	—	8	404	4328
Alaska [3-111]	240	5	7	8	3	260	1040
Arizona [4-209]	638	12	21	—	47	711	4354
Arkansas [5-167]	216	—	—	—	—	216	2516
California [6-663]	9547	574	55	453	508	10875	53455
Colorado [7-205]	1212	28	—	—	20	1243	6627
Connecticut [8-248]	1015	16	—	—	13	1031	7307
Delaware [9-139]	154	9	—	—	—	163	1034
D.C. [10-138]	2686	551	10	28	81	3288	7004
Florida [11-448]	2403	90	7	—	191	2521	18173
Georgia [12-242]	1190	131	—	—	11	1321	8835
Hawaii [13-162]	143	—	—	141	17	288	1563
Idaho [14-85]	164	—	5	—	11	175	1333
Illinois [15-268]	3795	349	—	38	49	4203	24853
Indiana [16-305]	680	38	7	—	—	725	6699
Iowa [17-188]	493	4	—	—	6	503	4198
Kansas [18-187]	438	9	—	—	—	447	4407
Kentucky [19-248]	507	13	—	—	7	520	4831
Louisiana [20-219]	865	80	—	—	10	945	7303
Maine [21-67]	280	—	—	—	—	280	1557
Maryland [22-249]	1757	313	—	27	5	2109	13235

continued

CHART C4. Continued

	White Female Lawyers	Black Female Lawyers	American Indian, Eskimo or Aleut Female Lawyers	Asian or Pacific Islander Female Lawyers	Spanish Origin Female Lawyers	Total Female Lawyers	Total Male Lawyers
Massachusetts [23-268]	2486	82	12	—	26	2597	13866
Michigan [24-370]	1877	195	5	—	13	2077	14275
Minnesota [25-212]	1225	12	4	—	6	1247	7268
Mississippi [26-167]	200	47	—	—	—	247	3053
Missouri [27-187]	928	103	6	—	—	1037	7000
Montana [28-111]	222	—	3	—	—	225	1282
Nebraska [29-154]	482	14	—	14	—	510	2947
Nevada [30-159]	200	—	6	—	—	206	1357
New Hampshire [31-84]	213	—	—	—	—	213	1326
New Jersey [32-473]	1904	179	5	35	69	2134	16807
New Mexico [33-153]	354	—	15	—	85	414	2004
New York [34-407]	7939	544	19	107	273	8695	53337
North Carolina [35-267]	618	145	—	—	6	763	5931
North Dakota [36-67]	83	—	—	—	—	83	818
Ohio [37-422]	1847	162	—	8	7	2024	17078

Oklahoma [38-214]	689	8	27	—	5	737	5095
Oregon [39-212]	857	2	3	16	6	878	4526
Pennsylvania [40-385]	2620	129	—	25	36	2781	18472
Rhode Island [41-124]	120	6	—	—	10	126	1591
South Carolina [42-242]	455	15	—	—	4	474	3462
South Dakota [43-111]	84	—	3	—	—	87	944
Tennessee [44-259]	699	71	8	—	5	778	5957
Texas [45-403]	3162	154	—	16	240	3407	24198
Utah [46-106]	226	—	—	6	13	232	2047
Vermont [47-67]	211	—	—	—	8	211	878
Virginia [48-294]	2283	101	—	—	72	2384	15038
Washington [49-286]	1147	26	2	30	18	1218	7504
West Virginia [50-145]	244	5	—	—	5	249	1981
Wisconsin [51-261]	906	23	—	—	19	929	7103
Wyoming [52-67]	77	—	—	—	—	77	744
TOTALS	63,158	4,272	230	952	1,913	69,268	432,541

1990 Census

The 1990 census information is from the 1990 census Population and Housing Equal Employment Computer File published by the U.S. Department of Commerce, Bureau of the Census, Data User Service Division (1993). The information regarding women and minorities is found in *Table (matrix number P.2)*, at 36 of the technical documentation included on CD ROM is also published in a hard copy "Data Dictionary" in *Census of Population and Housing, 1990: Equal Employment Opportunity File* (Bureau of Census: Washington, D.C., 1992). The *Table (matrix number P.2)* is titled "Detailed Occupation by Sex by Hispanic Origin and Race." As constructed, the chart includes only women by race as identified in the chart totaled by state. The total of males combines all races and is not broken out as the data on women is. The total for male lawyers in the population of individual states is race cumulative.

	Hispanic Female Lawyers	White Female Lawyers	Black Female Lawyers	American Indian, Eskimo or Aleut Female	Asian or Pacific Islander Female Lawyers	Other Race Female Lawyers	Total Female Lawyers	Total Male Lawyers
Alabama	1	986	150	0	0	0	1137	5856
Alaska	7	670	6	6	0	0	689	1495
Arizona	124	2022	32	11	22	0	2211	6764
Arkansas	10	635	16	8	11	0	680	3174
California	1616	23784	1243	82	1625	29	28379	75452
Colorado	103	2945	44	35	28	0	3155	9141
Connecticut	99	3391	117	5	20	0	3632	9910
Delaware	9	384	20	0	0	0	413	1453
D.C.	107	3831	706	0	83	0	4727	7155
Florida	887	6815	442	10	30	8	8192	28149
Georgia	43	2972	415	7	22	0	3459	12546
Hawaii	0	456	7	10	350	0	823	2736
Idaho	0	274	0	2	0	0	276	1826
Illinois	288	8502	517	13	115	0	9435	31478
Indiana	9	1885	95	0	19	0	2008	7334
Iowa	6	1055	20	0	0	0	1081	4473
Kansas	26	1223	55	0	7	0	1311	5062
Kentucky	9	1503	18	0	0	0	1530	5656
Louisiana	70	2267	322	0	0	0	2659	9741
Maine	0	711	0	0	0	0	711	2073
Maryland	50	5324	907	0	112	0	6393	17604

continued

CHART C5.   Continued

	Hispanic Female Lawyers	White Female Lawyers	Black Female Lawyers	American Indian, Eskimo or Aleut Female	Asian or Pacific Islander Female Lawyers	Other Race Female Lawyers	Total Female Lawyers	Total Male Lawyers
Massachusetts	163	7186	328	7	112	7	7803	17663
Michigan	24	3570	448	0	7	0	4049	16665
Minnesota	36	2815	37	14	23	0	2925	9265
Mississippi	28	710	117	0	14	0	869	3873
Missouri	37	2221	137	0	7	0	2402	9382
Montana	18	294	0	4	0	0	316	1602
Nebraska	0	697	9	0	21	0	727	2850
Nevada	18	485	36	0	7	0	546	2297
New Hampshire	0	624	8	0	18	0	650	1879
New Jersey	225	6282	578	5	142	0	7232	23169
New Mexico	132	977	0	28	10	0	1147	2695
New York	912	21297	1705	24	608	7	24553	65238
North Carolina	9	1946	217	9	14	5	2200	7599
North Dakota	0	221	0	3	0	0	224	828
Ohio	62	4822	325	19	18	0	5246	20060
Oklahoma	13	1458	70	57	0	5	1603	6726

Oregon	2	1583	8	7	25	0	1625	5533
Pennsylvania	60	6799	512	0	76	0	7447	23634
Rhode Island	7	503	19	0	0	0	529	2457
South Carolina	0	1236	95	0	0	0	1331	4499
South Dakota	0	200	0	12	0	0	212	958
Tennessee	19	1733	199	7	7	0	1965	7292
Texas	818	9154	573	38	96	0	10679	34866
Utah	5	477	3	10	14	0	509	2920
Vermont	0	390	0	0	0	0	390	1135
Virginia	184	6075	356	6	142	0	6763	19165
Washington	7	3125	41	0	92	0	3265	10273
West Virginia	9	501	0	0	0	0	510	2335
Wisconsin	20	1860	53	6	0	0	1949	7569
Wyoming	10	168	0	0	0	0	178	827
TOTALS	6,282	161,044	11,006	445	3,897	61	182,745	564,332

Contributors

Adjoa Artis Asantewaah Aiyetoro (1946–) is a 1967 graduate of Clark University in Worcester, Massachusetts. In 1969, she earned a Master of Social Work from the George Warren Brown School of Social Work at Washington University. In 1978, Aiyetoro earned a law degree *cum laude* from St. Louis University School of Law. From 1978 to 1982, she worked in the Civil Rights Division of the U.S. Department of Justice specializing in rights for the institutionalized and thereafter for eleven years with the National Prison Project of the American Civil Liberties Union Foundation. Aiyetoro is presently the Director of the National Conference of Black Lawyers and a leading spokesperson against injustice of blacks in the criminal justice system. She was admitted to the Missouri bar in 1978.

Sadie Tanner Mossell Alexander (1898–1989) was a 1918 graduate of the University of Pennsylvania and a 1927 law graduate of its law school. She was the first black woman to graduate from the law school and the first black woman to serve on the *University of Pennsylvania Law Review*. Prior to attending law school she earned a Ph.D. in economics at the University of Pennsylvania. She joined her husband's (Raymond Pace Alexander) law firm where she specialized in estate and family law. In 1928 she was appointed as Assistant City Solicitor in Philadelphia, a post that she held until 1930. She served on many committees and boards, including President Harry Truman's Committee on Human Rights. She later joined a major black law firm before retiring in 1982. She served with distinction as secretary of the National Bar Association for many years. Alexander is a second generation lawyer. She was admitted to the Pennsylvania bar in 1927.

Helen Elsie Austin (1910–) is a 1928 graduate of the University of Cincinnati University and a 1930 graduate of its law school. She is the first black woman law graduate of the University of Cincinnati. After passing the Ohio bar in 1930, the first black woman to do so, and the Indiana bar in 1932, she entered private practice until she was appointed assistant attorney general of Ohio in 1937, at age 27. She is the first black woman in the nation to be so appointed. She taught law in the late 1940s and early 1950s at the all-black Robert H. Terrell Law School in Washington, D.C. In 1948, she was the first black woman to work for the National Labor Relations Board. She also initiated the first women's activities programs as a foreign officer at the U.S. Information Agency in Africa. She is a past National President of Delta Sigma Theta Sorority and a leader in the Baha'i Faith.

Mary Frances Berry (1938–) is a graduate of Howard University, where she earned both her B.A. and M.A. degrees in 1961 and 1962, respectively. Berry earned the Ph.D. degree in History from the University of Michigan in 1966 and a law degree from the same university in 1970. Berry's career has been concentrated in the academic and public service areas. Berry has taught American and Constitutional History at Howard University, the University of Maryland, and the University of Pennsylvania, where she has been the Geraldine Segal Professor of American Social Thought since 1987. She was appointed Provost at the University of Maryland in 1974. From 1970–72, Berry was the director of the Afro-American Studies at the University of Colorado where she subsequently served as Chancellor in 1976. From 1977–80, during the Carter administration, Berry held the post of assistant secretary of education. She has been a member of the U.S. Commission of Civil Rights since 1980. A prolific author, Berry has published several books on race, gender, and class. Among her many honors, in 1990 Berry was elected president of the Organization of American Historians. She was admitted as a member of District of Columbia Bar in 1972.

Goler Teal Butcher (1925–93) was a 1946 graduate of the University of Pennsylvania and a 1957 honor law graduate of Howard University, graduating first in her class. She received a master of laws degree in international law in 1958 from the University of Pennsylvania Law School. She was Editor-in-Chief of the Howard Law Journal, the first woman to hold that post at the law school. From 1958 to 1959, she clerked for William Henry Hastie Sr., a federal circuit judge, the first black woman to clerk in the federal system. Between 1960 and 1963, she worked for the Legal Aid Society in the District of Columbia and for the Library of Congress Reference Service. In 1963 she joined the Department of State staff as a legal adviser, a first for a black lawyer at State. In 1971, she broke new ground again when Congressman Charles C. Diggs appointed Butcher as a consultant to the House Foreign Affairs Committee and counsel to the Subcommittee on Africa. In 1974 she went into private practice. In 1977, President Jimmy Carter appointed Butcher as Assistant Administrator of the Agency for International Development with principal responsibility in Africa. In 1981, she joined the law faculty of Howard University, where she taught international law until her death in 1993. She was admitted to practice in the District of Columbia in 1958.

Jean Camper Cahn (1935–91) was a 1957 graduate of Swarthmore College and the Yale Law School in 1961. Cahn commenced law teaching in 1968 as an adjunct professor at Howard University and as a Visiting Full Professor at George Washington University in 1968. She was the first black woman to teach law at a white law school in the history of the nation. In 1972 she was the cofounder and Co-Dean of the Antioch School of Law in Washington, D.C., a post that she held until the school closed in 1988. The Antioch School of Law was the seed for what is now the District of Columbia School of Law. She was admitted to practice in Connecticut in 1961.

Jean Murrell Capers (1913–) is a 1932 graduate of Western Reserve University and a 1945 law graduate of Cleveland Law School. She taught in the Cleveland public schools from 1932 to 1937 and entered private practice in 1945. She held various public posts in Cleveland. In 1949, she was elected to the Cleveland city council, on which she served until 1959. She served on the Municipal Court of Cleveland from 1977–86. She retired from active law practice in 1995. She was admitted to practice in Ohio in 1945.

Mary Ann Shadd Carey (Cary) (1823–93) was educated by the Quakers in Pennsylvania. She was an 1883 law graduate of Howard University. During her formative years, Shadd Carey fought against the evils of slavery and for the right of women to vote. She worked as a journalist and as a publishing agent, and she lectured on race issues. When the Civil War began, she was teaching in Michigan. After the war ended she continued to teach until late in her fifties when she enrolled in law school in 1881. She was admitted to practice in the District of Columbia in 1883.

Daisy G. Collins (1937–) is a 1958 graduate of Ohio State University and a 1970 law graduate (with honors) of Howard University, where she served on the *Howard Law Journal*. She served as an Assistant U.S. Attorney in the Department of Justice (Ohio) from 1975 to 1977 and taught law at the Capital University School of Law as a visiting professor from 1981 to 1982. She worked for the Equal Employment Opportunity Commission from 1986 to 1990. She is an administrative law judge in the Cleveland District of the Office of Hearings and Appeals of the Social Security Administration. She was in private practice at various times throughout her career. She was admitted to practice in Ohio in 1971.

Ollie May Cooper (1887–1981). It is not known where Ollie May Cooper attended college, but she was an honor graduate of the Howard University School of Law in 1921. She was one of two women in her class. In 1929, Cooper and Isadora A. Jackson Letcher opened the first law firm headed by black women in the nation's history. Cooper also was the first black woman to move the admission of another black woman's admission before the D.C. Court of Appeals in 1932. Cooper practiced law at night. During the day she served as secretary to the dean at Howard Law School. Over forty years as secretary to the dean, she served at least ten deans, including Charles Hamilton Houston. Cooper is the first woman attorney that Thurgood Marshall ever met, and Marshall admired "Ollie May." Cooper helped found and organize Epsilon Sigma Iota, the first black legal sorority. She served as secretary of the National Bar Association. In 1929, Cooper became the first woman to teach a law course at Howard's law school. She was admitted to the bar of the District of Columbia in 1926.

Mahala Ashley Dickerson (1912–) is a 1935 graduate of Fisk University, a historically black college, and a 1948 law graduate of Howard University. Prior to attending law school, Dickerson was a high school teacher and a clerk at the Tuskegee Air Field in Alabama, her native state. She has practiced law since 1949 in Indianapolis, Indiana, and Alaska. In 1983, she was installed as President of the National Association of Women at its annual meeting in Atlanta, Georgia, the first black woman to hold this post since the founding of that group in 1899. In 1994, she received the Margaret Brent Award from the American Bar Association, named for America's first woman lawyer. She has practiced law in Alaska for over thirty years. She is the first black woman lawyer in that state. She is also one of the first black women admitted to the bar in Alabama. She was admitted to practice in Alabama and Alaska in 1948 and 1959, respectively. She is the mother of triplets.

Marian Wright Edelman (1939–) is a 1960 graduate of Spellman College, a historically black college, and a 1963 law graduate of Yale Law School. From 1963 to 1964, she was a staff attorney for the NAACP Legal Defense and Education Fund, and she directed that office until 1968. From 1968 to 1973, she was associated with the Washington Research Project of the Southern Center for Public Policy and simultaneously associated with the Center for Law and Education, at Harvard University, from 1971 to 1973. In 1973, she became the president of the Children's Legal Defense Fund, a post that she holds presently. She is a member of several organizations and has won many awards and prizes, including the MacArthur Fellow Prize in 1985. She was admitted to practice in 1963 and the first black woman admitted to the bar of Mississippi in 1965.

Georgia Huston Jones Ellis (1892–1953) was a 1922 graduate of Sumner Teachers College, St. Louis, Missouri, and a 1925 law graduate of John Marshall Law

School. In 1925, she was one of about twenty-five black women lawyers in the nation. After her admission to the bar she became an attaché of the domestic relations branch of the Municipal Court of Chicago. She was the first black woman to hold a quasi-judicial post in Chicago's judicial system. In 1929, she was elected vice president of the National Bar Association, the first high-ranking woman officer in a national bar group. She joined a black law firm in Chicago in the early 1940s. She was admitted to practice before the U.S. Supreme Court in 1941. She was admitted to practice in Illinois in 1925.

Frankie Muse Freeman (1916–) is a 1937 graduate of Hampton University, a historically black college, and a 1947 law graduate of Howard University. In 1949, she opened a law office in St. Louis, Missouri, where she was a general practitioner, but soon became a civil rights specialist in public housing discrimination. She joined the St. Louis Land Clearance and Housing Authority to help implement a court decision won by Freeman. She served as associate general counsel and general counsel for the Housing Authority until 1970, when she returned to private practice. In 1964, President Lyndon Johnson nominated her to the U.S. Civil Rights Commission. She is the first woman to serve on the Commission, where she served terms under three other presidents. In 1979 President Jimmy Carter nominated and the U.S. Senate confirmed Freeman as Inspector General of the Community Services Administration, where she served until 1981. She returned to private practice in St. Louis. She was admitted to practice in the District of Columbia in 1947.

Linda Sheryl Greene (1948–) is a 1970 graduate of California State University (Long Beach) and a 1974 law graduate of the University of California (Berkeley). From 1974 to 1977, she was a staff attorney for the NAACP Legal Defense and Education Fund. She has taught law at several schools: Temple University (1978–81), Oregon University (1981–86), Georgetown (1985–86), and Wisconsin University (1989–). From 1986 to 1989, she was Counsel to the U.S. Senate Judiciary Antitrust Subcommittee. In 1992, she served as chair of the Minority Group Section of the American Association of Law Schools and, in 1996 to 1997, as President of the Society of American Law Teachers. Professor Greene is the author of several law review articles. She was admitted to practice in California in 1975.

Lani Guinier (1950–) is a 1971 graduate of Harvard (Radcliffe College) and a 1974 law graduate of Yale Law School. She was a law clerk for Judge Damon Keith, a U.S. District Judge for the District of Michigan from 1974 to 1976. Later, she served as a special assistant to the Assistant Attorney General of the civil rights division at the Department of Justice (1977–81). From 1981 to 1988, she worked for the NAACP Legal Defense and Education Fund in New York City, where she was involved in groundbreaking voting rights cases. She joined the law faculty at the University of Pennsylvania Law School in 1988. In 1998, she joined the faculty of the

Harvard Law School as its first black tenured professor. She has written extensively on civil rights and women's issues and has authored a book on voting rights. She was admitted to practice in Michigan in 1975 and the District of Columbia in 1981.

Mabel Dole Haden (1915–) is a 1940 graduate of Virginia State College for Negroes and a 1948 law graduate of Howard University. She enrolled in Howard Law School's evening program and taught in the public schools during the day. In 1956, she received a Master of Laws degree from the Georgetown Law School, becoming the first known black woman to earn a law degree from that University. Haden also opened a law practice in 1956, the year that she was admitted to the District of Columbia bar. She has practiced law in the District since then. In 1972, Haden cofounded the National Association of Black Women Attorneys.

Patricia Roberts Harris (1924–85) was a 1945 graduate (Phi Beta Kappa) of Howard University and a 1960 law graduate of George Washington University, where she graduated first in her law class. She was a member of the *George Washington Law Review*. From 1960 to 1961, she was one of the first black women to work at the Department of Justice and one of the first women to teach law at the Howard University. She joined the law faculty as a lecturer in 1961 and was made an assistant professor in 1963. Public service dominated most of Harris's life: In 1965, President Lyndon B. Johnson appointed her as ambassador to Luxembourg, a first for a black American, and as an alternate delegate to the United Nations (1966–67). In 1977 and 1980, respectively, President Jimmy Carter appointed Harris as Secretary of Housing and Urban Development and as Secretary of the Department of Health, Education, and Welfare. She held many other important positions, including the deanship at the Howard University School of Law (1969), the first black woman to head a law school in the nation. Prior to her death, she was a law professor at George Washington University. She was admitted to practice in the District of Columbia in 1960.

Margaret Austin Haywood (1912–) attended a business college and is a 1940 graduate of the Robert H. Terrell Law School, a black law school founded in the District of Columbia in 1937. Haywood was engaged in the general practice of law from 1940 to 1972. During the mid-1940s, Haywood also taught law at the Robert H. Terrell Law School. In 1967, she was appointed to the District of Columbia City Council, a post that she held until 1972, when President Richard Nixon appointed her as an associate judge on the Municipal Court of the District of Columbia. She held this post until she took senior status in 1987. She was the court's expert on Wills and Estate law. She was admitted to practice in the District of Columbia in 1940.

Anita Faye Hill (1956–) is a 1977 graduate of Oklahoma State University and received her law degree from Yale University in 1980. Her career has been marked by a steady climb. She has practiced corporate law in Washington, D.C., at two law firms and worked for Clarence Thomas as a special assistant from 1981 to 1982 and as an attorney adviser at the Equal Employment Opportunity Commission during the chairmanship of Clarence Thomas (1982–83), against whom she testified (1991) for sexual harassment when he was nominated by President George Bush to become a justice on the U.S. Supreme Court. She taught law at the Oral Roberts University (1986–90), when she joined the law faculty at the University of Oklahoma. She resigned from the University of Oklahoma Law School in 1997. In 1995, a law chair was established in her name by the Board of Regents at the University, the first chair named for a black woman in the history of legal education. She was admitted to practice in the District of Columbia in 1981.

Arnette Rhinehart Hubbard (1935–) is a 1957 graduate of Southern Illinois University at Edwardsville and a 1969 law graduate of John Marshall Law School. She is the first woman president of the National Bar Association (1981) founded in 1925. She has held several public posts in Chicago, including membership on the first Chicago Cable T.V. Commission and leading the local black bar association in Cook County. She has headed her own law firm and was a Commissioner on the Board of Elections in Chicago. In 1997, she was appointed to the Circuit Court in Chicago. She was admitted to the Illinois bar in 1969.

Joyce Anne Hughes (1940–) is a 1961 graduate (Phi Beta Kappa) of Carleton College and a 1965 law graduate (Order of Coif) of the University of Minnesota. She then worked for a major law firm in Minneapolis. She is the first black woman to receive a law degree from the University of Minnesota. She was selected as law clerk to Judge Earl L. Larson, a member of the U.S. District Court in Minnesota, the first black to clerk in the federal court system in Minnesota. She is the first black woman, ten re-track, professor at a white law school in the history of the nation. She joined the University of Minnesota's law faculty with the rank of associate professor in 1971 and resigned this post in 1975. In 1975 she joined the law faculty of Northwestern University School of Law, where she presently teaches. She was admitted to practice in Minnesota in 1965.

Jane Edna Harris Hunter (1882–1971) received a diploma in nursing from the Dixie Hospital and Training School for Nurses, at Hampton Institute, Virginia, around 1904. She is a 1925 law graduate of Western Reserve Baldwin-Wallace Law School. From 1910 until she entered law school, Hunter dedicated her life to building a Working Girl's Home (later named the Phyllis Wheatley Association), a home established in 1913 to protect black women living away from home. She never practiced law per se, but used her knowledge of the law to realize her goals for black women about which she wrote in *A Nickel and a Prayer* published in 1940. She was admitted to the Ohio bar in 1925.

Issie Lee Shelton Jenkins (1934–) is a 1956 graduate of Indiana University and a 1959 law graduate of Boston University. She also received a master of law degree from George Washington University in 1967. Jenkins has spent her career in government service. She has worked for the internal revenue service as a tax specialist and for the Department of Justice. She joined the staff of the Equal Employment Opportunity Commission in 1976. She has held many important positions at EEOC. In 1981, she was the first woman appointed as the acting executive director of that agency, which was created by Congress in 1964. She is active in several women's organizations, such as the National Council of Negro Women. She was admitted to practice in the District of Columbia in 1962 and in Pennsylvania in 1981.

Elaine Ruth Jones (1944–) is a 1965 graduate of Howard University, a historically black College, and a 1973 law graduate of the University of Virginia. She was the first black woman admitted to the law school. She was first employed at the NAACP Legal Defense and Education Fund (LDF) for a short while before the Secretary of Transportation, William T. Coleman Jr., appointed Jones as his special assistant. In 1977, she rejoined LDF becoming its chief spokesperson before the U.S. Congress. She is responsible for the confirmation of several federal judges of all races whose nominations were opposed by conservative members of the U.S. Senate. She was the chief monitor of nominations for federal judgeships and high positions in the U.S. Department of Justice. In 1988, she was made deputy director of LDF; in 1993 she became counsel director of LDF, the first woman to hold this post since it was created in 1940. She was admitted to practice in the Commonwealth of Virginia in 1970.

Barbara Charline Jordan (1936–96) was a 1956 graduate of a historically black college, Texas Southern University, and graduated from Boston University School of Law in 1959. In 1966, she became the first black and first woman elected to the Texas Senate since 1883. In 1972, with the support of former President Lyndon B. Johnson, Jordan was elected to the House of Representatives, one of two black people elected to Congress from the South since Reconstruction, a post that she held until 1977, when she joined the faculty of the University of Texas to teach in the Lyndon B. Johnson School of Public Affairs. She was admitted to practice in Texas in 1959.

Arthenia Lee Joyner (1943–) is a 1964 graduate of a Florida A&M University, and its law school in 1968. Florida A&M is a historically black college. She has been in the general practice of law since 1969. She was the first black woman lawyer in Tampa. She is a leading voice in the South on questions of racial justice and equality for women. She has been active in a host of community activities, such as the NAACP, Urban League, the Association of Women Lawyers, and the black bar association movement. During the 1980s, she was one of the activists in opposition to the apartheid system in South Africa. In 1984, she was elected as president of the National Bar Association, becoming the second black woman to lead this group since it was founded in 1925. She was admitted to practice in Florida in 1969.

Patricia A. King (1942–) is a 1963 graduate of Wheaton College and a 1969 law graduate of Harvard Law School. In 1969, she served as a special assistant to the chairman of the Equal Employment Opportunity Commission, a post that she held until 1971. From 1971 to 1973, she served as the deputy director of the Office for Civil Rights and the Department of Health, Education, and Welfare. She joined the faculty at the Georgetown Law School in 1973, where she has taught until the present, except for one year (1980–81) when she served as Deputy Assistant Attorney General at the Department of Justice. Her interest is in the field of law and medicine. She was admitted to the District of Columbia bar in 1969.

Jewel Rogers Stradford Lafontant (Mankarious) (1922–97) was a 1943 graduate of Oberlin College and a 1946 law graduate of the University of Chicago Law School. She was a third generation lawyer. She commenced her law career as an attorney for the Legal Aid Bureau (1947–54). From 1955 to 1958, she served as an Assistant U.S. Attorney in Chicago, possibly the first black woman to hold such a post in the U.S. Department of Justice. She was a partner in a firm founded by her father during the 1960s and 1970s. She served as national secretary to the National Bar Association from 1956 to 1961. Her career path was impressive: she was associated with several major corporate law firms and sat on the boards of major American corporations. She was appointed by Richard Nixon as a representative to the United Nations in 1972. The following year, she became deputy solicitor general under Solicitor General Robert Bork at the Department of Justice (1973–75). In 1983, President George Bush appointed Lafontant as ambassador-at-large and U.S. coordinator for refugee affairs. She was admitted to practice in Chicago in 1947.

Jane Cleo Marshall Lucas (1920–) is a 1941 graduate of Howard University and a 1944 law graduate of the University of Michigan. She first worked in the law offices of Arthur Davis Shores in Birmingham, Alabama, in the mid-1940s before relocating to Maryland, where she was admitted to the bar in 1946, becoming the first black woman admitted to that bar. In 1946, she joined the law faculty at Howard University becoming the first woman hired to teach in the law school. She was a member of the law faculty until 1951. During the 1960s, she worked for a brief period for the U.S. Equal Employment Opportunity Commission, where she worked on race and gender issues. She was admitted to practice in Michigan in 1944.

Lutie A. Lytle (1871–?) was a 1897 law graduate of all-black Central Tennessee Law School (Nashville), finishing its three-year course of instruction. She was a native of Topeka, Kansas. Prior to attending law school she worked as a compositor at a black newspaper in Topeka. From 1876 to 1878 she taught school in Chattanooga. In 1897, she joined the law faculty at Central Tennessee Law School, becoming the first woman of any race to teach law in a chartered law school in the history of the nation. She was active in the Negro National Bar Association, Women's Federation of New York, and National Council of Negro Women. She was the first black woman admitted to practice in Tennessee and Kansas in 1897.

Julia Cooper Mack (1921–) is a 1940 graduate of Hampton University, an historically black college, and a 1951 law graduate of Howard University School of law. After she graduated from law school, she worked for the Department of Justice for several years before joining the Equal Employment Opportunity Commission as Deputy General Counsel from 1963 to 1973. She has also worked on the legal staff of the General Services Administration and the Office of Price Stabilization. In 1975, President Gerald R. Ford appointed Mack to the District of Columbia Court of Appeals, a post that she held until she reached senior status in 1989. She is the first black woman to sit on the highest court of a court of last resort in the history of the nation. She was admitted to practice in the District of Columbia in 1952.

Consuelo Bland Marshall (1936–) is a 1958 graduate of Howard University and a 1961 law graduate of this university. She was a member of the *Howard Law Journal*. From 1962 to 1967, she was a deputy city attorney in Los Angeles and entered private practice from 1968 to 1970. She has been a judge since 1971. From 1971 to 1976, she served as a judge in the Juvenile Court in Los Angeles; from 1976 to 1977, as judge on the Inglewood Municipal Court, Los Angeles County; and from 1977 to 1980, as judge on the Criminal Court, for the Superior Court of California, Los Angeles County. In 1980, President Jimmy Carter appointed Judge Marshall to the U.S. District Court, where she became one of a handful of black women serving on this court in the nation. Judge Marshall was admitted to practice in California in 1962.

Juanita Jackson Mitchell (1913–92) was a 1931 graduate of the University of Pennsylvania and a 1950 law graduate of the University of Maryland. She was a member of the *Maryland Law Review*. She was the second black woman to be admitted to the bar in Maryland and the first woman to practice law in that state. After she graduated from law school at the age of thirty-seven, she used her legal training to fight against segregation and to desegregate everything public and private (such as restaurants) in the city of Baltimore, where she and her husband Clarence Mitchell II lived with their children. She was an active and dedicated member of the NAACP from a very early age. She was admitted to practice in Maryland in 1951.

Zephyr Abigail Moore (Ramsey) (1893–?) was a graduate of Pasadena High School and Knox College, and a 1922 law graduate of Howard University. She attended Howard University Teacher's College for two years. During World War I, she was employed by the War Trade Board and Bureau of War Risk Insurance. She received a certificate of efficiency for services rendered during the War Trade Board. After graduation, Moore was admitted to practice in California. She returned to the District of Columbia where she worked for the Federal Emergency Relief Administration. She returned to Los Angeles to practice law. She was the second black woman lawyer admitted to practice in California (around 1930).

Carol E. Moseley-Braun (1947–) is a 1969 graduate of the University of Chicago and a 1972 law graduate of that university. She worked for the Department of Justice as an Assistant United States Attorney in Chicago from 1974 to 1977. She began her political career as a member of the Illinois House of Representatives to which she was elected in 1977, serving the 26th Legislative District until 1988. She was the chief sponsor of the first minority public contract set-asides for minorities and women. In 1988, she was elected to the Cook County Recorder of Deeds, a post that she held until 1992, when she was elected to the U.S. Senate. She is the first black woman to be elected to the U.S. Senate. She was admitted to practice in Illinois in 1973.

Constance Baker Motley (1921–) is a 1943 graduate of New York University and the Columbia University School of Law in 1946. Her first job after law school was to work for the NAACP Legal Defense Fund under the tutelage of Thurgood Marshall. Motley is the first black woman to be elected to the New York Senate (1964), the first woman to serve as president of the Borough of Manhattan (1966), and the first black woman confirmed as a U.S. District Court Judge. Her clients include Dr. Martin Luther King Jr. (in defense of his civil disobedience) and James Meredith (in his quest to be admitted to the University of Mississippi). She has argued several cases before the U.S. Supreme Court. In 1982, Judge Motley became chief judge of the U.S. District Court in New York City until 1986 when she took senior status on the court. She was admitted to practice in New York in 1948.

Pauli Murray (1910–85) was a 1933 graduate of Hunter College and received her law degree with honors in 1944 from Howard University. She was one of the first black women to apply to Harvard Law School graduate program. She was turned down because she was a woman. In 1945, she received a master of law degree from Boalt Hall. Years later (1965), she earned a Doctor of Juridical Science degree from the Yale Law School. She practiced law in New York City in the 1950s. She was a founding member of the National Organization for Women. In 1977, Murray became one of three women first ordained as priest in the Episcopal Church. Her academic experiences include a professorship at Brandeis University and a senior lectureship at the Ghana School of Law in Accra. In 1946, she was appointed as an assistant attorney general of the state of California, the first black woman to hold that post in California. In 1945, Murray became the first black woman to publish a lead article in a law review of an American law school. She was the author of several books and was a poet. She was admitted to practice in California in 1946.

Eleanor Holmes Norton (1937–) is a 1960 graduate of Antioch College and a 1964 law graduate of Yale Law School. The year she graduated from law school, she clerked for Judge A. Leon Higgenbotham, who was a judge on the U.S. District Court in Philadelphia. Her career has been marked by an impressive involvement in civil rights work, starting as a lawyer for the American Civil Liberties Union in 1965, then as the first woman to head the New York City Commission of Human Rights (1970). In 1977, President Jimmy Carter appointed her as Chair of the Federal Equal Employment Opportunities Commission, a post she held until 1981. In 1983 she joined the law faculty at Georgetown University. In 1991, she was elected as a delegate to the House of Representatives from the District of Columbia, the first woman to hold this post. She was admitted to practice in the District of Columbia in 1965.

Glendora McIlwain Putnam (1927–) is a 1945 graduate of the all-black Bennett College and received her law degree from Boston University in 1948. She has served as assistant attorney general of Massachusetts, as Chief of the Division of Civil Rights and Liberties from 1963 to 1969, and as Chair of the Massachusetts Commission Against Discrimination from 1969 to 1977. She was elected national president of the YWCA of the United States in 1985. She was admitted to practice in Massachusetts in 1948.

Edith Spurlock Sampson (1901–79) attended the New York School of Social Work and is a 1925 law graduate of the John Marshall Law School. In 1927, she became the first woman to earn a master of law degree from Loyola University. She opened her own law firm and practiced in Chicago until the mid-1940s specializing in domestic relations and criminal law, while also serving as a referee for the Juvenile Court system in Cook County, Illinois. In 1947, she was appointed assistant state's attorney in Cook County. In 1950, President Harry S. Truman appointed Sampson as an alternate U.S. delegate to the United Nations. She continued to hold that post under the Eisenhower administration. She traveled extensively around the world under the auspices of the Department of State lecturing on a variety of issues. She was elected as associate judge on the Municipal Court of Chicago in 1962. She was admitted to the Illinois bar in 1927.

Althea T. L. Simmons (1924–90) was a 1945 graduate of Southern University, a historically black college, and a 1956 law graduate of Howard University. She earned a master's degree from the University of Illinois (Urbana) in 1951. Her life was dedicated to civil rights. She held many positions in the NAACP, heading voting rights drives and supervising the branches of the NAACP. She succeeded Clarence Mitchell II as chief lobbyist for the NAACP in 1979, a post that she held until her death. She testified before Congress on many occasions on civil rights matters and won many battles to secure the rights of black people to participate in the political processes in the nation. Simmons was the first woman to hold the post of chief lobbyist for the NAACP.

Lucia Theodosia Thomas (1917–) is a 1936 graduate of Xavier University (New Orleans) and a 1940 law graduate of the Robert H. Terrell Law School, a historically black law school. After graduating from law school, she worked for the law dean, George A. Parker, for one year before moving to Chicago to attend John Marshall Law School. In 1941, she worked in a major black law firm headed by Richard E. Westbrooks. In 1942, she received a master of patent law degree from John Marshall Law School, the first black woman to earn this degree. From 1943 to 1947, she became a lawyer-investigator for the Chicago Metropolitan Office of the Office of Price Administration before becoming an associate at a major black Chicago firm. She worked in other government posts in Chicago. From 1965 to 1969, she was an assistant state's attorney in Cook County, an assistant to a juvenile court judge (1969–73), and assistant corporation counsel (1974–77) before being appointed as a Circuit Court Judge in Cook County in 1977. She retired from this judgeship in the late 1980s. She was admitted to practice in Chicago in the early 1940s.

Gloria E. A. Toote (1931–) attended Howard University and is a 1954 graduate of Howard University School of Law. She also earned a master of law degree from Columbia University in 1956. From 1954 to 1971, she worked for the national affairs section of *Time* magazine and also practiced law during the same period. She headed her own publishing businesses and from 1973 to 1975 served as assistant secretary of the Department of Housing and Urban Development in the Nixon administration. In 1976, she seconded the nomination of Ronald Reagan as the Republican candidate for president. She was admitted to practice in New York in 1956.

Cora T. Walker (1926–) is a 1945 graduate of St. John's University and its law school (1946). She entered the private practice of law in 1947 and currently practices law in New York City. She has been a member of numerous commissions, boards, and civic groups. Her attempt to become the first black woman to be elected to the New York Senate was cut short losing to Constance Baker Motley in 1964. She has been an active member of the National Bar Association (founded in 1925) and a strong advocate for black lawyers, especially those in the private practice of law. She and her son practice law in New York City. She was admitted to practice in New York in 1947.

Barbara Mae Watson (1918–83) was a 1943 graduate of Barnard College and a 1962 law graduate of New York Law School. Watson was a second generation lawyer. She had a broad and varied career before she became a lawyer. During World War II she made a number of broadcasts in French and English for the Office of War Information designed to reach the peoples of Africa, Asia, and the West Indies, and for several years headed a modelling agency. After she became a lawyer, she served in several jobs for the New York City government, including employment as an Assistant Corporations Counsel. In 1968, Watson was appointed as Administrator of the Bureau of Security and Consular Affairs with the rank of Assistant Secretary of State in the U.S. Department of State, a post that she held until 1974. In 1977 President Jimmy Carter appointed her as Assistant Secretary of State for Consular Affairs. She is the first black American to hold a post that carried the rank of assistant secretary of state. She was the Ambassador to Malaysia for a short period between 1980 and 1981. Upon her retirement from the State Department, she continued to be a consultant. She was admitted to the bar in New York in the 1960s.

Ruth Whitehead Whaley (1901–77) was a 1921 graduate of Livingston College, a historically black college, and a 1925 law graduate of the Fordham Law School. She was the first black woman graduate of this law school. She entered the private practice of law in 1926. She practiced law in New York until around 1950, when she was appointed to the Board of Estimates in New York City becoming one of the first black women to hold a major public post in New York City. She retired from this post in 1973. She was the first black woman lawyer to engage in the active practice of law in New York and to file major civil rights actions to redress racial discrimination. She was admitted to practice in New York in 1926, and in North Carolina in 1933. She was the first black woman admitted to the North Carolina bar.

Karen Hastie Williams (1944–) is a 1966 graduate of Bates College and a 1973 law graduate of the American University. She is a second generation lawyer. Williams earned a master's degree at the Fletcher School of Law and Diplomacy in 1967. She was a law clerk to Spottswood W. Robinson III, a circuit judge of the D.C. Circuit Court of Appeals (1973–74), and to U.S. Supreme Court Justice

Thurgood Marshall (1974–75). In 1975, she entered private practice in a major Washington, D.C., law firm, where she worked until 1977, when she became chief counsel of the U.S. Senate Committee on Budget. In 1980, she joined the Office of Federal Procurement Policy in the Office of Management and Budget. In 1981, she returned to private practice in another major law firm in the District of Columbia, where she became a partner in 1982. She was admitted to practice in the District of Columbia in 1973.

Margaret Bush Wilson (1919–) is a 1940 graduate of a historically black college, Talladega College, and a graduate of Lincoln University School of Law, a black law school (1943). In 1945, she became the first black woman member of the Federal Bar Association. Wilson's career has been diverse. She has worked for the federal government and in various important jobs in local government in St. Louis. She has practiced law in St. Louis, fought for equal rights for black Americans and against racial discrimination, and once ran for Congress (first black woman to do so from the state of Missouri in 1948). She has been a major leader in the National Association for the Advancement of Colored People. In 1958 she became the first woman to lead the St. Louis branch of the NAACP. In 1975, she was elected chair of the National Board of Directors of the NAACP, the first black woman to hold this post since the group's founding in 1909. She was chair until 1983. She taught law at St. Louis University through the Council on Legal Education Opportunity Institute (CLEO) in 1971. She is admitted to practice in Missouri (1943) and Illinois (1947).

Veva Izelle Young (1914–) is a 1938 graduate of LeMoynes/Owens College, a historically black college, and a 1947 law graduate of Howard University. Prior to enrolling in law school Young was a social reporter of the *Atlanta World* (Memphis), a black newspaper, and worked for the Memphis Housing Authority. She also worked for the Navy Department and the D.C. Housing Authority. In 1947 she went to Chicago, where she opened a law firm. In 1948 she joined the law firm of Brown, Brown, Cyrus and Greene. She has been either a sole practitioner or associated with black law firms since 1948, with the exception of two years during the 1960s when she went to Tennessee to help in the civil rights movement as a lawyer. She retired from the full-time practice of law in 1988, but continues to practice law on a small scale. She has served on the Committee on Character and Fitness committee of the Illinois Supreme Court from 1985 to 1997. She was admitted to practice in two jurisdictions: Illinois (1948) and Tennessee (1963).

Index

Jacket photographs, clockwise from upper left: Women at Howard Law School, 1949–51. (*Left to right, top*), Annie E. Brown (Kennedy), Shirley E. Jones, Charlie M. Lovett; (*middle*), Julia P. Cooper (Mack), Romae L. Turner, Ida I. Stephens, Dovey I. Roundtree; (*bottom*), Leona Pouncey, Lucille J. Williams, Peggy S. Strauss (Griffith). *Upper right:* Lutie A. Lytle. *Lower right:* Black Women Lawyers at the Annual National Bar Association convention, 1947. (*Top to bottom*), Lucia Theodosia Thomas, Wilhelmina Jackson (Rolark), Helen Elsie Austin, Isadora Augusta Letcher. *Lower left:* Ollie May Cooper. *Photographs courtesy of Ollie May Cooper and Mr. and Mrs. Paul F. Cooper.*